Course Design

Third Edition

Course Design
A Guide to Curriculum Development for Teachers

George J. Posner
CORNELL UNIVERSITY

Alan N. Rudnitsky
SMITH COLLEGE

Longman
New York & London

Executive Editor: Raymond T. O'Connell
Senior Editor: Naomi Silverman
Production Editor: Pamela Nelson
Cover Design: Joseph DePinho
Production Supervisor: Judith Stern
Compositor: Pine Tree Composition, Inc.
Printer and Binder: Interstate Book Manufacturers, Inc.

Course Design: A Guide to Curriculum Development for Teachers, Third Edition

Longman Inc.
95 Church Street
White Plains, N.Y. 10601

Associated companies:
Longman Group Ltd., London
Longman Cheshire Pty., Melbourne
Longman Paul Pty., Auckland
Copp Clark Pitman, Toronto
Pitman Publishing Inc., New York

Library of Congress Cataloging-in-Publication Data

Posner, George J.
  Course design.

  Bibliography: p.
  1. Curriculum planning.   2. Education, Secondary—
Curricula.   I. Rudnitsky, Alan N.   II. Title.
LB1570.P645   1987   375′.001   86–7290
ISBN 0–582–28666–2

    89   9 8 7 6 5 4

**To Adrienne, Sue, Rebecca,
Rachel-Anne, Robin, and Kim**

Contents

Figures and Tables   **xi**

Preface   **xiii**

1   Getting Oriented   **1**

The Approach   1
The Project   3
Some Guidelines for Getting Started   4
A Framework for Course Design   6
Curriculum Development and Teacher Thinking   11

2   Setting a Direction   **14**

Generating Initial Ideas   14
Developing a Tentative Course Outline   15
Intended Learning Outcomes (ILOs)   16
Formulating Central Questions   20
Conceptual Maps   25
Flowcharts   31
Finding Out Where the Students Are   35
Related Material   37
Answers to Exercises   38

3   Developing a Course Rationale   **41**

Values and Assumptions   42
Rationale and Entry Point in Planning   44
Components of a Course Rationale   45
Summary   51
Rationales for Elementary School Units   54

4   Refining Intended Learning Outcomes   **57**

ILO Statements: Form and Function   57
Categorizing ILOs   61
Guidelines for Clarifying ILOs   67
Priority of ILOs   78
Overall Balance of ILOs   80
Summary   80

5   Forming Units for the Course   **83**

Clustering ILOs into Units   84
Forming Units Around Instructional Foci   89
Titling the Units   101
Organization and Sequence for Elementary Unit Planning   101

6   Organizing the Course's Units   104

Alternative Sequencing Principles   104
Organizing the Units   112
Alternative Organizations: Some Examples   115
Answers to Exercises   123

7   Developing General Teaching Strategies   **127**

Cognitions   131
Cognitive Skills   137
Psychomotor-Perceptual Skills   139
Commonalities   141
Affects   142
Some General Ideas about Teaching Affects   142
Some Examples   147

8   Planning a Course Evaluation   **152**

Perspectives on Evaluation   152
Gathering Evidence on Main Effects   155
Gathering Evidence of Educational Results   161
Gathering Evidence on Side Effects   162
Troubleshooting   165
Summary   167

Epilogue   **169**

Appendixes   171

A   A Metric Measurement Unit for Grades One and Two   172
B   American Poetry: Female Voices   189

Glossary   206

Selected Bibliography   208

Figures & Tables

Figures

1.1 A Curriculum Instruction Model (adapted from Johnson, 1967)   9
1.2 Relationship between the Model and Components of *Course Design*   12
2.1 Cooking with Heat   26
2.2 The Causal Factors Affecting Rice Growing (adapted from Collins, 1977)   27
2.3 A Conceptual Map for a Course on Freshwater Habitats   28
2.4 One Possible Arrangement of Physics Terms (adapted from Champagne, Klopfer, Solomon, and Cahn, 1980)   30
2.5 Procedure for Addition of Fractions (adapted from Greeno, 1976)   33
2.6 Flowchart of Skills for Ice Hockey   34
3.1 Components of a Course Rationale   49
4.1 The Relationship between ILOs and Behavioral Indicators   60
4.2 Categories of ILOs   62
4.3 Conceptual Map for "Our Federal Government"   71
4.4 (Untitled)   72
4.5 (Untitled)   76
8.1 (Untitled)   157
A.1 Conceptual Map for "A Metric Measurement Unit for Grades One and Two"   175
B.1 Conceptual Map for "American Poetry: Female Voices"   191

Tables

5.1 Chart for German, Level III   95
5.2 Selecting Instructional Foci (IF): Ecosystems   100
5.3 Selecting Instructional Foci (IF): Language Manipulations   101
7.1 A Checklist for Planning Teaching Strategies   145

Preface

Course Design attempts to bridge theory and practice in curriculum development. Intended primarily for secondary and postsecondary teachers and teachers in training, it presents the skills and concepts of curriculum development and applies them to actual course planning. The overriding goal of the book is to enable the reader to become flexible yet systematic in planning by developing a greater awareness of the alternative courses of action available at each decision point.

We begin with a set of guidelines for developing an actual course. By working through this book you will produce a design for an actual course. We guide you through this process by providing relevant design theory, frequent exercises, representative examples, a glossary of terms, bibliographic references, and, finally, two sample course designs completed by students.

These materials have been field-tested in beginning curriculum development courses over a thirty-month period at Cornell University and Smith College. Those enrolled in the courses have been primarily undergraduate and graduate students planning to teach in public schools, two-year colleges, and nonformal educational settings. The students have designed a wide variety of courses whose diverse subject matter includes beekeeping, propaganda analysis, creative writing, communication media, second-year algebra, developmental psychology, ecology, reading for parents of nonreaders, and hockey. Many refinements and revisions in this book have come about as a result of student comments and the student-developed course designs.

Course Design has four principal functions: (1) as a textbook for undergraduate courses in curriculum development and instructional design or as a supplement to a "methods" course, (2) in inservice workshops for classroom teachers at secondary and postsecondary levels, (3) for individual teachers desiring to increase their professional competence, and (4) as a self-instructional "lab" portion of beginning graduate-level courses in curriculum development or instructional design.

In the second edition we incorporated some recent developments in cognitive psychology into Chapters 2, 4, and 7. These new developments emphasize the information processing aspects of human learning. We also substantially broadened our definition of what can be considered an intended learning outcome. Here, we have focused on these same two changes but have gone further. In particular, Chapter 2 has been reorganized and expanded to include recent work on student preconceptions. Chapters 4 and 7, as well as most other chapters, have been more modestly revised.

In this third edition we have tried to preserve the general format of the book and at the same time improve its quality, increase the number of examples, and update the discussion and guidelines. Throughout, we have tried to clarify the methods for using the text with elementary teachers and teachers in training.

Every time we use this book we think of changes that would improve it. We are fortunate to have the opportunity to publish new editions, continuing to refine a basically sound approach.

We believe that these additions, modifications, and extensions of the basic approach to curriculum development are a substantial improvement for the reader.

A book such as this comes into existence more through a process of evolution than through creation. The sources of ideas are difficult to identify because they are numerous and have been incorporated into our general orientation to curriculum development. Nevertheless, we will attempt to acknowledge the major contributors.

The intellectual source of most of the book stems from the theoretical work of Mauritz Johnson. Although he did not participate directly in the preparation of the manuscript, Johnson's clarity of thought about curriculum and instruction has been both an inspiration and a conceptual guide.

Kenneth Strike contributed significantly to two chapters of the book. James Stewart, Verne Rockcastle, Karen Block, Meredith Gall, and Charles Elliott reviewed preliminary versions of the first edition of the text and provided valuable suggestions.

SUNY's Central Awards Committee, in cooperation with the Office of Instruction in the College of Agriculture and Life Science at Cornell University, provided funds for the original development, field testing, and refinement of a pilot version in 1974–1976.

Fred Finley provided valuable comments throughout the development of this edition. Graduate and undergraduate students at Cornell University and Smith College contributed innumerable significant suggestions and many of the examples provided.

Dorothy Bruscoe, Carol Grills, Marj Hulin Young, and Berni Oltz typed and retyped revision after revision.

These substantial contributions are greatly appreciated, although any errors or shortcomings are the authors' alone.

George J. Posner
Alan N. Rudnitsky

Chapter 1

Getting Oriented

After completing this chapter, the reader should:

1. Understand the format of a course-planning project and why it has been selected as a focal point for learning the concepts and skills of course planning.
2. Understand the distinction between processes and products of planning.
3. Understand the distinction between curricular and instructional matters.
4. Understand the following terms and their interrelationship: values, educational goals, curriculum, instructional plan, instruction, actual learning outcomes, and evaluation (see the Glossary for definitions).
5. Know what the three basic needs for course design are and be able to perform the preliminary research necessary to begin planning.

The Approach

This book is based on two assumptions about you, the reader. The first assumption is that you want to learn the basics of course design. The second is that you already have in mind or can come up with a particular course that you want to plan.

The first assumption is the critical one. This book can teach you how to plan courses, regardless of subject matter, institutional setting, or educational level. *Course Design* attempts to show you how to get started, to give you a sense of direction in the planning process, to make you aware of what goes into the design of courses and curricula, to help you ask the right questions at the right times, to offer alternatives at each decision point, to suggest some concepts that will serve as useful tools, and to provide examples that can expand the way you think about courses.

The second assumption stems more from the means employed in *Course Design* than from the ends. Planning is a process that requires time, energy, and commitment by the planner; learning how to design courses and curricula is similarly demanding. In order to make course planning meaningful to you, we have focused the activities of *Course Design* on a project that consists in the planning of an actual course. The project provides for the application of each concept and skill presented in this book to the particular subject matter, institutional setting, and educational level that interests you.

Focusing the learning activities of this book on your own project has important pedagogical value. If you want to learn the concepts and skills of course planning but do not have a particular course in mind, we suggest that you arbitrarily decide on a course in a familiar subject matter that can serve as a focus.

Keep in mind that the project is primarily a means to an end. The skills and concepts of course planning are primary, and the project is intended to help you acquire them. The steps followed in working through the book do teach how to plan courses, but, given the time constraints usually present, the approach may appear at times too detailed and systematic for actual course planning. This is to be expected. The approach has been designed to teach course planning but not necessarily to guide the course-planning process once the skills and concepts have been learned. Learning long division serves as a useful analogy. When we learn long division, we learn a series of specific steps to follow. But once we learn the process, we skip steps and generally divide in a more flexible and intuitive way than when we were learning it.

It is too much to expect a single approach to curriculum development to work always and for everyone. Such factors as audience, setting, subject matter, and grade level place their own particular constraints on teachers. You should feel free to modify our general approach to suit your particular circumstance.

Planning at the elementary school level has its own unique constraints. Fundamentally, elementary teachers tend to plan in unit-sized rather than course-sized sections. Elementary school units vary in scope and duration but typical units may last from two to six weeks and cover topics such as fractions, time, punctuation, myths and fairy tales, animals in winter, oceans, the Revolutionary War, and elections, to name a few.

The emphasis on unit planning is not to suggest that this is the only kind of educational planning elementary teachers can or should do. On the contrary, elementary teachers need to engage in a broader form of planning in which they consider their overall program. Units should be planned in context with other units. Units in a particular content area are preceded and followed by other units; typically, these units are related. The sequence of units is something that should be planned, not simply allowed to happen haphazardly or because publishers sequence their material in a particular way. In addition, units in one content area are taught concurrently with units in other content areas. Teachers should consider which units work particularly well together, which units conflict or are difficult to teach at the same time, and which units may depend on learning in another content area. In any case, steps that may not at first seem appropriate for elementary unit planning can prove crucial for planning that is broader in scope.

The following suggestions may prove helpful for elementary teachers:

1. Intended learning outcomes are likely to be fewer in number. Try to teach a few important ideas and skills well rather than cover too many intended learnings.
2. Some suggested course-planning steps such as formulating central questions, and sequencing and organizing a course's units may not be appropriate. We suggest that you think about all the course-planning steps and consider various alternatives, but do not become a slave to them.

At times in the text we address the particular concerns of elementary teachers. At all times, we hope you will use our suggestions flexibly and with imagination. (Some specific suggestions for elementary unit planning are included in Chapter 5; the Appendix contains a sample elementary unit design.)

The need to modify may also arise from the fact that different projects have different needs and requirements and thus will have different emphases. Teachers who have taught topics for a long time but never really considered what particular learnings they were seeking will likely put greater emphasis on clarifying their intended learning outcomes. Teachers wishing to introduce totally new types of courses will have to concentrate on the courses' justification and thus emphasize the rationale. Do not think that every component of the design process you encounter in the book requires equal emphasis and attention. Flexibility and adaptation will help make your project more meaningful.

The Project

If you complete each course-planning step in this book, you will finish with the following products:

1. A *rationale* for the course, including the overall educational goals.
2. A *curriculum plan* describing intended learning outcomes for the course categorized according to type of learning and prioritized according to importance, to be expressed in the following formats:

   a. Lists of statements and paragraphs,
   b. Maps of major ideas,
   c. Flowcharts of skills.
3. An *instructional plan* describing what each unit is about, what learning outcomes each unit is intended to accomplish, and what general teaching strategies could be used in each unit to accomplish the intended learning outcomes.
4. An *evaluation plan* describing behavioral indicators for each high-priority intended learning outcome (main effects), together with a list of some unintended, undesirable learning outcomes (side effects) to be on the lookout for.

You will make other products along the way, such as course outlines and central questions. For the purposes of this book, these are considered instrumental products, used mainly to improve the major components listed above. Instructors using this text in class may or may not require that these instrumental products be part of a final project.

In the appendixes you will find two completed course designs that might give you some idea of our aim.

Some Guidelines for Getting Started

Now that you have an idea what this book is about, you can start planning a course as a focal point for learning the basics of curriculum development. Decide on a course you want to plan. In making your decision consider the following points: (1) Your course may run as long as a whole year or it may be as short as a four-week "minicourse." (2) Choose a course for which you know the subject matter well. It is difficult to plan something that is unfamiliar to you. (3) Create a course to answer some educational need, whether it be a learner or a societal need, a "felt" or an "unfelt" need. (4) Don't be afraid to create a unique course; you may want to give a traditional course a different emphasis, combine diverse subject matter, or adjust a course usually taught to one audience so that it can be taught to a different (for example, older, more heterogeneous, more "turned off") audience.

Motivation for Planning

When you begin to plan a course you may have any number of ideas, resources, or restrictions fixed in your mind. You may have received a mandate from an administrative source (for example, the State Education Department) specifying goals or requiring a certain level of student achievement. An existing course may not be producing satisfactory results. Students may not be taking with them the math they need for next year's work. You may want to implement a new teaching technique and may find the existing course inappropriately organized for such a technique. A school may provide a new language laboratory, a nature trail, a computer terminal, or sophisticated audiovisual equipment that will extend the capabilities of teachers, and courses will have to be created or re-created to use these new resources. Courses at a two-year college may not be attracting students, and new courses may be needed to attract students to the college. Courses previously considered appropriate for a particular kind of student may have to be redesigned as the student population becomes more mature or more heterogeneous. A new middle school may require courses specifically designed for its population and institutional purposes.

All sources for course planning provide "givens" that affect the start of the planning process, and they should be made explicit from the beginning if the course-planning process is to proceed in an open and systematic manner rather than on the basis of some hidden agenda.

Audience for the Course

Right at the outset and, indeed, all the way through the planning process a guiding principle should be to consider the students at every stage. It is necessary to consider carefully their maturity, needs, interests, abilities, and knowledge. If you are unfamiliar with the characteristics and background of your intended audience you will have some preliminary work to do before beginning to plan the course. The following resources may help you learn about your audience:

1. Texts in educational psychology covering both the psychology of human learning and human development.
2. Observations or practice teaching at a local school or college with a student population similar to yours.
3. Interviews with teachers who have taught students similar to yours.

We will have more to say about understanding your students in Chapter 2.

Current Approaches to the Subject

Another requisite for course planning is a thorough understanding of the subject matter. One part of this understanding is an ability to identify and explain the details and relationships in the subject. Another part of this understanding is a familiarity with current curricular approaches to the subject matter. If you are unfamiliar with the current approaches, you may want to do some preliminary work before you begin course planning. The following suggestions may be useful:

1. Collect as many current textbooks and syllabi in the subject as you can. Skim through each of them and study their contents pages in particular in order to get an idea of what is currently being taught in the subject.
2. Try to find out (from texts, teachers, or syllabi) what the students usually study in the subject or related subjects before they get to your course. Also try to determine what they may study in the subject after they complete your course.
3. Talk with teachers in your subject in order to identify topics, approaches to the subject, resources, exercises, and activities that seem to have the potential for stimulating interest.

Course planning begins with and is based on three things: a clearly recognized motivation or source; a recognition of the capacities, needs, and interests of the students; and a familiarity with current approaches to the subject matter.

Questions for Discussion: Getting Started

1. In what general area do you want to plan a course (civics, English, dance, filmmaking, reading, gardening, biology, ecology)?
2. Can you make a list of courses you have taken (or taught) specifically in this or a related area?
3. How might those courses differ from the courses you want to plan? How might they be similar?
4. Do you have something special in mind for your course (a new technique, a special audience, new equipment)?
5. What are five questions an interested party might ask about your course?

COURSE-PLANNING STEP 1.1.   Write a brief paragraph describing your course.

With these initial thoughts in mind, it may be helpful to get an overview of *Course Design* before proceeding further with your project.

A Framework for Course Design*

Any systematic approach to course planning must be considered within the context of a theoretical framework. At the least such a framework must identify important aspects of the planning process and must show

---

*Much of the following discussion has been adapted from Johnson (1967). The reader is encouraged to read his paper for a deeper understanding of the conceptual framework underlying this book.

how these aspects are interrelated. This section presents such a framework.

The basic concept such a framework must deal with is *curriculum*. There are almost as many definitions of curriculum as there are writers, and we do not claim that any one definition is correct. Nevertheless, certain conceptual distinctions are useful in course planning, and certain definitions of curriculum make these important distinctions. One such distinction is that between processes and products of planning. Another distinction is that between curricular and instructional matters.

Process-Product

A process consists of one or more events. A product is something produced by a process. Planning is usually a highly complex process, and a plan is the product of that process.

In order to make several points regarding this distinction, let us examine a noneducational but relatively familiar planning situation. A blueprint for a proposed building is a plan developed by an architect. In the planning (a process) the architect considers architectural form, building materials, characteristics of the proposed site, intended use of the building, energy efficiency, and many other factors. The blueprint is the result (a product) of the planning and it guides the process of construction. A blueprint specifies what the product of construction should be but does not specify how the process of construction (the construction schedule) should proceed. This analogy illustrates how a plan may (but does not have to) be for an anticipated process (for example, construction). Also, a complex process such as building houses may be broken down into discrete component processes, such as preparing blueprints, preparing a construction schedule, and constructing the house according to the blueprint.

Curriculum-Instruction

Instruction is obviously a process—a series of events intended to lead to some learning outcomes. As such, it is analogous to the process of house construction. Instruction consists of providing activities, overt or covert, for some content or subject matter. Instructional matters, then, have to do with the nature of the activities and content that make up the process of instruction. The process of instruction is guided by a plan analogous to a construction schedule, termed the *instructional plan*.

It is important to distinguish instruction from curriculum. Curriculum is not a process. Many (if not most) books on education consider curriculum as consisting of experiences or the activities that engender these experiences. But this usage confuses curriculum with instruction. A more precise view of curriculum—and the common understanding of curriculum among laypeople—is that it is what is taught in school or what is intended to be learned. It does not refer to what is to be *done* in school or what is to *happen* in the learning process. Curriculum represents a set of *intentions*, a set of intended learning outcomes. Consequently, curricular matters have to do with the nature and organization of those things we as course planners want learned in our courses. Curriculum development results in a design specifying the desired learnings (the intended learning outcomes); thus, curriculum is analogous to a blueprint or an architectural design. Instructional planning, on the other hand, results in a plan outlining the intended process of instruction; thus, an instructional plan is analogous to a construction schedule. A curriculum and an instructional plan are as different as a design for a new house and a plan giving the steps in its construction. Yet they are related in that a blueprint is a necessary guide for planning a construction schedule.

Curriculum development entails selection and organization of a set of intended learning outcomes. Selecting intended learning outcomes is made more rational by basing them on the educational goals to be served. Educational goals should indicate what the learning should lead to, not what it consists of; they describe intended educational results in much the same way curriculum describes intended learning outcomes. (See Chapter 3 for more details on educational goals.) Educational results derive from the complex, interactive, and cumulative effects of actual learning outcomes, intended and unintended, both in school and outside school, in addition to maturation and other forces acting on students. Educational goals describe desired results of the entire educational process. The selection of intended learning outcomes (i.e., curriculum development) represents the best guess as to what needs to be learned to achieve the educational goals. Using our terminology, if a statement is in terms of things to be learned it is curricular; if it is in terms of attributes of the well-educated person it is an educational goal; if it is in terms of teaching strategies, it is instructional.

Thus, the *curriculum* indicates *what* is to be learned, the *goals* indicate *why* it is to be learned, and the *instructional plan* indicates *how* to facilitate learning. None of these three planning processes—curriculum development, goal setting, and instructional planning—results in any learning. Only the instruction process does that.

Figure 1.1 depicts the major processes related to course planning and their resulting products. The arrows in the figure should be interpreted as processes, the boxes as products. Moving from left to right on the chart, one answers various implementation questions. How do we implement our values? By aiming at a particular educational goal. How do we implement our educational goal? By having students learn par-

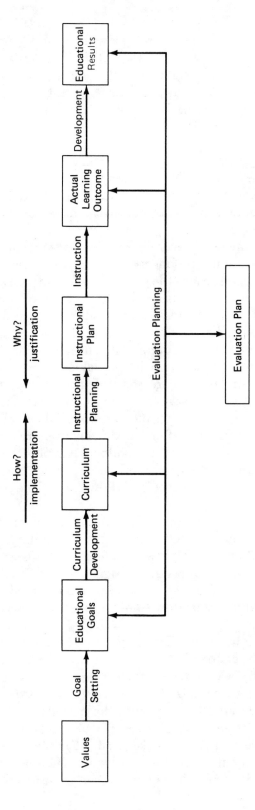

Figure 1.1. A Curriculum Instruction Model (adapted from Johnson, 1967).

ticular things (a particular curriculum). How do we implement our curriculum? By providing particular activities (that is, a particular instructional plan). Moving from right to left, one answers justification questions: Why this instructional plan? Because instructional planning was guided by this curriculum. Why this curriculum? Because we are aiming at this educational goal. And so on.

Notice in Figure 1.1 that an additional process is included—that of evaluation. For the purposes of this book, evaluation planning will consist of specifying a set of sample indicators that can be used to analyze actual learning outcomes and educational results. The approach used will emphasize evaluation for course improvement rather than for grading individual students.

Although this framework generally clarifies for students the logical relations among educational products and processes, it also misleads in several significant ways. Perhaps the greatest danger in using this framework is that people interpret it as a guide to the *steps* of course design. At times the framework will function adequately as such a guide, but generally it is counterproductive to assume that this conceptual overview is also a procedural model. For example, it is usually wrong to insist on developing curriculum only after goals and values have been specified. Goals and values do underlie our reasons for including particular curricular content, but it is not always necessary to specify those goals and values first. Actually, it is often possible to think productively about abstract topics (such as goals) only after thinking about more concrete matters (such as curricular content and instructional techniques). Therefore, it is important when using the framework to remember that it is a conceptual overview rather than a procedural flowchart of the course design process.

Related to this issue is the assumption by some readers that course design is a fairly straightforward linear process. If anything, the authors have probably contributed to this belief by depicting a linear framework in Figure 1.1 and by presenting course design in a step-by-step manner. We have obviously oversimplified the process and the reader should be careful not to fall into the trap of thinking about course design in a strictly linear manner.

A linear approach is one in which each step is completed before the next one is begun. In course design, no steps are ever completed once and for all. Generally, we move to the next step after making a rough approximation because we realize that we will be in a better position to continue our work on an early step with the insights that a later step provides. A course design evolves as a series of successive approximations. In fact, course designs are never really completed. Rather, we "abandon" further planning for the time being. The same can be said of our course-planning steps. There is no reason to insist on any degree of finality to a course-planning step so long as we remember that we will be returning to that step at a later time equipped with new ideas and clearer thinking.

With this general framework in mind, it may be useful to specify the relationship between process/products and the corresponding chapters of *Course Design*.

Generally speaking, values and educational goals are described in the course's rationale. This component is developed in Chapter 3. Curriculum is described, in part, in the course's statement of intended learning outcomes and the conceptual map(s) for the course. The intended learning outcomes are selected and their organization analyzed in Chapter 2, and they are further refined in Chapter 4. The instructional plan is described in the unit outline of the course developed in Chapters 5, 6, and 7. The approach to evaluation is described in the course's evaluation plan, a component of course design developed in Chapter 8. Figure 1.2 summarizes the relationships between the model and components of course design as presented in this book.

Questions for Discussion:
The Conceptual Framework

1. What are the advantages and disadvantages of defining curriculum as "an organized set of intended learning outcomes"?
2. Although ends and means are relative, isn't there an ultimate end? What happens when we ask the question "Why?" of an underlying value?
3. What questions (other than "Why?", "What?", "How?", and "Was it successful?") should a course design help to answer?
4. The analogy between curriculum development and the design of houses is not perfect. In what ways does the analogy break down?
5. Do values ever influence curriculum development and instructional planning directly rather than indirectly through educational goals?

Curriculum Development
and Teacher Thinking

The teaching environment, as Yinger (1978) notes, is characterized by complexity, a fast pace, and unpredictability. Teachers must think constantly about managerial concerns, covering the material, how students are doing, what is coming next, and what has transpired, to name a few. Teachers must respond quickly to a tremendous variety of situations and events. In such an environment careful planning can have substan-

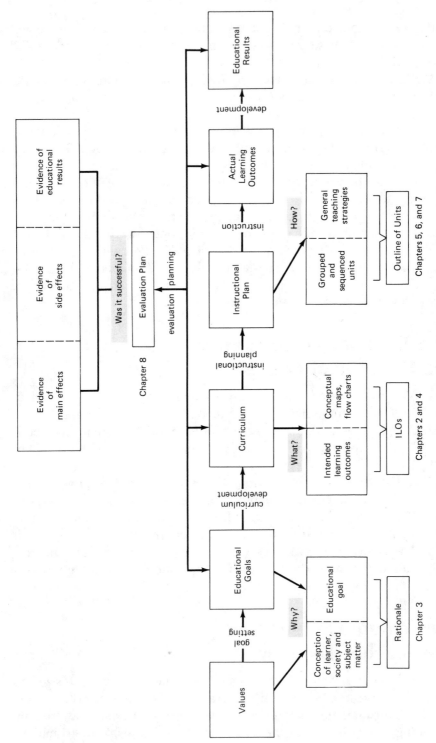

Figure 1.2. Relationship between the Model and Components of *Course Design*.

tial benefits. However, no instructional plan can anticipate the unexpected. An instructional plan tells teachers what materials to use, what learning activities students should engage in, what sequence these activities should take, and more. But, of course, an instructional plan cannot tell a teacher how to respond to spontaneous classroom interactions. These unpredictable yet commonplace occurrences are significant aspects of instruction and can thus have significant effects on the outcomes of instruction. The ways in which teachers respond to these events depend to a great extent on what and how they are thinking.

A curriculum is commonly thought of as a guide to instructional planning. If it only guided instructional planning, a curriculum would be important but of limited direct significance in day-to-day classroom teaching. However, we have found that the curriculum, or at least the curriculum development process, can also guide teachers in their responses to daily unexpected classroom events. Our experience with *Course Design* is that it has a significant effect on teachers' thinking and on how they act in the classroom. Teachers report that the design process, as a whole, has given them a clear conception of what they want learned and this conception has directly affected their teaching. Teachers find themselves better able to respond to questions and comments in a focused way, to ask pertinent questions, to react to various types of student errors, and to take advantage of unplanned teachable moments. As a result of engaging in the design process, teachers have found that their judgments about their own teaching effectiveness become increasingly based on what and how students learn, not just on how smoothly the day went.

A clear conception of what is to be learned in a course is, perhaps, the major goal of *Course Design*. This clear conception is more than statements of outcomes; it is bound up in a design process that includes justification for learnings and how these learnings will be actualized and evaluated. As you work through the various steps of *Course Design*, keep in mind that this process is intended to affect your everyday thinking as well as your planning.

References

Johnson, M. "Definitions and Models in Curriculum Theory." *Educational Theory* 17, no. 2 (1967): 127–139.

Yinger, R. J. *A Study of Teacher Planning: Description and a Model of Preactive Decision Making* (Research Series No. 18). East Lansing, MI: Michigan State University, Institute for Research on Teaching, July 1978.

Chapter 2

Setting a Direction

After completing this chapter, the reader should be able to:

1. Comprehend the meaning and significance of intended learning outcome (ILO).
2. Generate an initial list of ideas for a course.
3. Develop a tentative course outline.
4. Generate one or more central questions for a course.
5. Distinguish ILOs from teaching strategies, materials, activities, and other initial ideas.
6. Identify ILOs implicit in desirable teaching strategies, materials, activities, and test items.
7. Categorize ILOs into skill and understanding categories.
8. Construct a flowchart for a course or a unit.
9. Construct a conceptual map for a course or a unit.
10. Use flowcharts and conceptual maps as a way of expressing ILOs for a course.

Generating Initial Ideas

It is important at the beginning of course planning to have something tangible with which to work. The first step is to create a list of "initial ideas." This list may take virtually any form and may consist of words and phrases or sentences identifying subject matter, content areas, specific facts, teaching techniques, and so on. It may contain the names of specific books; it may list other resources. Anything important to the course should go on an "ideas" list. At this point it is not important that the list be consistent or balanced.

COURSE-PLANNING STEP 2.1. Jot down any and all ideas you have for your course on a list of initial ideas. The following example illustrates the form these initial ideas may take for an environmental science course. Absolutely no restrictions are placed on this list.

the relationships of various environmental systems
respect and care for the environment

forest succession
ecosystems
food chains
producers, consumers, decomposers
field trips to forest, field, pond
Sapsucker Woods Bird Sanctuary
individual project
plant and animal identification
how one affects environment
pollution
niches
become better individuals
blindfolded walk
build terrarium
nature trail

Once you have made an initial list, your course should be given a title. A title may be creative and novel or it may be traditional. A good way to formulate a title is to consider your list of initial ideas and see if an appropriate title emerges. Planners sometimes have a title for a course in their minds at the outset of planning. If this is true in your case and if this title does not conflict with your initial ideas, use it.

COURSE-PLANNING STEP 2.2. Give your course a title. To title your as yet incompletely specified ideas, you must consider whether or not these ideas are coherent. This is the primary purpose of supplying a title at this point. It is the first of many considerations of the relationship of the parts to the whole, a consideration that gives an initial focus for the course.

With your initial ideas and tentative title in hand, you are ready to elaborate on your ideas. Developing a tentative course outline will contribute to this ongoing process.

Developing a Tentative Course Outline

A course outline contains the major ideas, components, or topics of the subject you are planning to teach. As mentioned in Chapter 1, the task of curriculum development presupposes subject-matter expertise on the part of the planner; and a course outline affords the planner an opportunity to lay out that subject matter concisely. This concise outline will be of help in making sure there are no gaps in the presentation of the subject matter, in making decisions about audience appropriateness, in identifying intended learnings, and in organizing the course content.

Course outlines vary depending on the nature of the course being planned. One aspect of this variation is the outline's degree of detail. Highly detailed outlines may include specific factual information. Less detailed outlines will include only major topics and subtopics. Relatively short units can be described in more detail than complete courses. Another factor to consider in deciding on how much to include is your own knowledge of and confidence with the subject matter. You may find it useful to outline in greater detail topics and/or subtopics for which your knowledge is less thorough.

The best way to produce a tentative course outline is to consult several good resource books on the topics. Some of your initial research on current curricular approaches will be relevant here (see page 6). The outline should be written as you peruse these references. The exact sequence of the topics in the outline is not particularly important at this stage. Decisions about whether particular content is appropriate for the intended audience need not be made now, unless these decisions are obvious. Of far greater importance is the outline's inclusiveness and that the format adequately represents the relative importance of the subtopics under each topic.

Courses that do not focus on traditional subject matter will have to have outlines suited to their content. The teaching of reading, writing, typing, or instrumental music, to name a few, are typically performance-oriented courses. A course outline for subjects like these should break down the overall performance into subtopics that can be separately addressed. A reading unit, for example, could be divided into the following subtopics: decoding using phonic cues, decoding using the context, decoding by structural analysis, reading for literal meaning, making inferences for news articles, and so on. Regardless of course type, an outline of the course is the planner's first chance to think systematically about the substantive elements of the subject.

COURSE-PLANNING STEP 2.3.   Develop a tentative course outline.

Intended Learning Outcomes (ILOs)

The primary product of this planning phase is a stated set of *intended learning outcomes*, or learning objectives. An intended learning outcome is a statement of what the student is to learn. It may be a statement about facts, ideas, principles, capabilities, skills, techniques, values, or feelings. A set of ILO statements may be altered, reconsidered, and refined, but it is an important part of almost every step in course planning.

Since the notion of ILO is crucial to all that follows, let us examine it in more detail. The use of the word "intended" emphasizes control and direction in the educational process. A course may result in many outcomes, and some of them may be quite accidental, whether good or bad. Course planning does not proceed on the hope of accidental learning but with lucid stateable intentions. The word "learning" is again used advisedly, for it emphasizes that the major purpose of planning a course is to affect student learning. Courses are for students, not for teachers or for testers. A student may learn more or less than a teacher has actually taught. Much of the content taught (for example, the use of examples) may be only instrumental for the learning of particular concepts, principles, attitudes, and skills. Similarly, for one reason or another a student may or may not meet the requirements of a certain test and still may have learned what was intended. Finally, the word "outcome" indicates that our major concern is what the student will gain after completing the course.

The next step in developing a focus is selecting intended learning outcomes from the initial list of ideas and the course outline; other ILOs will be added later. The process of selecting important material to be learned is, in part, a process of "drawing a ring" around the course's learning objectives. This consists of deciding what the course will and will not be about. After this decision has been reached, the material can be further specified so that all the learnings important to the course are included.

Identifying ILOs

The first step in the process of selecting intended learnings is to decide which items on the list of initial ideas and in the course outline represent intended learning outcomes. These ILOs may be facts, ideas, theories, or other types of information that the student is expected to learn as a result of the course. Ecosystems, food chains, the causes of World War II, and the characteristics of a good diet are examples of content to be learned. ILOs may also be skills, competencies, or values. Touch typing, math computation, clear speaking, and proper grammar are examples of skills to be learned. Intended learnings may also include values such as respect for the environment, for honest advertising, and for the rights of others. Specific teaching strategies are not intended learning outcomes. Special materials, such as particular books, film strips, videotapes, or programmed instruction units, are not intended learning outcomes. We must also leave out field trips, group projects, and oral reports. Nevertheless, all these things must be examined carefully to ascertain what specific intended learnings they suggest. For example, if a field trip is on the list of initial ideas or in the course outline, consider why a field trip is important. What will students be expected to learn from the trip (for example, an ability to apply ecological concepts in a natural setting)?

An ILO comes into being because you think an item in your list of initial ideas or course outline is something to be learned. Use your judgment and imagination. Do not omit potentially important ILOs because an item "doesn't look like an ILO." Some ILOs are obvious and explicit; others, however, are implicit and require thinking if they are to be identified. It is better to have too many rather than too few ILOs. Later course-planning steps will help you refine your ILOs.

EXERCISE 2.1.* The lists below represent what might be lists of initial ideas. Identify obvious and explicit ILOs in the lists with a check mark.

1. *Creative Cooking*
   types of kitchen tools
   ? the student knows what a frying pan is for
   Rombauer's *Joy of Cooking*
   ability to test cake to see if done
   trip to local restaurant
   how to bake bread
   cooking not a specifically female thing
   desserts
   knowledge of menu planning
   manual cooking skills: kneading, sautéing, flipping crepes, stir-frying
   how to plan before you cook
   meats
   vegetable protein
   each student prepares own dish—bring-a-dish meal
   safe use of knives

2. *English Grammar and Composition*
   complex and compound sentences
   parts of speech (verb, noun, article, adjective, adverb, etc.)
   correct punctuation
   recognizes sentence fragments
   choice of words
   learns from reading
   appreciates own good writing
   uses commas with nonrestrictive relative clauses
   avoids run-on sentences
   doesn't use dialect forms in formal writing
   use of exercises as teaching device
   assign compositions every week
   short stories
   spelling tests weekly

*Answers to Exercises appear at the end of each chapter.

3. *Social Studies*
   small-group discussions
   knowledge of what constitutes an institution
   institutions are self-perpetuating
   enlightened self-interest in relationship to society
   essay on democratic vs. autocratic institutions
   cooperatives
   media as used by social forces
   recognizes institutional interests
   extensive use of library sources
   films
   types of institutions: social, religious, commercial
   how institutions change

4. *American History—The Post-Revolutionary Period*
   knows significance of the dates: 1776, 1803, 1812
   Jefferson, Adams, Madison
   debates
   understands the causes of the War of 1812
   can describe the attack against Tripoli
   can describe why Hamilton accepted a duel with Burr
   film: *The Burr Conspiracy*
   the U.S. Constitution
   economic trends
   America takes her place among the nations of the world
   the situation with Britain and France at the time
   projects
   the Embargo Act of 1807
   description of the burning of Washington
   knows the origin of the national anthem

EXERCISE 2.2. In Exercise 2.1 you selected the ILOs already apparent in the lists. For this exercise, go back to the lists and develop possible
ILOs that are implicit or suggested rather than explicit

COURSE-PLANNING STEP 2.4. All ILOs, either explicit or implicit,
in your list of initial ideas and course outline should now be written on
a separate list, "the list of ILOs."

Categorizing ILOs

For the purposes of curricular and instructional planning, it is often useful to categorize learning into types. Categorization is useful because
different types of learning require different types of instruction, differ-

ent considerations when sequencing and organizing the course, and different types of evaluation. At this point in the planning process, ILOs are grouped into two categories: skills and understandings. Generally speaking, understandings comprise the information and beliefs with which we think. Understandings can be thought of as "knowing that" (including "knowing" in a deep sense, not just memorizing). Ideas, concepts, facts, principles, theories, and generalizations are some of the things that can be known. Skills can be thought of as "knowing how." Skills are things students are able to do at the end of a course. Skills include mental abilities, such as problem solving, reading, arithmetic computation, interpretation, analysis, application; and physical abilities, such as bicycling and ball throwing.

For most courses, some balance between skills and understandings is desirable. A course stressing only skills is more characteristic of training than of education. Such a course aims at having students learn how to do things but not at learning the principles behind what they are doing. For example, a good physical education course teaches the rules of the game and the basis for good sportsmanship. On the other hand, a course stressing only understandings may equip students with a set of ideas but may leave them without any competencies. A course of this type may not provide students with the ability to use what they have learned. A good English literature course, for example, teaches the skills of literary criticism.

COURSE-PLANNING STEP 2.5.   Categorize your ILOs into skills and understandings.

This is the first time in the planning process that items are categorized under specific headings (skills/understandings), but you will be called on to perform this type of operation again. This is a part of the process of giving your course direction and assists you in planning and determining such things as completeness and balance. This categorization is not just an exercise, but an instrumental step in the planning process.

Formulating Central Questions*

Initial ideas, a course outline, and a list of tentative ILOs describe the scope of your course. Central questions, questions that are fundamental to the course and that identify the focus of the course, help to give these elements coherence. In order to develop central questions, formulate the

---

*We are indebted to the work of Gowin (1970) for this idea, although he used the term "telling questions."

most important questions addressed in the course. Different courses have different focal points and, therefore, different types of appropriate central questions. In some cases the central questions can be answered correctly by a student successfully completing the course. In other cases, such as those in philosophy or literature, the questions may be open-ended, and the student who completes the course should be able to deal with these questions independently, rather than be able to answer them correctly. Courses range from ones emphasizing understanding and appreciations, to those emphasizing problems or decisions, to those emphasizing skill acquisition and personal growth.

Inquiry Orientation

In general, an inquiry orientation aims at understanding. In some inquiry-oriented courses the teacher and students explore topics in a search for underlying reasons for, meanings of, or implications of events. Inquiry-oriented courses might also investigate the structure or function of living things, objects, systems, or social organizations. Or they might study the meaning of particular concepts, such as humanity, reality, truth, or equality. Inquiry-oriented courses would be best summarized by questions such as the following:

What is X?
What are (or were) the causes of X?
What are the implications of X?
What is the structure (or function) of X?
What does X mean (what is its nature or essence)?
Why does (did) X occur?
How does (did) X happen?

These general questions are only intended to suggest the form some central questions might take, rather than to limit you in formulating central questions for your course.

Appreciation Orientation

Appreciation-oriented courses help the student develop taste, whether that taste is in literature, music, fine arts, dance, or theater. In such courses students typically experience art through reading, viewing, listening to, or participating in the creation of an art product. While doing so, students develop personal preferences and also learn the criteria that experts use in critiquing a piece of art. Central questions for such courses are of the sort, "What do I like, and why do I like it?"

Problem Orientation

Some courses focus on developing the students' ability to solve problems. For example, philosophers of science have described the training of physicists as instruction in how to categorize physical phenomena (such as pulleys) as a type of problem (an equilibrium-of-forces problem), and how to solve a variety of these problem types. Mathematics (for example, elementary algebra) can be similarly characterized, though being problem oriented does not mean that a course cannot also be inquiry oriented. The range of courses that focus on problems is very broad. Business courses focusing on management problems, interdisciplinary courses focusing on environmental problems, psychology courses focusing on coping with personal problems, and courses aimed at teaching general problem-solving methods represent only a sample of possibilities. In problem-oriented courses, the central questions would be of the type, "How does one solve problems X, Y, and Z?" Probably a listing of the major problems or problem types is the best central question format for these courses.

Decision Orientation

Decision-oriented courses provide the student with information or frameworks on which to base decisions, and sometimes even with a step-by-step method for arriving at a decision. Decisions such as what career to pursue, what types of energy conservation measures to take, and what kind of used car to buy are typical. Included here would also be courses aimed at helping individuals with moral decisions. Some courses allow the decisions to be open-ended, whereas other courses assume a prespecified decision. A course in car buying may or may not be biased toward fuel efficient cars but a drug education course is very likely to be biased toward a decision not to use (or, at least, not to abuse) drugs. Decision-oriented courses are best represented by central questions that simply list the decisions.

Skill Orientation

Still other courses are most appropriately described as skill-oriented. A skill orientation emphasizes improving performance in carrying out physical tasks. Skill-oriented courses emphasize "how to do it," whether "it" is driving a car, typing, or playing ice hockey. Central questions for such courses will typically be of the type, "How does one (or what is the proper way to) do X?" Often such questions include qualifiers for X such as "safely," "efficiently," "critically," and "with good sportsmanship."

Personal Growth Orientation

Though not entirely distinguishable from some of the other orientations, a personal growth orientation attempts to help the student define a personal goal (typically a psychological state, such as "self-actualization") and then to develop ways to work toward that goal. Such courses are usually grounded in theories of psychological counseling. Appropriate central questions are of the sort, "What are my goals and how do I work toward them?"

It should be obvious that any real course is unlikely to represent only one of these types. Some courses might even be inquiry, appreciation, problem, decision, skill, and personal growth oriented all at once. The important point is that your central questions should reflect the central concerns of *your* course. How many and what kinds of central questions naturally depend on the course. The following course titles accompanied by central questions serve as illustrations:

1. Driver Education
   What is the proper way to drive an automobile safely?
2. American History 1700–1800
   What political, social, and economic forces shaped America during this period? What was "revolutionary" about the United States?
3. Environmental Science
   How should I, as an individual, interact with my environment in a mutually beneficent way? What elements make up an ecosystem, and what is the nature of their interaction?
4. Philosophy
   What is the nature of reality? How do I give meaning to my life?
5. Social Studies (from *Man: A Course of Study*)
   What is human about human beings? How did they get that way? How can they be made more so?

Central questions do not include all the interesting or important questions for a particular course, but they should concern what is most fundamental to it. Central questions represent the "heart" of a course. They are the questions that, once discovered by a student, serve as the focus for study. That is, a student who discovers a course's central questions might remark, "Aha! Now I see what this course is about. Now I see what the purpose is."

Obviously, the more central questions you specify, the less focused your course will appear. If you have a large number of central questions (more than five), you might attempt to organize them into major questions, each with associated subquestions. Such a procedure will maintain the scope of your course, while forcing you to examine its coherence.

One way to generate central questions is to imagine that you are developing a final examination for your course consisting of less than six essay questions. What would these questions be? This might be a good time to write out your ideal answers to these questions.

COURSE-PLANNING STEP 2.6.   Examine your list of initial ideas, ILOs, and tentative course outline and write down the central questions that give coherence to your course. Now reconsider your ILOs in light of these questions.

Thinking about central questions at this stage of course planning should help you in identifying the central or unifying theme of your course. You may find that your course will need revision in order to achieve a focus. In general, thinking about central questions is another way to evaluate and continue to develop your course. These questions are only one of several tools you will be taught for thinking about your course.

Questions for Discussion: Central Questions

1. What do your central questions tell you about the focus of your course?
2. Are one or two of your questions the real focus of your course and the others secondary or subquestions? From your list of central questions, which ones truly represent the "heart" of your course?
3. What would be unacceptable answers to some of your central questions?
4. What kinds of questions are you asking? Are you more interested in "where" and "when" or in "why" and "how"?
   a. If you are more interested in "where" and "when" questions, what does that suggest about your course?
   b. If you are more interested in "why" and "how" questions, what does that suggest about your course?
5. What are some of the evaluative words you have used in your questions (good, bad, useful, beneficial, harmful, efficient, growth, interest)? What does this suggest about your course?
6. Are there some central questions that might appear relevant to your course, but which you would reject? Explain why you would reject them.
7. To what extent do these questions take the student into consideration? The society in which the student lives? The subject matter?
8. Show your questions to an expert in the field. Does the expert agree with your focus? How do you account for any discrepancies?

COURSE-PLANNING STEP 2.7. Expand your list of ILOs keeping the central questions (above) in mind.

Although central questions, lists of ILOs, and course outlines are useful tools for thinking about the scope and coherence of your course, they are not sufficient. More schematic tools such as charts are needed. Two schematic tools will be discussed in this chapter: conceptual maps and flowcharts. Conceptual maps are appropriate for representing understandings; flowcharts are most useful for analyzing skills.

Conceptual Maps

The technique you will learn in this section is called conceptual mapping. You already know about maps as diagrammatic representations of geographical regions. Maps of this type show where you are in relation to other geographical points. For example, road maps help you to "get your bearings and to proceed to your destination" (Anderson, 1979, p. 17). Conceptual maps are like road maps, but they are concerned with relationships among ideas, rather than places. Conceptual maps also help you to "get your bearings" in designing a course—to clarify the kinds of ideas you want taught—so that you can proceed toward your destination of real student learning.

This is the first stage of conceptual mapping. Here we will focus on identifying key ideas and arranging them in a reasonable pattern. In Chapter 4 we will elaborate on this technique further, identifying and representing specific relationships among ideas. The reader may want to continue with the discussion of maps in Chapter 4, temporarily skipping Chapter 3.

In a conceptual map, ideas are depicted as related to one another. These ideas include concepts, theories, facts, rules, propositions, principles, and generalizations. Maps may depict relationships among ideas as simple or complex, clear or indefinite.

Figure 2.1 is a simple map. It is definite and clear but gives us only limited information. The first thing the chart indicates is that each labeled node represents a subcategory under the category "cooking with heat." Reading down from the top of the chart shows us that there are two major subcategories for "cooking with heat," one using the stove top and one using the oven. If the oven is used, two methods can be employed; indirect heat and direct heat. This is a hierarchical map. It specifies only two things, but it does this definitely and exhaustively: subcategory identification and membership. For example, simmer, boil, and steam are all members of the subcategory water. Likewise, oil and water are members of the subcategory stove top. This method of mapping is simple, definite, and complete. It specifies precisely every relationship it sets out to. Nevertheless, it is important to note that many other re-

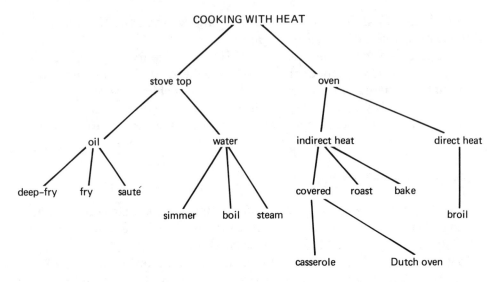

Figure 2.1. Cooking with Heat.

lationships are not specified. For example, the relationship between bake and roast is seen here only as membership in the same subcategory. Likewise, the similarity of boil to deep-fry is not shown in the diagram. This simple hierarchical diagram simply does not have the capacity for showing these relationships. A hierarchical diagram is a graphic presentation of conceptual structure in terms of the relationship of classes to constituency.

But maps do not have to be hierarchical diagrams. Ideas may be related in ways other than class membership. One idea (a) may *cause* another (increased inflation is one *consequence* of government spending), (b) may be compared with another with regard to magnitude (the amount of solar radiation the earth absorbs *equals* the amount it radiates), and (c) may be a *property* of another (hurricanes have *high* winds and torrential rains). These are only examples of the many possible relationships among ideas.

For example, Figure 2.2 is a conceptual map for a social studies unit on rice growing. Instead of a hierarchical arrangement, causal relations seem more appropriate for this content. According to this map four factors affect rice growing: fresh water, a flat area, fertile soil, and warm temperature. Other concepts could be added through more detailed analysis. For example, irrigation could be added between "river or lake" and "supply of fresh water." Collins (1977) discusses in detail how such a map could guide the teaching of a student using Socratic questioning.

When you construct a conceptual map you do not have to choose which one of the many possible relationships your map will feature. A

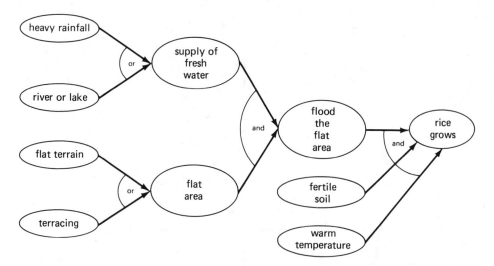

Figure 2.2. The Causal Factors Affecting Rice Growing (adapted from Collins, 1977).

map may employ several kinds of relationships. For example, Figure 2.3 illustrates three factors that *influence* freshwater habitats, and two *aspects* of the adaptation of freshwater inhabitants to their habitats.

Obviously, the kinds of relationships featured in your conceptual map will depend primarily on the subject matter and the relationships within that subject matter that concern you as a planner. Making those relationships more specific and explicit will be one of the topics treated in Chapter 4.

One issue that almost always surfaces when constructing maps concerns the appropriate level of detail. Using our earlier comparison of conceptual maps with geographical maps, we might think of a map as "view" of the "conceptual terrain" in a course. In a sense, there is a trade-off between the level of detail (the "resolution") and the scope (the "field of vision") of information included in a particular view of the terrain. The broader the "field of vision" we wish for our view, the less "resolution" we can provide. Similarly, the higher the resolution of our view (the "finer grained"), the more restricted our field will be.

It is very difficult to represent all the major concepts of a course on one map. Instead, a series of maps with varying degrees of detail is probably a more fruitful approach. This approach is similar to that followed in atlases. A world atlas might contain maps of the world, maps of continents, maps of countries, and even maps of provinces and states. Maps of states may even contain "inserts" depicting major cities within a state. Although the level of complexity of an atlas is far greater than the complexity of a conceptual map for a course, the general approach may be

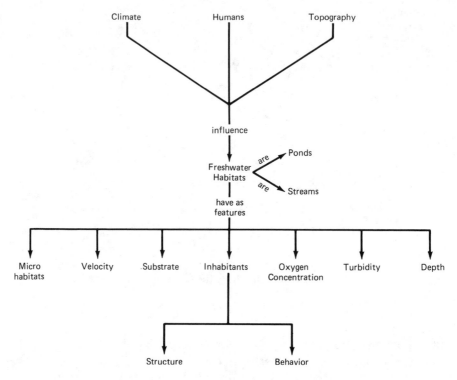

Figure 2.3. A Conceptual Map for a Course on Freshwater Habitats.

useful. For example, some students have found it useful to construct a general conceptual map for their course, then to detail portions of their general maps for each of their units or even for each of their lessons.

COURSE-PLANNING STEP 2.8. Analyze the important terminology contained in your skill and understanding ILOs and course outline, and list all terms you feel are representative of the major ideas you want your students to understand.

The following list of words might represent the major ideas in one teacher's physics course on mechanics:

Mechanics	Direction
Kinetics	Force
Dynamics	Mass
Particle	Rest
Body	Acceleration
Motion	

COURSE-PLANNING STEP 2.9.   Arrange the list of words signifying ideas and add interconnecting lines until you have a diagram or set of diagrams illustrating the interrelationships among the ideas particular to the course. Add any ideas that you feel are needed to make your map(s) meaningful and complete.

Figure 2.4 shows the arrangement of terms produced by one university faculty member. Other "correct" arrangements are possible.

COURSE-PLANNING STEP 2.10.   Evaluate the map(s). Have you depicted major relationships clearly? Can the map(s) be simplified and still effectively communicate the relationships you consider most important?

Conceptual maps are useful for thinking about your course. In fact, mapping is an important step toward acquiring a clear conception of what you want learned. Understandings are, in many ways, more adequately expressed as a map than as a set of ILO statements (to be discussed further in Chapter 4). Knowledge has meaning in context and part of context is how ideas are interrelated. These interrelationships can be, at least partially, expressed by a map.

Maps can illuminate many important issues at this stage of planning. For example, a map that includes only discrete and specific facts may indicate a need for more inclusive ideas. On the other hand, a map may show only inclusive and abstract ideas without the applications and examples that make these ideas understandable and useful. Noticing that a map lacks relationships among certain ideas may point out the need for additional ideas to make those relationships possible. These are only a few examples of the information a conceptual map may provide during planning.

As a sort of shorthand representation of a teacher's conceptual ILOs, maps often prove useful during instruction. Knowing how ideas relate should help teachers to respond to questions and comments in a more focused way. Remarks made by students can be seen as instances of a concept, and the teacher can try to help students understand the desired relationships. A teacher's cueing, questioning, and supplying of new information is apt to be more targeted when accompanied by a clear notion of the ideas and relationships the teacher wants learned. (See Collins, 1977, for several useful examples.)

The mapping process is flexible and a map for any given set of concepts can take many forms. Too often teachers worry about the "correctness" on their maps. Correctness is a secondary concern here. You, the teacher, will be teaching the course, and you undoubtedly have some view of the relationships among the course's ideas. Whatever framework you possess is likely to affect your teaching. Mapping allows you to make this framework explicit, revise it, and, generally, be more conscious of

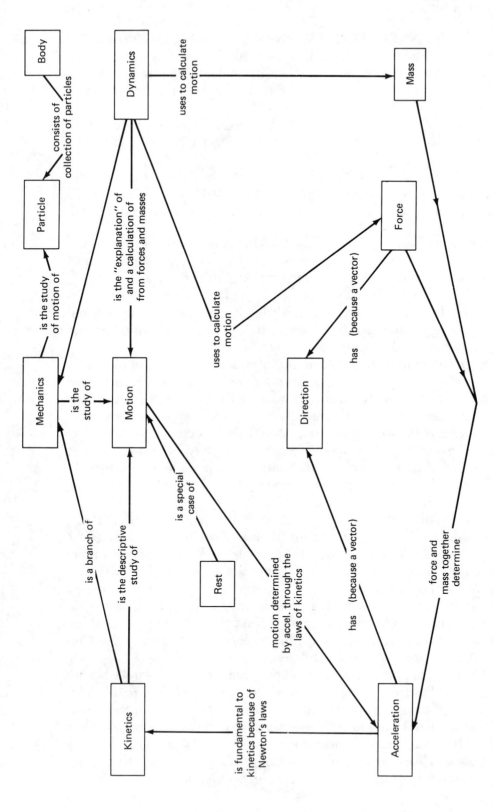

Figure 2.4. One Possible Arrangement of Physics Terms. Note the advantage to the reader when the mapmaker labels the arrows (adapted from Champagne, Klopfer, Solomon, and Cahn, 1980).

it. Therefore, in constructing a conceptual map, your initial attempts should be made with the goal of getting this framework on paper and with the expectation that the framework will require revision. Relating, in two dimensions, all the important ideas in a course is a difficult task. However, mapping is usually worth the effort and will prove useful in thinking about and planning your course.

Questions for Discussion: Mapping

1. If your map has lines connecting terms, do the lines mean different things?
2. Compare those terms that are connected to many other terms with those terms connected to just one other term. Does this comparison help you identify the important or central ideas in your course?
3. Was your map instrumental in finding any new ILOs?
4. Do you feel your course lent itself well to mapping, or did you find mapping inappropriate? How do you account for this?
5. Would your map help students find their way through your course? If so, you might want to use it as a hand-out, a kind of two-dimensional course outline.
6. Show your map to an expert in the field. Does the expert understand and agree with you regarding your map? Are any changes in order?

Flowcharts

Arithmetic computation, reading, writing paragraphs, editing films, and parking a car are all complex skills in the sense that they each require a set of subskills, and understandings for their performance. If we want to teach any of these skills we must do so by teaching the necessary subskills and understandings. Therefore, it is important to identify the components of these complex skills. So long as important aspects of a desired skill remain unidentified and untaught, achievement of the skill will be impeded. Identification of subskills and understandings enables them to be specified as course ILOs and subsequently taught using appropriate teaching strategies.

One tool for identifying such subskills and understandings is a cognitive task analysis utilizing flowcharts. Let us look at an example.

$$\frac{3}{5} + \frac{1}{5} = ?$$

$$\frac{3}{5} + \frac{2}{15} = ?$$

These two problems require the addition of fractions that can be represented in a general form as:

$$\frac{a}{b} + \frac{c}{d} = ?$$

Addition of fractions is a complex skill. Try to solve these two problems and analyze your thinking process at the same time. That is, think the steps through aloud as you do each of them. Note what you are doing and compare it with the flowchart in Figure 2.5.

In the first problem $b = d$ (both are 5) so we can add a and c (that is, 3 + 1) and get 4/5 as an answer. Notice, however, that this flowchart begs the question of how we add 3 and 1. Do we count on our fingers, or in our heads, or do we just know the answer? Clearly, these analyses can be performed at different levels of depth.

In the second problem $b \neq d$, but d is a multiple of b (15 is 3 times 5). As in the first problem, each step in the procedure could be reanalyzed as a subskill for which we could identify additional and necessary subskills, facts, principles, etc. The depth of our analysis will depend on what learning outcomes we can assume our students have already achieved.

In a similar way we could analyze each of our skill ILOs by asking the question, "What do I go through when I perform this skill, and, specifically, what skills and understandings does the ILO entail?"

This analysis could be done at a general level for the whole course by analyzing the course's ILOs. For example, Figure 2.6 presents the skills and understandings entailed in playing a game of ice hockey. Then, at a more specific level, each of the skills in this general flowchart could be analyzed in greater detail.

In the analysis of most skills, the skills (or "tasks" as they are typically called) can be best described in terms of a series of internal and/or external actions performed on available information. Many cognitive psychologists distinguish between data or "information" and the operations or actions we perform on the data, termed "processes." These psychologists are concerned with how humans act on (process) data (information); thus, they use the term "information-processing analysis."

There are several additional points to keep in mind as you construct flowcharts for your skill ILOs:

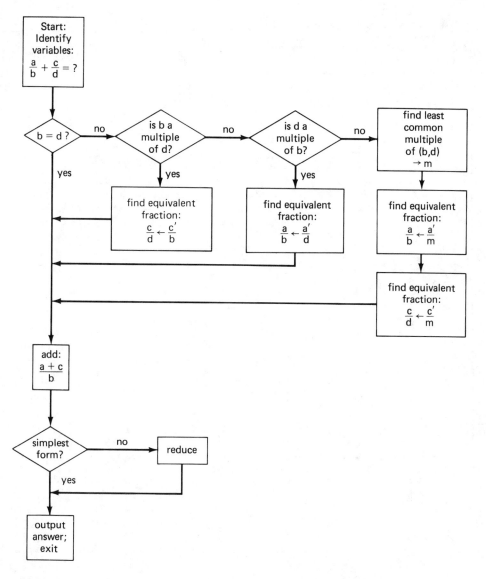

Figure 2.5. Procedure for Addition of Fractions (adapted from Greeno, 1976).

1. Many of the subskills you identify during the analysis may be internal thought processes rather than observable behaviors. This is to be expected.
2. It is usually best to think of the steps in the procedures as occurring serially (one at a time).
3. The analysis should include the identification of both understand-

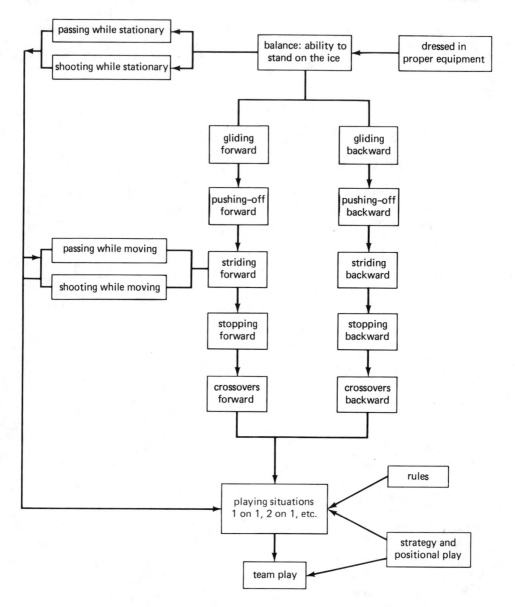

Figure 2.6. Flowchart of Skills for Ice Hockey.

ings (information and data) and other subskills (processes or operations on the data).

4. Any flowchart represents an hypothesis regarding the processes
   and information necessary in performing skills. There is usually
   more than one possible flowchart for a skill. Which of several
   candidates is correct is a matter for psychological research. How-

ever, the one you construct should be consistent with your own introspective experience when you ask yourself "What do I go through when I perform this skill?"

5. As a set of subskills and understandings that need to be taught in the pursuit of a particular skill ILO, a flowchart can be considered an expression of intended learning outcomes.

6. A flowchart is only one way to represent the subskills and understandings necessary for the performance of a skill. Skills that are very complex or not highly structured do not easily lend themselves to flowcharting. Nevertheless, these skills can and should be analyzed. As an alternative to flowcharting, the subskills and understandings resulting from this analysis can be expressed as a list. Skills that are not complex need not be analyzed at all.

COURSE-PLANNING STEP 2.11. Construct a flowchart or list of subskills and understandings for any of your ILOs representing complex skills.

Finding Out Where the Students Are

The charts and lists developed up to now have been concerned with your view of what the course should cover, what students should learn, and what questions students should address. Now we will reconsider your view of the course in light of the students' capabilities and conceptions.

Preconceptions

Of course, we would not want a course to cover the same ground as previous courses, except for review purposes. But the fact that students have or have not been exposed to certain ideas does not tell us what they do or do not understand. In fact, students' existing knowledge is not typically an all-or-nothing situation. Students do not come to any of a course's topics completely empty-headed. They may not know the terminology or have a precise understanding of the topic, but they usually have some ideas about it. Whether the course includes the study of how plants get their food, how to write an academic essay, the meaning of a fraction, the dangers of drug abuse, or how to "head" a soccer ball, students typically come to most courses with well-developed preconceptions.

Although much of the research on student preconceptions has been conducted in science education (see Driver, 1983; Resnick, 1983), there is enough research to suggest that students generally are not empty vessels into which we pour knowledge. Instead, they actively try to make sense of their experience (including classroom experience) based on what they already know or believe. When students' preconceptions are either incorrect or only partially true, instruction may become a task of changing people's ideas rather than instilling fresh knowledge.

Before we can adjust a course's ILOs and instructional method to the students, we must know in fairly specific terms what particular students know or believe about the topics we intend to teach. The best way to find out this crucial information is to talk with them in open-ended interviews and group discussions asking them for their explanations or descriptions while listening to them very carefully. In these diagnostic settings, we can find out the extent to which their views are idiosyncratic or common to the other learners; whether their ideas derive from prior instruction, mass media, life experience, or their own "spontaneous reasoning" (Viennot, 1979, p. 205); and possibly how deeply held their beliefs are and, thus, how difficult they will be to change.

Without the opportunity to study students directly, the course planner has to settle for secondhand knowledge, for example, the observations of experienced, perceptive teachers. Although there are times when this type of information must suffice, firsthand knowledge of students gained from observations and discussions both inside and outside of the classroom is highly preferable.

It is important to find out what students know because the course planner can determine not only which of their ideas the course needs to correct or extend, but also what resources students can bring to their understanding of the new material. The course can act as a bridge between what students already know and what the course planner wants them to understand. Analogies, metaphors, and examples are some of the instructional devices teachers use as bridges between familiar and unfamiliar ideas. We used the analogy between course design (unfamiliar) and building construction (familiar) in order to introduce this book in Chapter 1. Without knowing what students understand and what experiences they have had, teachers may use these potentially powerful strategies inappropriately and ineffectively.

One way to represent students' preconceptions is to construct a conceptual map describing which ideas and which relationships between ideas students seem to understand. In fact, you might try giving students a list of words representing the major ideas in the course after you complete Course-Planning Step 2.8. You could then ask the students to try to complete Course-Planning Step 2.9. While the students talk you through their maps by explaining the relationship between each pair of connected words, you develop a stronger sense of their understandings, misconceptions, and gaps in knowledge about the subject matter. As a result, you are in a better position to decide what aspects of the course need to be added, omitted, delayed, and emphasized.

COURSE-PLANNING STEP 2.12. Revise your course outline and ILOs in light of what you have learned about your students' existing knowledge.

Entry-Level Skills

Much of the previous discussion about preconceptions is also applicable to skills students bring to courses (their "entry-level" skills). Students base their approach to the learning of new skills on their current repertoire of skills. This fact suggests a view of students' current skills both as obstacles to learning (things to unlearn) and as foundations of new learning. Giving students tasks to perform and carefully observing their performance are the best means for diagnosing the skills they have and thus for determining the starting point of the course.

The flowcharts developed in Course-Planning Step 2.11 provide one basis for this diagnosis. You can use these flowcharts to identify which of the subskills students can and cannot perform, which ones need some polishing, and which ones are performed incorrectly. As in the case of preconceptions, this diagnosis provides an informed basis for reexamining the course outline and ILOs.

COURSE-PLANNING STEP 2.13. Revise your course outline and ILOs in light of what you have learned about your students' entry-level skills.

You now have a course outline, a list of ILOs, a set of central questions, one or more flowcharts, and one or more conceptual maps that, taken together, represent the skills and understandings to be acquired by students in your course. These lists and charts represent what you intend the student to learn and will be the foundation for a large part of subsequent course planning. They will influence the selection of materials, the design of teaching strategies, the development of evaluation techniques, and even the actual process of instruction. While there will be many opportunities to revise and edit them, it should now be clear how crucial they are to the process of course planning.

COURSE-PLANNING STEP 2.14. Look over your ILOs and think carefully about them. Review the process by which you developed them. Make any changes you think are appropriate at this time.

Related Material

This chapter completes the initial phase of selecting and clarifying statements of intended learning outcomes. The criterion of clarity for this phase is whether or not the ILO statement communicates clearly to you, the planner. The second phase of this process is the subject of Chapter

4, where a great deal more attention is given to the clarification of ILO statements. The criterion of clarity in Chapter 4 is whether or not the ILO statement communicates clearly to other planners, to teachers, and to students.

Chapter 8 shows how to translate each type of ILO into behavioral indicators that can be used to determine if the course's intended learning outcomes have actually been achieved. One criterion for an adequate behavioral indicator of an ILO is whether or not it is observable.

But before proceeding further with course planning on the basis of the ILOs you have produced so far, Chapter 3 asks you to give some thought to justifying these ILOs and thus giving your course an overall purpose.

Answers to Exercises

2.1

1. *Creative Cooking*
   the student knows what a frying pan is for
   ability to test cake to see if done
   how to bake bread
   knowledge of menu planning
   manual cooking skills: kneading, sautéing, flipping crepes, stir-
       frying
   how to plan before you cook
   safe use of knives

2. *English Grammar and Composition*
   correct punctuation
   recognizes sentence fragments
   appreciates own good writing
   uses commas with nonrestrictive relative clauses
   avoids run-on sentences
   doesn't use dialect forms in formal writing

3. *Social Studies*
   knowledge of what constitutes an institution
   enlightened self-interest in relationship to society
   recognizes institutional interests

4. *American History—The Post-Revolutionary Period*
   knows significance of the dates: 1776, 1803, 1812
   understands the causes of the War of 1812
   can describe the attack against Tripoli
   can describe why Hamilton accepted a duel with Burr
   knows the origin of the national anthem

2.2

1. *Creative Cooking*
   recognizes and names types of kitchen tools
   believes that cooking is not a specifically female thing
   knows how to prepare desserts
   knows how to prepare meats
   understands the importance of vegetable protein

2. *English Grammar and Composition*
   distinguishes between complex and compound complex sentences
   recognizes and names parts of speech in a sentence
   carefully chooses words when writing

3. *Social Studies*
   knows that institutions are self-perpetuating
   understands how cooperatives operate
   recognizes that media is used by social forces
   distinguishes among the types of institutions
   knows how institutions change

4. *American History*
   understands the role played by Jefferson, Adams, and Madison in
       shaping early America
   familiar with U.S. Constitution
   explains the economic trends occurring in early America
   understands America's relationship with Britain and France
   comprehends the impact of the Embargo Act of 1807 on trade

References

Anderson, T. H. *Techniques for Studying Textbook Materials in Preparation for Taking an Examination.* Urbana, IL: University of Illinois at Champaign-Urbana, Center for the Study of Reading, 1979.

Champagne, A. B., Klopfer, L. E., Solomon, C. A., and Cahn, A. D. *Interactions of Students' Knowledge with Their Comprehension and Design of Science Experiments* (LRDC Publication No. 1980-9). Pittsburgh: University of Pittsburgh, Learning Research and Development Center, 1980.

Collins, A. "Processes in Acquiring Knowledge." In R. C. Anderson, R. J. Spiro, and W. E. Montague (eds.), *Schooling and the Acquisition of Knowledge*, pp. 339–363. Hillsdale, NJ: Lawrence Erlbaum Associates, 1977.

Driver, R. *The Pupil as Scientist?* Milton Keynes, England: The Open University Press, 1983.

Education Development Center. *Man: A Course of Study.* Cambridge, MA, 1968.

Gowin, D. B. "The Structure of Knowledge." *Educational Theory* 20, no. 4 (1970): 319–328.

Greeno, J. G. "Cognitive Objectives of Instruction: Theory of Knowledge for Solving Problems and Answering Questions." In D. Klahr (ed.), *Cognition and Instruction*, pp. 123–159. Hillsdale, NJ: Lawrence Erlbaum Associates, 1976.

Resnick, L. B. "Mathematics and Science Learning: A New Conception." *Science* 220, April (1983): 477–478.

Viennot, L. "Spontaneous Reasoning in Elementary Dynamics." *European Journal of Science Education* 1, no. 2 (1979): 205–222.

Chapter 3

Developing a
Course Rationale

After completing this chapter, the reader should:

1. Understand the relation between a rationale and a set of ILOs.
   a. Know that a rationale guides curriculum development by providing overall direction.
   b. Know that a rationale serves to justify a set of intended learning outcomes.
   c. Know why a particular rationale may justify many different sets of ILOs and a set of ILOs may be justified by many different rationales.
2. Know that a rationale incorporates a set of values within three frames of reference (that is, the learner, the society, and the subject matter), together with a statement of educational goals. This knowledge should include an understanding of how each frame of reference provides distinct bases for justifying the educational goals.
3. Be able to construct a rationale for a given set of ILOs. This rationale should include all component parts.
4. Be able to analyze a statement of the rationale for a course into its component parts, to determine whether or not the goals are well stated, and to identify the values and assumptions implicit in the statement.

"Why do we have to learn this stuff?" "What good is this going to do me?" "This is a waste of time, I'm never going to use this!" Such expressions, if not frequently voiced by students, are frequently thought by them. And answers are all too often not readily available or are unsatisfactory to both students and teachers. This lack of purpose and justification is also reflected in the conduct of a course. As a teacher, you should always be thoughtful about your work, able to articulate your goals and to justify the time and resources spent striving for those goals. This chapter is about justification. It is not just an exercise in rationale writing but a framework for dealing with the "why" questions that could and should be asked about the course.

A course rationale is a statement that makes explicit the values and educational goals underlying the course. The rationale serves the purpose of justifying the learnings that students are to acquire during the course as well as justifying the methods and procedures employed in teaching the course. The rationale also serves the related purpose of guiding the planning of other course components. The values and educational goals expressed in a rationale reflect the rules and expectations that will underlie the way the course will be taught; they express the emphasis and tone that the teacher will give to the course. Lastly, the rationale serves as a check on the consistency of the various course components in terms of these values and goals. The values and goals expressed in a rationale are related; that is, goals are desirable only as they reflect certain values of the planner.

Values and Assumptions

As any parent of a preschooler knows, the answer to a "why" question can be followed by another "why" question *ad infinitum*. Although an educational goal answers the "why" question for a given set of ILOs, we can always ask the question "why these educational goals?" and follow the answer to that question with another "why" question. Our answers to successive "why" questions are framed in terms of more and more basic values and assumptions regarding education and, ultimately, life in general. Rarely do course planners examine these basic values and assumptions; nevertheless, they underlie the course's rationale.

The values and assumptions underlying the rationale concern the role of the individual in society, the societal role of education, the nature and purposes of society and human beings, the relation of the future to the present, the question of what knowledge is most useful, and the purpose for which it should be useful.

Questions for Discussion:
Values and Assumptions*

1. Individual–Society

Is education an investment that should pay off to the society or is its main purpose to increase self-realization?

What is the individual's proper role in society—passive participant, rebel, agent for encouraging rationally directed change,

*Adapted from Grobman (1970, pp. 107–108).

middle-class conformist, rugged individualist, warrior, peaceable resister, employed person, parent, competitor, cooperator?

2. Societal Role of Educational Institutions

Is it the job of educational institutions to perpetuate present society or to encourage a restructuring of society? If the latter, what direction should the restructuring take?

3. Societal Purposes

What is it that makes a good society? Are free enterprise and capitalism as we now know them essential to democracy?

What constitutes progress—technological advances, increased Gross National Product, improved social conditions, increased knowledge?

4. Present–Future Orientation

Is education preparation for adulthood or should education help individuals live their present life to the fullest? Is the future predictable? Can it be used as a basis for planning?

5. Gratification of Needs

Should needs be gratified when they arise or should gratification be delayed?

6. Termination–Recurrence of Education

Should education terminate or should it recur throughout life as needs arise?

Should education before adulthood be devoted to the pursuit of individual interests rather than providing basic skills? Can the individual afford to wait for these basic skills?

7. Utility of Subject Matter

Is a subject matter useful if it enables the individual to solve a relatively narrow range of problems and perform a relatively narrow range of skills?

Is a subject matter useful if it influences the way an individual experiences things, as the arts often do by enriching the individual's imagery?

Is a subject matter useful if it enables an individual to interpret the world by providing concepts for use in processing information?

Is a subject matter useful because it is helpful to adults in today's world? because it will probably be of use to the individual in the future? because it will be of use in further learning? because it can be applied in everyday practical situations?

Which is of more utility, an exposure to, and an understanding of, the popular culture or the classics?

8. General–Specialized Education

Are liberal studies less or more useful to those secondary school students least likely to pursue them further in college?

As the level of necessary training increases with an increasing technology, does the level of general education required to profit from training (and probable retraining) increase or decrease?

These questions are obviously difficult for an individual to answer, let alone for a group of individuals to achieve consensus on. No wonder, then, that value differences and disputes about goals underlie much of the debate about what our educational institutions should teach. Although it would be overly ambitious to attempt a conclusive answer to these questions, a careful consideration of the purposes and significance of a particular course at this point in planning can contribute greatly to the coherence and validity of that course.

Rationale and Entry Point in Planning

Logically, the rationale comes first in course planning. This is the often-cited position taken by Ralph Tyler (1950).* Nevertheless, other factors may influence what comes first in course planning. The "entry point" (that point at which the actual process of course planning begins) may be determined by any number of considerations. As we mentioned in Chapter 2, motivation to develop a course may come from a mandate or a philosophy. A grant, materials, the availability of an expert, or physical facilities such as a laboratory or special audiovisual equipment may suggest that the course-planning process be begun.

In the absence of other compelling factors, the statement of the rationale fits best as a course-planning step immediately after the initial thinking about ILOs and before the step in which ILOs are refined. This is true for several reasons. First, anyone planning a course has a notion, however vague or unarticulated, about the overall aims of the course. The task of clearly articulating this rationale is best accomplished after some thought has been given to the particulars of the course. Second, a well-articulated rationale provides a guide to the refining of course ILOs as well as to other steps in the planning process. This guide can serve to help keep the course components consistent and focused. In the writing of a rationale you will probably make decisions or confirm implied aims. Subtle or even major alterations in your viewpoint may make some ILOs no longer consistent with the rationale. In this case, it will be most appropriate to consider the ILOs a second time. In any event, a carefully constructed rationale, one that accurately represents your overall purposes and shows how the ILOs express those purposes, is essential in helping you to refine your ILOs.

---

*But note that Tyler (1975) now recognizes the need to be flexible with regard to entry point in planning.

Components of a Course Rationale

Every person holds values that express conceptions of people, practices, and institutions, as well as other aspects of that person's world. A course rationale, if it is to be useful and complete, should express a planner's values at least in terms of the learner, the society, and the subject matter. These valuative considerations, expressed in a rationale, are the "determinants" (Gwynn & Chase, 1969), "sources" (Tyler, 1950; Zais, 1976), "influences" (Tanner & Tanner, 1980), "data-sources" (Goodlad, 1966), or "criterial sources" (Johnson, 1967, 1977) for the course. Historically, a major curriculum issue has been what values shall underlie the purposes of American education. Proponents for a society-centered, child-centered, or subject-matter-centered curriculum have at times opted for their value position to the exclusion of all others. Our view is that course planners must give careful consideration to all three of these value areas, although a completed rationale might emphasize only one or two of the areas.

The Learner

Values regarding the learner express conceptions of what individual learners are like and what they need. Smith, Stanley, and Shores (1957) identified two variations in conceptions of learners. The first one emphasizes education that prepares the individual for achieving maximum social and economic success. The second conception views individual needs and interests in terms of developing a well-balanced person. These two sets of values would probably underlie different sets of educational goals.

Expressing a conception of the learner gives you the opportunity to deal with the issue of the individual learner's unique interests, abilities, learning style, and needs. It is important to specify the intended audience for the course and what you assume to be their unique needs and interests. The following examples illustrate conceptions of the learner as expressed in actual course rationales.

Literature, High School: Students may be seen as people working through life, looking for satisfaction, for pleasure, and for value. Every person needs to find beauty and meaning in their world. Beauty and meaning—these elements make the world more enjoyable in good times, more tolerable in bad. The worst situation is seeing life devoid of sense and without aesthetic pleasures. Many studies provide access to beauty and meaning (including science and religion, for example) but the study of literature, because it may be written about anything (including science or religion, for example), affords the student a direct and broad approach. Not every student may find interesting questions or tentative answers in literature, but if a literature course opens that form of art and knowledge (often depreciated in our technological society) to a few students, it is worthwhile. For young people trying to make sense of the world and themselves, reading works of literature may provide some insights. This means that students must have the opportunity to bring their own meanings to the text; a course that depends on the use of secondary sources and simply presents literature as others have read it will distance the works from the students.

Basic Math, Ninth Grade: Basic math is intended to help the individual gain self-confidence through success in math and take pride in the ability to meet or exceed societal standards for performance, including job-related uses. Most important, a knowledge of mathematics increases an individual's versatility in communicating with others, and in understanding the world through observations and through the media.

The Society

The assignment of societal values might involve informed voting, environmental awareness, rapid social change, racial intolerance, uncontrolled technology, and so forth. Values with respect to the society concern conceptions of social responsibilities or societal constraints and how the course can help the individual meet these responsibilities or deal with these constraints. The attitudes, knowledge, and skills learned in a course are, from this perspective, those required for participation in the social group.

Societal values vary and may be directed toward socialization, preservation of the social order, or preparation for citizenship. Occupational or vocational preparation is a societal value when implemented as a means to supply the work force with the skilled people needed by society at any particular time. Conceptions of society also include those views that express the need for a restructured social order or the "destructuring" of present institutional arrangements. Whatever conception of society is implied by your course, it should be articulated in the course rationale. It should make clear your explanation as to why the course goals are of value to society. The following examples are illustrative of conceptions of society as expressed in actual course rationales.

Indian Music, High School: The U.S. is a young nation. Speed and practicality are her watchwords. There is no time for waiting. Instant tea, instant success, instant art, instant culture, instant salvation . . . these are the hallmarks of life here. The stress is more on "reaching outness," and "out-goingness" than on introspection or self-knowledge. A dash of orientalism through the music of India, if made available to the young, may inject a badly needed counter-influence to the speed of life here.

English for Speakers of Nonstandard English, High School: If these symptoms (reading problems) do not have a pathological cause, perhaps the problem is social in nature. The job situation is one example that points to this possibility. Studies have demonstrated a high correlation between reading failure and supposed "speech irregularities," especially extraordinary slurring and deletion of consonants. And statistics indicate that candidates for employment who do not speak "standard English" (and, therefore, cannot read "standard English") are shunned by the nation's employers. Clearly, this is a social judgment, since many jobs do not entail reading or writing.

Although most courses serve both individual and societal needs, the distinction between the two is important and may reflect significantly different curricular emphases. For example, an occupational education course may view work or a career primarily as a means to self-sufficiency and self-fulfillment and thus respect individual purposes and life-styles. However, another occupational education course may view as its primary purpose the supplying of society with workers in the proper number and with the proper qualifications. Such a course may attempt to produce an "organization man" and may derive its curriculum solely from labor data and task analyses. Some courses (for example, literature and art) may aim exclusively at self-fulfillment with society receiving only the indirect benefits attributable to being populated by fulfilled individuals. Other courses (for example, social studies) may aim solely at "good citizenship" with the individual receiving only those benefits that all citizens gain from living in a stable or progressive society. Whatever the emphasis, the rationale should clearly indicate the planner's values with respect to the individual learner and to the society in which the learner lives.

The Subject Matter

The conception of the subject matter is the third area of values that needs explication in a course rationale. Values with respect to subject matter reflect the way you are approaching a particular subject and your conception of why that subject matter and that approach is significant enough to warrant a course. The rationale may stress the importance of a particular topic or discipline. Ancient history as the vehicle of our cultural heritage, mathematics as a necessary way of ordering the physical world, and literature as a storehouse of humanity's great thoughts are examples of the manner in which a rationale may treat subject matter. The balance of nature in science, the inquiry approach to history, and the Renaissance as the most magnificent period in art are examples of approaches to subject matter that might be justified in the rationale.

A rationale should express the value of the subject matter to its particular audience. Tyler (1950, pp. 27–33) asks, "What can this subject contribute to the education of young people who are not specializing in it?" In part, your answer to this question will express the value of the subject matter.

The following examples illustrate conceptions of subject matter expressed in actual course rationales:

Poetry Unit, High School: Poetry is the speech of a man speaking to men, in the words of the poet William Wordsworth. In a sense, at its inception, language itself was poetry. The poet Karl Shapiro states, "Poems are what ideas feel like." And in this light, every word at its birth is a new flash of poetry by which an individual sees a thing in a new way. Thus, poetry has always been a method of discovery as well as a way of knowing. What we seek to know through poetry is the world and ourselves, perhaps mainly ourselves.

Film Making, High School: This course attempts to introduce the language of film in much the same way that a parent might introduce a child to English; the course focuses on the problem of getting the student to speak. Thus, the course is more interested in helping students *express* themselves adequately through film, that it is, say, in filling their heads with notions of proper cinematic diction or syntax. Just as a parent might steer a child away from obviously incoherent phraseology, this course will attempt to steer the student away from the use of unintelligible images or image groups.

Thus the rationale should include a description of what the course is about. However, equally important is a description of what the course is not about.

Wildflowers Unit, Sixth Grade: This should *not* be considered a course in floral biology or botany. The children will be studying wildflowers as organisms—not the flower as the reproductive part of a plant. Therefore, parts of a flower, pollination, and seed formation are not covered in great detail. Rather, the emphasis is on ecological relationships and man's interest in wildflowers. (If the

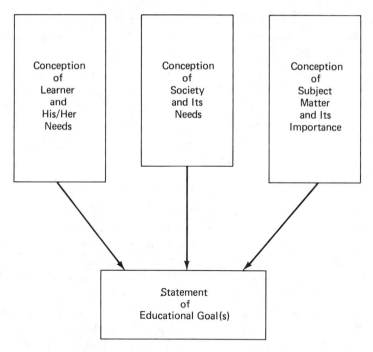

Figure 3.1. Components of a Course Rationale.

other topics are to be covered, the course will have to be expanded considerably.)

As Figure 3.1 indicates, conceptions of the learner, the society, and the subject matter form the framework for the course's educational goals.

The Educational Goal

Goals found in a course rationale should be educational goals. In considering what distinguishes educational goals from other types of goals, it is useful to consider the distinctions Zais (1976) makes. Zais distinguishes between curriculum aims, goals, and objectives. Aims are described as "life outcomes, targets removed from the school situation to such an extent that their achievement is determinable only in that part of life well after the completion of school" (p. 306). Goals refer to "school outcomes," which are long-range and reflect schooling in general rather than specific levels of school. Objectives are viewed as specific outcomes of classroom instruction. Zais's description of goals and objectives corresponds closely to our notions of educational goals and ILOs, respectively. The goals expressed in a rationale should capsulize the intentions of the course and thus should be more general and inclusive than learning objectives (that is, ILOs); yet they should remain school related, the cumulative effect or result of many learnings. Goals describe anticipated educational results. *Goals are attributes or characteristics of the well-educated person rather than the specific skills or knowledge that constitute that education.* Furthermore, the educational goal stated in the rationale must be consistent with the planner's conception of the learner, the society, and the subject matter.

The following guidelines should help you to state appropriate educational goals:*

1. Educational goals should describe the desired product. What units should be offered, what instructional procedures should be used, and what environmental conditions should be maintained to achieve those results should be determined later. This means that a statement of goals should not advocate the "opportunities" to practice this or experience that. It should describe the consequence of such practice and experiences, preferably in general terms of what the students should be like as a result of education.

2. Educational goals should be stated as desirable characteristics attributable to *learning*. Educational institutions may well be expected to achieve certain social goals, such as racial balance, reduction of dropout rate, and nutritional supplementation, but these are not *educational* goals because they are not achievable through learning.

3. If more than one goal is stated, priorities should be indicated. If all goals cannot be fully achieved, which goals should be given preference?

4. The goals should indicate what each *individual* should derive. Let society's benefit be indirect and implicit. Individuals with certain characteristics result from education. They, not the schools or colleges, will create the good society. Let not the "good citizen" be a stereotype; the properly educated *individual* is the best kind of citizen a democracy can have.

5. The scope of educational goals is an important consideration. Goals should not be so broad that they give purpose and justification to anything and everything and thus mean nothing. A statement such as "a person needs to be well educated" provides no guidance, purpose, or meaningful justification for any set of learnings. On the other hand, goals should not be as narrow as ILOs. A statement such as "a person should know the names of

*Adapted from Johnson (1972 pp. 4–8).

the major world capitals" is too restrictive to serve as a justification; it is more appropriately an ILO. Considering the proper scope for educational goals is a way to make sure that the rationale is more than educational rhetoric.

The following are examples of brief goal statements extracted from actual course rationales:

This course is designed for adults who are active in local voluntary organizations and is aimed at improving their confidence and skill in dealing with their local mass media.

Specifically, this course will provide good management and personnel for the parts function of the machinery business. Furthermore, this course will provide customers who are more knowledgeable as to what the parts function of a machinery dealership should be, so that they can make intelligent choices as to which dealerships to deal with.

The purpose of this course is not immediately to reject or regard as suspicious everything we read, but to learn how to understand the implications of what we read.

The curriculum hopes to provide parents with the necessary incentives to cultivate advantageous reading environments at home.

Summary

Logically a rationale comes first in course design, but other considerations may put it in a different position in the actual planning procedure. In the absence of other compelling factors, the rationale should follow the initial thinking about ILOs (which it serves to justify), and should come before the refinement of ILOs (for which it acts as a background).

A rationale contains a general statement of educational goals. Conceptions of the learner, the society, and the subject matter form the framework within which the planner articulates these goals. The rationale serves as a guide and a check for all later steps in course planning.

A Sample Rationale

The following example is an actual course rationale developed by a teacher in training. It is not perfect, but it does illustrate one approach used in course rationales.

*Writing from Experience, a One-Semester Course for College Fresh-men.** Individuals who know who they are in a deep and secure way will be able to lead lives that are meaningful to themselves and probably useful to other people. Education should encourage the growth of people in this direction of self-knowledge, self-confidence, and self-direction; it should not force people to grow in ways that are twisted or unnatural for them.

One place where many students are "twisted" is in traditional English classes. In reading literature, students are all too often forced to accept, without believing, a more mature and sophisticated interpretation of the work than they ever could have developed on their own, and which they find far-fetched. Their need to look into and explain their own responses to written work in any depth is usually ignored. Students are forced to write about things about which they know very little and sometimes care less; thus they develop the ability to hedge and a sense that writing—at least as far as they are concerned—is a matter of superficialities.

Writing from Experience is a course whose purpose is putting students in touch with their own thoughts, feelings, and experiences, and encouraging them to develop their sense of themselves, through writing and through reading other students' work.

Writing is a way of helping people think clearly. Almost all people who use writing regularly and seriously will say that writing helps them clarify their thoughts. Their descriptions of the process differ—some speak of fragmented thoughts on a topic coming together on paper; some of metaphors that suggest new possibilities; some of rough drafts whose ambiguities force the writer to rethink what he wants to say. In any case, good writers find a real connection between clear writing and clear thinking.

Similar processes take place when writers deal with their feelings as when they deal with their ideas. Since feelings cannot always be laid out as explicitly as ideas, a writer may have to work toward a kind of clarity that is not entirely verbal; he may have to establish a personal symbolism to deal with his feelings, for example, or he might find that he can best communicate by presenting a situation in a new and different form. However he writes about his experience, though, the writer uses writing to discover and develop himself in a way that goes below the surface.

*This rationale is taken from a course design produced as a term project by Carol Lamm, Cornell University, 1974.

Questions for Discussion: Sample Rationale

1. Having read the rationale, discuss how it conceptualizes the learner, the subject matter, and the society.
2. Is equal emphasis placed on all three considerations? If not, which conception is emphasized?
3. What are the educational goals stated in this rationale? Does it seem to strike a balance between generality without being grandiose or elusive, on the one hand, and specificity without being trivial, on the other?
4. What kind of course does this rationale imply? See if you can describe the ILOs and the instructional plan that might follow from it. How would this course differ from other possible freshman writing courses?
5. What assumptions does the rationale make with respect to the role of the individual in society, the societal role of educational institutions, the nature and purposes of society and of human beings, the relation of the present to the future, the question of what knowledge is of most utility and the purposes for which it should be useful? What would you like to ask the planner about her course in order to identify these assumptions?

EXERCISE 3.1. Below are four sets of statements, expressions, or words. Each set represents initial thinking about ILOs, and each set is for a different course. Read each list, then consider what a rationale for a course based on each list might include. Formulate for yourself (not necessarily in writing) conceptions of the individual, the society, and the subject matter, as well as goals that may be included in such a rationale. Lastly, try to justify these courses with another rationale that differs from the first and determine the ways in which the alternative rationale implies a different kind of course.

1. *Child Raising*

rewards	protection from the cold world
discipline	
attention	overprotection
sister/brother	the spoiled child
older/younger	permissiveness
family get togethers	imagination
privacy	stifling the child
fights	home medical care
everything begins at home	"shut up" and "you're really bad"

good citizenship   divorce
fights between parents   child abuse

2. *Team Games*
football   team games vs. individual
practice   sports such as swimming
good physical well-being   and running
part of a health program   praise/cheers
physical coordination   pride
    taught by games   injury
a healthy body and a   medical attention
    healthy mind   teamwork
lacrosse   the need for play as a part
baseball   of growth

3. *Consumer Buying*
bargains   where can you haggle over
what is a bargain? (It's not   the price?
    a bargain unless you   waste not—want not
    need it)   making use of leftovers
buy in season   our sometimes wasteful
be sure to buy the sales   economy
    sensibly   returnable bottles
quality vs. quantity   recycling
buying on time   tools can be investment
guarantees   using the public library

4. *The Environment*
pollution   the pond
food chain   life cycles
ecology   human beings in
balance of nature   relationship to
cows   their environment
insects   people should be aware of
role of the predator   the consequences of their
industrial waste   actions on the environment
farming in India   field trip

Rationales for Elementary School Units

Many people planning elementary units find a complete rationale for
each unit unnecessary. The term "rationale" as explained in this chapter
is more descriptive of the justification needed for a semester's or full

year's worth of planning. For an elementary unit, we suggest that you consider including an "introduction." An introduction should contain the following: (1) educational goals for the unit; (2) where the unit fits into the overall curriculum, that is, what should precede or follow it and how it fits in with the rest of the year's work; (3) your view of the learners, what they should know going into the unit, and why this content is interesting and appropriate; and (4) comments or suggestions that convey the manner in which the unit should be taught. The introduction is your chance to tell others what you might say to them if they were going to teach your unit. You should certainly use this opportunity to think about your goals and values. You may want to write the introduction to your unit as a final course-planning step.

COURSE-PLANNING STEP 3.1.   Write a rationale for your course on the basis of your initial ideas and your thoughts about the course's focus. The rationale should clearly state the course's educational goals within the framework of the learner, the society, and the subject matter.

Questions for Discussion: Course Rationale

1. Have your capabilities of the learner been taken into consideration sufficiently?
2. Is your course slanted more toward making the student conform to societal values or more toward arming the student against aspects of the society? Why have you given it that orientation?
3. Is your treatment of the subject matter in any way different from standard treatments? How do you defend this difference?
4. Do you consider yourself an educational conservative, moderate, liberal, or radical? What about your course shows this?
5. Does your rationale suggest other courses that would express the same general philosophy?
6. Where would the student get the skills needed in order to finish your course successfully?
7. For what activities does your course prepare the student?
8. What would the student have to learn if the course's educational goals were to be achieved?
9. Are there any ILOs suggested by your rationale that are missing from your list of ILOs?
10. See if you can find the educational goals of *Course Design*. What rationale (if any) is offered for the book?

COURSE-PLANNING STEP 3.2.   Revise your list of ILOs from Chapter 2 in view of your course rationale.

References

Goodlad, J. I. *School Curriculum and the Individual.* Waltham, MA: Blaisdell, 1966.

Grobman, H. *Developmental Curriculum Projects: Decision Points and Processes.* Itasca, IL: F. E. Peacock, 1970.

Gwynn, J. M., and Chase, J. B. *Curriculum Principles and Social Trends* (4th ed). New York: Macmillan, 1969.

Hines, V. A. A Critical Study of Certain Criteria for Selecting Curriculum Content. Doctoral dissertation, University of Illinois, 1950.

Johnson, M. "Definitions and Models in Curriculum Theory." *Educational Theory* 17, no. 2 (1967): 127–139.

Johnson, M. *Stating Educational Goals: Some Issues and a Proposal.* (A background paper prepared for the New York State Commission on the Quality, Cost, and Financing of Elementary and Secondary Education.) Albany, NY: State University of New York at Albany, 1972. Mimeographed.

Johnson, M. *Intentionality in Education: A Conceptual Model of Curricular and Instructional Planning and Evaluation.* Albany, NY: Center for Curriculum Research and Services, 1977.

Lamm, C. Writing from Experience. Unpublished design for a course produced as a term project. Cornell University, Ithaca, NY, 1974.

Smith, B. O., Stanley, W. O., and Shores, J. H. *Fundamentals of Curriculum Development,* New York: Harcourt Brace Jovanovich, 1957.

Tanner, D., and Tanner, L. N. *Curriculum Developmnt: Theory into Practice,* (2d ed). New York: Macmillan, 1980.

Tyler, R. W. *Basic Principles of Curriculum and Instruction.* Chicago: University of Chicago Press, 1950.

Tyler, R. W. "Specific Problems in Curriculum Development." In J. Schaffarzick and D. Hampson (eds.), *Strategies for Curriculum Development,* pp. 17–34. Berkeley: McCutchan, 1975.

Zais, R. S. *Curriculum: Principles and Foundations.* New York: Harper & Row, 1976.

Chapter 4

Refining Intended Learning Outcomes

After completing this chapter, the reader should be able to:

1. Categorize ILOs into four classes: cognitions, cognitive skills, psychomotor-perceptual skills, and affects.
2. Write clear ILO statements for a course.
3. Check a set of categorized ILOs for balance.
4. Decide on the relative priority of each ILO in a set.

Chapter 2 helped you develop a set of intended learning outcomes initially categorized as skills and understandings, with little attention given to ILO format. This chapter presents guidelines for refining statements of ILOs based on your previous work. Your ILOs will become more useful for you, the course planner, and for others associated with the course. The result will be a set of clearly stated ILOs categorized according to the type of learning involved. This refined set of ILOs will be coherent, comprehensive, and consistent with the products of the preceding chapters. The ILOs will be important in later steps of course planning—in organizing the course into units, in selecting general teaching strategies, and in planning an evaluation strategy.

ILO Statements: Form and Function*

If you were to ask different groups of educators how ILOs should be stated, you would probably get several different answers. Educators with backgrounds in programmed instruction, educational measurement, or vocational education might list characteristics such as the following:

1. A subject: the learner
2. A verb: behavior, or behavior product

---

*This discussion is based on Posner and Strike (1975).

3. Given conditions: the situation in which the behavior occurs
4. Standards: of quality or quantity

Example: The learner will solve nine out of ten equations containing two unknowns. The equations must be solved within twenty minutes. (Schutz, Baker, & Gerlach, 1971)

1. The overall behavior act
2. The important conditions under which the behavior is to occur (givens, restrictions, or both)
3. The criterion of acceptable performance

Example: Given a human skeleton, the student must be able to correctly label at least 40 of the following bones; there will be no penalty for guessing. (List of bones inserted here.) (Mager, 1962)

1. The situation faced by the pupil
2. The learned capability
3. The object of the performance
4. An action verb
5. Tools and other constraints: how must the performance be carried out

Example: Given instructions to interpret the meaning of Hamlet's soliloquy in simple terms generates an alternative communication of the soliloquy by writing sentences of simple content. (Gagné & Briggs, 1979)

Differences among these writers are apparent both in terminology and in the precise number of elements considered important. But, they agree on at least one point: A well-stated objective must specify the observable behavior that a student would exhibit if the objective was achieved. Because of this emphasis on behavior, we call objectives satisfying this requirement *behavioral objectives (performance objectives* is an equivalent phrase).

If, however, you were to ask your question on stating ILOs of educators with a primary interest in the humanities, particularly in the arts or with an allegiance to existentialism and phenomenology, you might get a hostile response to the idea of using a set of predetermined intended learning outcomes as a basis for planning instruction (see Macdonald, 1965).

Viewed in the context of this broad range of positions, much of the current debate on ILO statements suffers from a fallacy of too few options. It is as though one must be either an advocate of behavioral objectives or anti-objectives. We hope to point the way to an approach that is more sound educationally than either of these two extremes and more consistent with prevailing value systems of teachers.

One way to approach this issue is to consider the functions an ILO statement should serve and the appropriate form of statement for those functions. There appear to be three primary functions that ILOs should serve: (1) they should guide instruction and instructional planning; (2) they should communicate to others (for example, students and the public) what we are using precious time, money, and facilities for; and (3) they should serve as a basis for developing indicators or evidence of success.

Instruction and Instructional Planning

Instructional planning should be based primarily, though not exclusively, on what we want students to learn. Other criteria, such as interest and personal involvement, are important, but if our teaching is not designed to lead to desirable learning outcomes, we are wasting our students' time and the valuable resources of the community. In order to serve this function, ILO statements should clearly specify the kind of learning outcomes involved so that appropriate instructional strategies can be designed to accomplish them. In addition, teachers should think about this during instruction, thus influencing their actions and responses in the classroom.

Communication

Students and other interested parties have a right to know what we hope to achieve when we ask them to cooperate with us and commit themselves to a presumably valuable educational program. It is even likely that if students understand a program's direction, they will learn more easily. To serve this function of communication, ILO statements should express the planner's intents in an unambiguous manner.

Planning Evaluation

It is not enough for us to want students to learn important ideas and skills; we must also find out whether or not they are achieving these desirable learning outcomes. If we find a discrepancy between what we intend and what students achieve, then we have a basis for course revision. But we do not want the evaluation tail to wag the dog. We do not want to teach in a way that atomizes and perhaps trivializes our ILOs by requiring them to indicate not only what we want learned, but also what sample behaviors we will accept as evidence that we have been successful. In order to help us plan an evaluation, an ILO statement must be stated only with enough clarity for us to generate from each ILO a set of observable behavioral indicators. Each behavioral indicator points to a piece of evidence that can be used to determine whether an ILO is, or is not, being achieved.

ILOs versus Behavioral Objectives

The important point is that the behavioral indicator is only evidence (and tentative evidence at that) of learning and should not be confused with the ILO to which it corresponds. In contrast to advocates of behavioral objectives, we believe that an ILO typically need not, and probably should not, be stated in terms of observable behaviors because many ILOs are understandings or unobservable skills. Here we are distinguishing between ILO statements and statements derived from ILOs for data collection. (See Figure 4.1.) These latter statements are more properly termed behavioral evidence or indicators, and their function is to guide our observations. These statements, in contrast to ILOs, must be stated in terms of observable behavior. Therefore, a "behavioral objective" represents a lumping together of two distinct concepts in curriculum, namely, ILOs or learning objectives (that is, what we want learned) and behavioral evidence (that is, how we will tell if the desired learning has occurred).

From this discussion it should be obvious that there are no hard-and-fast rules for stating ILOs irrespective of audience, subject matter, and the particular approach to the subject matter. What can be claimed is that, by indicating the kind of learning involved and by choosing words that are not ambiguous, an ILO statement should be expressed clearly. Clarity does not typically require stating behaviors in observable, highly specific terms.

Remember, course planning is not a strictly linear process but consists of constant revisions and improvements of earlier ideas as our thinking progresses. A final set of clear ILO statements cannot be written once and for all by simply working through this chapter. Instead, you will find that your course ILOs will be improved by a series of successive approximations. Chapter 2 resulted in your first approximation of ILO statements. The present chapter should help you through a second and

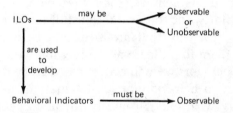

Figure 4.1. The Relationship between ILOs and Behavioral Indicators.

better approximation. Subsequent chapters dealing with instructional and evaluation planning will result in more revision. When and if your course is ever taught, still further revision will be required. A cyclical process of course planning is the one most likely to lead to an educationally sound course design.

With this rationale for our approach in mind, let us proceed to refining the ILOs you developed in Chapter 2.

Categorizing ILOs

The first step in refining ILOs is categorizing them further according to the kind of learning involved. This additional categorization will have a significant impact on general teaching strategies (Chapter 7) and evaluation (Chapter 8) because each category entails special considerations for instructional planning and evaluation. Moreover, by classifying ILOs into these categories, gaps and redundancies will become evident, and revising, deleting, and generating new ILOs will become necessary. These are all aspects of the refining process.

Categorization is an instrumental step in course planning. You may not always categorize ILOs when you plan a course. But the categories we use in this chapter will compel you to think more clearly about what you want learned in your course. It is these conceptual tools that we hope you learn in this chapter.

For the purposes of course planning, four categories of ILOs appear useful;* they represent a refinement of the understanding/skill categories discussed in Chapter 2. The "Skill" category is subdivided into "Psychomotor-perceptual skills" (roughly speaking, physical skills), "Cognitive skills" (mental skills), and "Affective skills." Similarly, the "Understanding" category is subdivided into "Cognitions" (conceptual knowledge) and "Affective understandings." Affective understandings and affective skills are then grouped together under the umbrella term "Affects." Figure 4.2 provides a graphic summary of the relationship between this four-category system and the two-category system used in Chapter 2.

---

*The categorization scheme proposed here is similar to categories of learning types or learning outcomes proposed by others. One set of categories familiar to many educators is that proposed by Bloom (1956), and Krathwohl, Bloom, and Masia (1964), among others, in their "taxonomies." Our psychomotor-perceptual category resembles the psychomotor domain described by Harrow (1972). Our affective category very roughly corresponds to the affective domain of Krathwohl et al. (1964). The cognitive skills in our scheme correspond to levels 2 through 6 of the Bloom (1956) cognitive domain. Our category of cognitions is a substantial expansion of level 1 of the cognitive domain (Bloom, 1956). Level 1 refers to memory of information, while our cognitions encompass the entire range of knowledge acquisition from memory to "deeper" levels of understanding. Gagné (1977) also describes categories of learning types. His "attitudes," "motor skills," "intellectual skills," and "verbal information" roughly correspond to our "affects," "psychomotor-perceptual skills," "cognitive skills," and "cognitions." Gagné's "cognitive strategies" represent a blend of our "cognitions and cognitive skills."

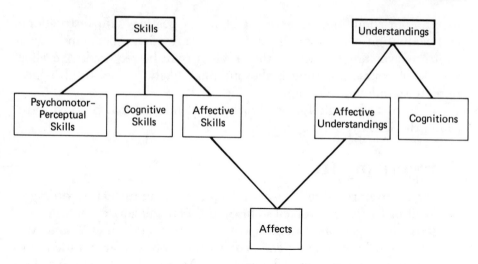

Figure 4.2. Categories of ILOs.

Categorizing Understandings

The ILOs classified as understandings in Chapter 2 are now further categorized as either cognitions or affects.

An important kind of learning in most schools and colleges consists of the ideas (that is, facts, concepts, generalizations) that teachers hope students will learn as a result of schooling. We label this type of knowledge or understanding *cognition*.

Cognitions, in contrast to skills, have no directly observable referent. (Nevertheless, as we will see in Chapter 8, observable behaviors such as explaining, listing, comparing, naming, discussing, and the like will have to be used as indirect indicators that cognitions have been achieved.)

Remember that your categorization should include all possible cognitions. Cognitions may be in the form of statements, lists of terms, or conceptual maps like those in Chapter 2.

The following are examples of cognitions:*

1. The student should realize that almost all written and oral language affects individual bias to some degree.

---

*A word about examples. Throughout this chapter you will find exercises and examples consisting of ILO statements. These ILOs are meant to elaborate the points made in the discussion. At this point in *Course Design*, the ILOs with which you are working are those you developed in Chapter 2. These ILO statements are rough and were formulated without a great deal of concern as to their wording. For this reason, many of the ILOs used in the examples are worded so that they are similar to the kinds of ILOs with which you will be working. These ILOs, therefore, are not necessarily exemplars of clearly stated ILOs.

2. The student should know that proper timing can affect media coverage and attention.
3. The student should understand that a proper diet is one that contains all the essential nutrients.
4. Set theory.
5. Associative property of addition.
6. Bill of Rights.
7. Minimalist art.

Affect is an umbrella term that could cover a wide range of outcomes. Here we will take a narrow view and treat affects in a manner appropriate for course ILOs. It is likely that underlying most affect is understanding or knowledge, and thus, one major subtype of affective ILO is affective understanding. Affective understandings are distinct from cognitions largely in the knowledge or content area with which they deal. Affective content focuses on the self or the interaction of self with others. ILOs of this type may be expressed with verbs such as "understand," "know that," or others commonly used to indicate cognitions. Whenever the *object* of these verbs reflects self-knowledge, however, they are more appropriately categorized as affects rather than as cognitions. ILOs embodying self as content include developing aspects of a positive self-concept, understanding how behaviors are self-serving, awareness of feelings and attitudes, and knowledge that one is a capable learner. ILOs embodying the interaction of self with others include knowledge or understanding of the factors motivating others' behavior, knowledge that questioning a teacher's authority often leads to conflict, and understanding how to interact with others to achieve certain goals.

The other major subtype of affective ILO is affective skill. Affective skill involves being able to behave in ways that reflect certain attitudes. Counselors have to be able to listen and respond with empathy. Teachers and parents must act with patience when working with children. Members of a school committee must listen tolerantly to complaints by citizens. There are many situations when we must behave in a manner that can be characterized by an affective skill. These skills can often be taught and may, therefore, form a portion of the ILOs for a course.

Some people include aspects of personality as affective ILOs. We disagree. We believe that aspects of personality refer to those traits or attributes that describe the kind of person someone should become, not what the person should learn. Attributes are distinguished from affective skill and understanding in that they are *general* characterizations of people, rather than specific teachable skills that can be applied at the student's discretion or specific teachable knowledge of some affective content. For example, being honest in an interview situation is more specific and more teachable than being an honest person. The same could be said about being able to listen empathically as opposed to being an empathic person. In these two examples, the first could be considered affective skills and the second might be viewed as attributes.

There are several reasons for not including attributes as ILOs. First, as we already pointed out, attributes can be modeled by a teacher, but they cannot be taught directly in the same sense that other ILOs can. Instead, students become more studious, honest, empathic, and the like as they develop intellectually and emotionally. Intellectual and emotional development involves both physiological maturation and the personal integration of things learned from teachers, parents, siblings, peers, and others. Even if we ignore the feasibility problems in teaching attributes, there may be serious ethical reasons for not considering attributes as ILOs.

We recommend that any attributes important to the course be incorporated into the rationale as educational goals. In this way their relationship to planning and teaching is more clearly defined. In addition, ethical and value issues are explicitly discussed in a rationale. While this approach doesn't eliminate the issues involved in teaching attributes, it does confront these issues more openly and directly, since a justification for these goals will be stated and thus be readily available to debate.

The categorization of an ILO as affective has important implications because planning for affects raises issues and presents problems unique to this domain of learning.

The following are examples of affective ILOs:

1. The student should realize that commercial messages affect perceptions and judgments.
2. The student should be able to listen to others, and to respond with empathy and without altering the content of the message.
3. The student should be able to avoid ethnic and racial stereotyping.
4. The student should be able to convey enthusiasm when talking.
5. The student should be able to treat children firmly and with warmth.

Notice that many of these ILOs can be achieved, in part, through cognitive learning. For example, "realizing that commercials have affected perceptions" can be taught by showing students a variety of real life situations where their perceptions have been shaped by commercial messages.

Affective and cognitive ILOs may be conceptually distinct but, frequently, teaching one type of ILO also entails teaching other types. This interrelatedness of cognitive and affective (and, we might add, psychomotor-perceptual) aspects of learning is not surprising when we remember that education involves teaching wholely integrated individuals whose thoughts and feelings accompany almost everything they do.

Categorizing Skills

The ILOs classified as skills in Chapter 2 are now further categorized as either cognitive skills or psychomotor-perceptual skills.*

Cognitive skills demonstrate the ability to use or apply cognitions. Learning ideas without acquiring corresponding competencies does not necessarily enable the student to *use* the ideas. That is, cognitions may be prerequisites for performing cognitive skills, but they are not always sufficient. Often it is also necessary to teach students how to *apply* their ideas when analyzing a situation, creating a communication, predicting the occurrence of an event, solving a problem, constructing a logical argument, or comparing similar ideas.

The following are examples of cognitive-skill ILOs:

1. The student should be able to recognize the outward signs of presupposition in English.
2. The student should be able to analyze the decisions made by editors in terms of the factors that influence those decisions.
3. The student should be able to develop a logical argument.
4. The student should be able to distinguish descriptive from judgmental statements.
5. The student should be able to analyze and solve work problems involving the use of algebra.
6. The student should be able to evaluate a potential apiary site.

As you will recall, the flowcharts you created in Chapter 2 include either cognitive skills or psychomotor-perceptual skills.

Psychomotor-perceptual skills encompass skills, abilities, and/or movements that are more observable than any of the other categories. The following kinds of learning are usually included in this category: fundamental and reflexive movements (for example, running, jumping, balance, and posture), perception and perceptual discrimination (for example, physical orientation, bodily awareness, visual tracking, and sound differentiation), physical qualities (for example, endurance, speed,

---

*For the sake of simplicity, our previous discussion assumed that *all* your affective ILOs were originally categorized as understandings. We then showed how these ILOs consist of affective understanding and/or affective skill ILOs. We will not discuss affective skill ILOs any further in this section, although, strictly speaking, they are skills.

strength, and agility), and complex skilled movements (for example, typing, sawing wood, playing golf, and performing trampoline stunts).

The following are examples of psychomotor-perceptual ILOs:

1. The student should be able to dodge a moving ball.
2. The student should be able to measure the volume of water using a 100 milliliter burette within a tolerance of 1 milliliter.
3. The student should be able to bisect a line with a compass and a straight edge.
4. The student should be able to move across the floor with grace.
5. The student should be able to adjust a carburetor's needle valve.
6. The student should be able to discriminate aurally among the calls of common local bird species.
7. The student should be able to pronounce correctly the r in *French*.

Blends of ILO Categories

Categorization will be useful in later planning steps. Nevertheless, one should not consider learning outcomes as belonging to one of four discrete categories. More often than not, an ILO represents a "blend" of several categories, rather than belonging to a "pure" category. In fact, it is probably more useful to think of the categories as continuous rather than discrete.

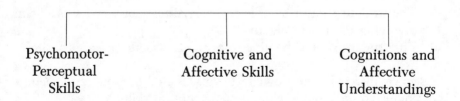

Psychomotor-Perceptual Skills	Cognitive and Affective Skills	Cognitions and Affective Understandings

It is difficult to think about a psychomotor-perceptual skill without a cognitive component. The sort of knitting one can do while watching TV comes close to being purely physical, since it requires little, if any, conscious thought. However, dismantling a carburetor or operating a 35-mm camera both have significant cognitive components and thus represent a blend of psychomotor and cognitive skill. Plotting a graph for equations of the type $y = 1/x$ is largely a cognitive skill but with the psychomotor-perceptual component of actually doing the plotting.

It is also difficult to think about a cognitive skill existing without accompanying knowledge (that is, an accompanying cognition). A person can rehearse and memorize information, and thus acquire the cognitive skill of being able to recall the information without knowing or understanding the information in any real sense. However, a cognitive skill, such as recall, is usually accompanied by some degree of comprehension. Being able to solve long division problems involves knowing some procedure for doing it. Being able to analyze a novel requires substantial knowledge of the genre and literature in general. Cognitive skill ILOs almost always must be accompanied by cognitions to be meaningful. Cognitions can also be taught in a rather "pure" state. A person can be taught to know or understand something without also being taught to use the knowledge in the performance of some skill. While it is likely that once a person knows or understands something, this knowledge will be used in a variety of ways, the point is that none of these uses were intentionally taught.

Our purpose in having you categorize ILOs is not to force every ILO into a "pigeonhole" but to help you consider the kind of learning you are trying to accomplish in your course. Therefore, while you should try to decide if an ILO is properly categorized as a psychomotor-perceptual skill, cognitive skill, cognition, or affect, you need not base your decision on a criterion of "pure" membership. Since our categories are not mutually exclusive but instead continuous, you may want to categorize and label ILOs as being blends or mixtures of more than one category.

COURSE-PLANNING STEP 4.1. Review the ILOs you have categorized as either skills or understandings. Understandings should now be categorized as cognitions or affective understandings. Skills should be categorized as psychomotor-perceptual skills, cognitive skills, or affective skills. If an ILO does not fit neatly into a category, do not hesitate to create an appropriate blend. If a psychomotor skill requires an accompanying cognitive component, write this component in. Similarly, if a cognitive skill requires an accompanying cognition, supply it. Remember, by categorizing ILOs you are making an important decision regarding the kind of learning you want your ILO statements to communicate.

Guidelines for Clarifying ILOs

You should be careful not to go overboard when stating ILOs. It is better to teach a few things well than to compile a long list of ILOs that may detract from a coherent course focus. It is likely that your conceptual map and accompanying statement, and your outline of the course content, taken together, provide an elegant and clear statement of cognitions. It may be superfluous to include a separate statement for each cognition. Similarly, a well-developed flowchart succinctly expresses a set of skills. In general, consider the overall goals of clarity, communication, and usefulness in working through the remainder of this chapter.

In the following guidelines for clarifying ILO statements, each category is discussed separately.

Expressing Cognitions

Cognitions involve the incorporation or storage of information in the brain. Describing the precise nature of this information storage—how information is acquired, remembered, and used—is a major task of the interdiscipline of "cognitive science." Most cognitive science descriptions of acquired information stress the interrelatedness, structure, and context of knowledge elements. Knowledge elements themselves vary and can include data about people (for example, their ages, occupations, traits), objects (for example, their size, color, shape), and events (for example, their sequence, time of occurrence), and a variety of more abstract information (for example, context and causes of events, purposes and life-styles of people). Thus, acquired information varies in its structure and the quality and quantity of component knowledge elements. (See the discussion of conceptual mapping in Chapter 2.) Numerous terms are used to characterize the structure and context of acquired knowledge elements. Examples included concepts, facts, principles, propositions, generalizations, and theories. Because these terms have no consistent and accepted usage, we will refer to these and similar cognitions by the everyday expression "ideas."

Ideas enable us to reduce the complexity of our environment through the use of abstractions. Abstractions make possible the grouping of objects, people, or events and thus enable us to respond to classes of things rather than to each and every thing that enters our awareness (Bruner, Goodnow, & Austin, 1956). When we acquire knowledge, we learn to make sense of our world, in contrast to the newborn child who perceives only "bloomin' buzzin' confusion." Ideas constitute our technical vocabulary and are our tools of thought; they are the units with which we think. The more fundamental and generative our ideas, the more potential we have for understanding basic processes (Bruner, 1960, 1966).

Acquiring knowledge enables us to analyze situations, solve problems, and discover relationships among events. While the acquisition of an idea may be necessary for the performance of such tasks, it is rarely sufficient. In addition to acquiring knowledge, we need to learn to use it; for the purposes of this book, such additional learning is considered cognitive skill rather than cognition. If acquiring an idea is supposed to result in certain capabilities, then those capabilities should also be made explicit as ILOs categorized as cognitive skills.

Ideas can be linked to form other ideas. For example, ideas about investment, ownership, and free market economy may be related to form an idea of capitalism. The space shuttle may become part of a person's idea of aircraft. Sometimes relationships between two or more ideas form statements of ideas that assert something. For example, the ideas of force (simply stated as a push or a pull) and acceleration (the rate of change in an object's velocity) can be combined to form an idea expressed as the following *assertion:* The acceleration of an object is directly related to the force exerted on it. Or the idea of bachelor may be used with the idea of "singleness" in the following two ideas that are assertions: All bachelors are single. All single persons are bachelors.

Note that the first statement is true and the second statement is false. Ideas that are assertions can be either true or false depending on the veracity of the relationships. This is not the case with all ideas. Many ideas such as aircraft, capitalism, and acceleration may be useful or useless, but they cannot be considered true or false.

Just as ideas differ in their structure, complexity, and truth value, they also frequently differ in the ways in which they are best taught. Some ideas are best taught through typical examples, through definitions (note the definitions of force and acceleration given above), and by showing the relationships between ideas (as in a map).* Other ideas (particularly those that are assertions) are taught through argumentation, experimentation, or, more generally, through convincing presentations of reasonable evidence (as in a geometric proof or a set of empirically derived data). Chapter 7 discusses this point further.

Learning the meaning of an idea that is an assertion also entails learning the ideas inherent in it. For example, learning that force equals mass times acceleration consists of learning what force, mass, and acceleration mean and learning the ideas of mathematical equality and multiplication. A teacher cannot reasonably expect students to learn the meaning of an assertion if the students do not know the component ideas.

Just as assertions can be considered as the relation of one set of ideas to another, assertions can also be linked together, making the structure of the acquired information increasingly interrelated. At some level, this information begins to characterize our general thought in a certain area. We refer to ideas structured in this way as a *conception.* The origin of species can be considered from either an evolutionist or a creationist conception. In either case a conception will influence how new information is interpreted and what new information is important. A pond observed by a biologist and by an elementary school child could lead to very different interpretations and even different observations. A child may have a conception of a pond as a place where frogs and other interesting creatures live. An artist may see a pond in terms of the interplay of light and shadow in the subtle shadings of reflection and shoreline vegetation. A biologist's conception could be dominated by energy transfer and eco-

*Chapter 7 refers to these ideas as "concepts."

logical ideas. As a result, the biologist may observe the particular network of related organisms in a pond environment, the artist may observe a perspective and location for a landscape, and the child may observe the hiding place of a large bullfrog.

Any set of terms for describing acquired knowledge is actually a set of rough labels referring to the acquired knowledge's depth, structure, extent, and complexity. Expressing cognitions clearly is difficult; we recommend several ways of expressing cognitions in order to achieve clarity. One way is to construct a conceptual map for the entire course, as well as for each unit. The maps should contain all the major ideas to be learned in the course. Relationships among ideas that correspond to assertions can be numbered. Two examples of the use of conceptual maps with lists of numbered assertions follow.

Our Federal Government, Sixth Grade Unit
1. The purpose of the federal government is to serve and protect its citizens.
2. The Constitution of the United States describes the rights of citizens and the structure and functions of the government.
3. The government has three branches—executive, legislative, and judicial.
4. The legislative branch enacts laws, the executive branch enforces laws, and the judicial branch interprets the Constitution.
5. The three branches are balanced, each checks the others' power, so that no single branch becomes too powerful.
6. Citizens influence government by electing representatives to the legislature and by participating in the election of the president (executive).
(See Figure 4.3.)

Energy, Eighth Grade Unit

Definitions

Energy   The capacity to do work; the property of a system that diminishes when work is done to another system.
Work   A transference of energy equal to the product of force times the distance through which the force acts.
Fossil fuel   Combustible matter comprised of organic compounds from the remains of living organisms, usually plants.
Solar power   Technology that uses the sun's energy directly to do work.

Assertions

1. The earth's energy comes from two major sources—either from substances on earth (nuclear energy) or from the sun.

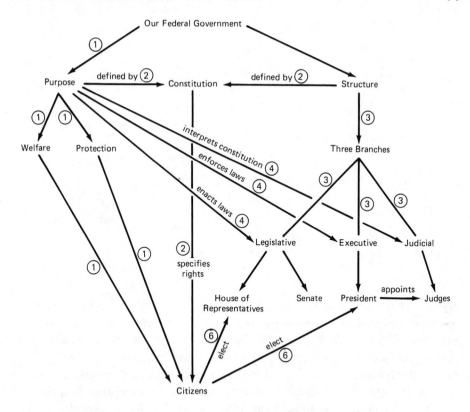

Figure 4.3. Conceptual Map for "Our Federal Government."

2. The sun's energy is used by plants directly. Others use the sun's
   energy indirectly by using plants or a plant product as fuel.
3. Living things use energy for growth and the maintenance of life.
   People use energy to do work.

Figure 4.4 is a map of a junior high-school science unit about how
and from where earth derives its energy, and how this energy is used.
(The map is incomplete.) Each term that signifies an important idea is
listed and accompanied by a careful, clear, and concise definition. (If
formal definition is not possible, the meanings of the terms can be explored using examples to help clarify them.) Ideas that are assertions
desired as course ILOs are also represented on the conceptual map. Another example can be found in the design for a poetry course presented
in Appendix B.

A *conception*, as stated earlier, is more than the sum total of the ideas
which comprise it. A conception constitutes a way of looking at the

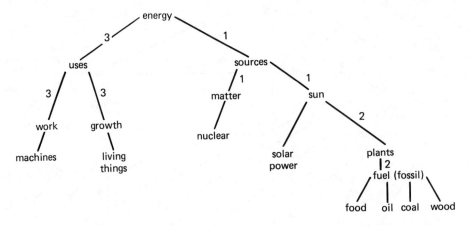

Figure 4.4.

world. It roughly corresponds to a person's theory or belief system regarding some set of phenomena (for example, a conservationist's view of offshore oil exploration). Entire conceptual maps, or, in some cases, major aspects of the maps, will serve as representations of conceptions. Characterization of one's thinking by a conception is, in part, a result of acquiring considerable knowledge. If such a conception is a desired result of the course, it should be reflected in the map. In addition, the conception might be described in the rationale as an educational goal.

One way of further clarifying what we mean by "learning a cognition" is to consider where the learner stands in relation to the knowledge. There are several properties that describe this relationship. One property is memory; knowledge can be retained in the mind. Another property is comprehension; one can grasp the linguistic and literal meaning of a statement expressing an idea. A third property is understanding and justified belief. Understanding involves going beyond literal or linguistic comprehension and grasping ways in which ideas are related to other ideas. Understanding ideas that are assertions involves justified belief. By justified belief we mean acceptance of an assertion as true based on good reasons. Each of these properties implies a different kind of learning and suggests a distinct instructional strategy and evaluation technique. Any particular cognition might embody one or more of these three properties. Note that being able to use knowledge to solve problems, interpret data or situations, generate questions, and critique a work of art are cognitive skill ILOs. Notice too that such ILOs are good illustrations of cognitive skills that must be accompanied by cognitions.

It is often wise to supplement a course's cognitions with explanations of their meaning, stipulating which of the three properties applies to each cognition. It is crucial for the planner not to shy away from ILOs just because clarity is difficult to achieve. Such a tendency can only harm the course by limiting its scope and perhaps rendering it trivial.

COURSE-PLANNING STEP 4.2. Using maps, a list of definitions of major terms, a list of assertions, and statements with supplementary explanations (when needed), express your course's cognitions.

Expressing Affects

Expressing affects in a manner that clearly communicates their meaning to others is not a simple matter. In part the difficulty arises from the fact that many verbs used in stating affects (particularly verbs for affective understanding, such as "realize," "be aware of," and "appreciate") have broad and overlapping meanings. Furthermore, the referent for the verb in a particular affective ILO (for example, "the opinions of others") may be clear in your mind even though there are many different ways to use that referent in a clearly stated affective ILO. For example, "to listen tolerantly to the expression of others' opinions that differ from the student's own," "to be able to evaluate one's ability to attend to views that differ from one's own," and "to be able to seek out the opinions of others as a means of personal growth and development" are all different ILOs that have essentially the same referent (the opinion of others). Therefore, the key ingredients of a clearly expressed affective ILO are (a) a carefully chosen verb describing the affect, (b) the identification of the referent (or object) of the verb, and (c) a thorough description of the specific context for the affect. Your rationale or introduction is an ideal place to set the context so that affective ILOs communicate clearly.

How might you improve the clarity of the following ILO by incorporating each of the three ingredients mentioned above?

The students should appreciate others' opinions.

One interpretation of this rather ambiguous ILO is as follows:

The student listens attentively (the verb) to views of others that are different from his or her own (the referent or object of the verb), particularly during discussions on controversial issues (the specific context).

The following illustrate other clearly expressed affective ILOs:

1. The student should understand how he or she responds to a literary work—what in the work and what in himself or herself leads to that response.
2. The student should be able to criticize another student's fiction writing objectively and constructively.
3. The student should view the claims made in TV advertisements with skepticism.

4. The student should know what he or she likes in commercial architecture and why.

COURSE-PLANNING STEP 4.3. Using the guidelines discussed above, review your affective ILOs. Rewrite any affects that need clarification.

Expressing Cognitive Skills

Cognitive skills can often be expressed clearly in a single sentence. The range of verbs that can communicate the kind of behavior intended in a cognitive-skill ILO is broad. The following verbs are useful in describing the behavioral aspect of cognitive skills: define, acquire, identify, recognize, translate, give in own words, illustrate, prepare, represent, interpret, reorder, differentiate, distinguish, draw, explain, demonstrate, estimate, infer, conclude, predict, determine, extend, interpolate, extrapolate, fill in, apply, generalize, relate, choose, separate, organize, use, employ, transfer, restructure, classify, distinguish, detect, identify, clarify, discriminate, assert, categorize, deduce, analyze, simplify, devise, write, tell, produce, constitute, transmit, originate, modify, document, propose, plan, design, specify, develop, combine, organize, synthesize, compute, formulate, judge, argue, validate, assess, decide, compare, contrast, standardize, appraise.*

Some verbs represent "higher order" or more complex cognitive skills than others (see Bloom, 1956). For example, "the ability *to distinguish* a valid from a faulty research design" is not as complex a cognitive skill as "the ability *to design* a valid research study for a particular problem." Likewise, "the ability to *organize* ideas and write an effective piece of expository prose" is a more complex cognitive skill than "the ability *to explain* a piece of expository prose in your own words." It is important in stating cognitive-skill ILOs to write them at a level of complexity appropriate for the situation.

Earlier in this chapter we noted that cognitive skills are often complex blends of cognition and skill. In Chapter 2 we discussed cognitive task analysis of skills that results in a flowchart of subskills and component understandings (that is, cognitions). Just as conceptual maps form an important part of clearly stated cognitions, flowcharts form an important part of clearly stated cognitive skills. Statements of "higher or-

---

*The guidelines for stating cognitive skills and psychomotor-perceptual skills list some verbs that are descriptive of behaviors often sought in these types of ILOs. You might want to use a thesaurus when searching for a verb that accurately communicates your intention. The appropriateness of any verb used in an ILO depends on that particular ILO. There is nothing inherently "good" about a particular verb.

der" or complex cognitive skills should be accompanied by a flowchart or list that represents major components of the skill. Keep in mind that you must determine the depth or level of detail that best serves to clearly state your cognitive skill ILO. The following examples illustrate complex cognitive skills stated with the help of a flowchart or list.

List
1. The student should be able to design a simple experiment given a hypothesis.
    a. Identify the variables of the hypothesis.
        (1) Determine which variables are presumed causes (independent) and which are effects (dependent).
    b. Operationalize the variables in measurable terms.
    c. Understand the idea of control and the need to vary variables one at a time (in a way that each variable's influence can be independently determined—thus one at a time or orthogonally).
    d. Form the set of all possible combinations of variables.
    e. Analyze the measured effect of independent variables on dependent variables in order to reach a decision about hypothesis.

Flowchart
2. The student is able to write a well-constructed narrative. (See Figure 4.5.)

Although the following cognitive skill ILOs consist of subskills and understandings, they are clear enough to guide further planning and thus do not have to be accompanied by a flowchart or list:

1. The student should be able to specify the information needed to calculate the trajectory of an object.
2. The student should be able to draw a Venn diagram illustrating a simple problem of set membership.
3. The student should be able to classify common foods into their appropriate nutritional group.
4. The student should be able to detect underlying racism or sexism present in commercial messages and advertisements.

COURSE-PLANNING STEP 4.4. Considering the guidelines for stating cognitive skills, review your ILOs. Make sure that all ILOs intended as cognitive skills communicate their meaning clearly. Rewrite any ILOs that are unclear and include flowcharts or lists for the most complex cognitive skills.

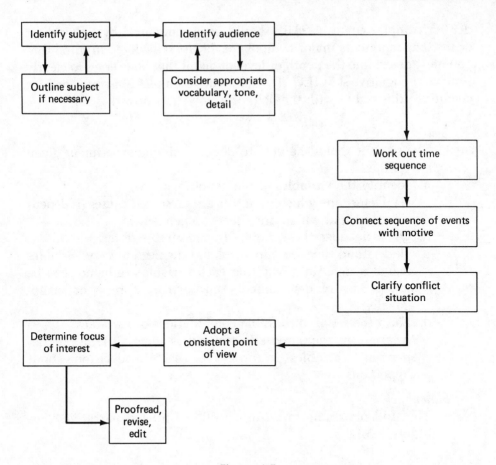

Figure 4.5.

Expressing Psychomotor-Perceptual Skills

Psychomotor-perceptual skills also can often be stated in a single sentence. Any verb that accurately describes the intended behavior can be used in stating psychomotor-perceptual skills. The following verbs are often used in ILOs of psychomotor-perceptual skill: run, jump, walk, repair, dismantle, construct, type, write, flex, stretch, pull, push, grip, handle, hear, discern, detect, follow, pronounce.

These examples illustrate some clearly stated ILOs of psychomotor-perceptual skill:

1. The student should be able to calibrate a triple-beam balance visually.
2. The student should be able to mount a pack and frame weighing 75 pounds correctly on the back.
3. The student should be able to focus correctly a microscope at 400×.

4. The student should be able to band a crate safely and securely.
5. The student should be able to apply wood stain so as to enhance the wood's grain optimally.

COURSE-PLANNING STEP 4.5. Considering the guidelines for stating psychomotor-perceptual skills, review your ILOs. Make sure that all ILOs intended to be psychomotor-perceptual skills communicate their meaning clearly. Rewrite any ILOs that are unclear. Add flowcharts as necessary.

Clarity: Some Examples

The preceding steps for expressing ILOs are all aimed at achieving clarity. A clear ILO accurately indicates the kind of overt or covert behavior being sought and the context for that behavior. Clear ILOs also identify the knowledge a learner is supposed to acquire in a way that makes the structure of that knowledge explicit. A clear ILO statement is neither so vague that it cannot guide planning nor so specific that it is trivial. Some ILOs can be expressed with sufficient clarity in a single statement. On the other hand, some ILOs require maps, charts, definitions of terms, or explanatory paragraphs in order to achieve clarity. This is particularly true for complex cognitive skills and cognitions. However, there is no hard-and-fast rule. Clarity is the goal toward which to work. The following examples may help to illustrate these points:

1. *The student should know the ten most frequently found trees in the northern hardwood forest zone.* The object or content portion of this ILO (that is, "the ten most frequently found trees in the northern hardwood forest zone") is clear. But the verb "know" is not clear. "Know" in this instance could mean "be able to recognize" (a cognitive skill), to "remember the names" (a cognition), or to "understand why these trees are the most numerous" (a cognition), among other things. Of these possibilities, only the last one, "understand why they are most numerous," would require an accompanying map. In any event, for this ILO to be clearly stated, "know" must be elaborated so that it is more descriptive of the desired behavior.
2. *The student should comprehend the expression "due process of law."* This ILO is a cognition. The verb "comprehend" is aimed at grasping the meaning of the expression and is clear. A map identifying the ideas that constitute "due process" should accompany this and other ILOs for this course. Since the content and the nature of the intended learning are clear, a teacher could plan instructional activities and evaluative measures for this ILO.
3. *The student should be able to explain the practicality of fad diets.*

The use of "fad" suggests that such diets are *not* practical, but the ILO requires the student to explain their practicality. If this statement is to express a cognitive skill, it might be clearly stated as "the student is able to evaluate fad diets for their practicality in terms of the body's nutritional requirements." If the ILO is to express a cognition, it could state that "the student should undersand the nutritional deficiencies of most fad diets." If the student is to evaluate fad diets, a flowchart describing how one proceeds to do this would be helpful. If this is a cognition, the ideas needed to understand nutritional deficiencies should be mapped.

4. *The student should be able to relate economics, sociology, politics, and geography to history.* As a cognitive skill, "ability to relate" is not an adequate description of desired behavior, and the content portion of this ILO is too general. If a cognitive skill is desired, the ILO might be expressed as "the student should be able to synthesize economic, political, sociological, and geographical factors in an analysis of an historical event." This is a very complex cognitive skill, one that assumes a great deal of knowledge on the part of the student. To state all this presumed knowledge is beyond the requirements of a clearly stated ILO.

5. *The student should be able to load a 35-mm camera correctly.* This ILO is a clearly stated psychomotor-perceptual skill. The behavior and the context are clear. A teacher should have little difficulty in understanding precisely what is intended here.

6. *The student should be able to fix a broken bone.* The psychomotor-perceptual skill might better be expressed as "the student should be able to fashion a temporary splint for a simple fracture of an arm or leg."

7. *The student should appreciate backpacking.* For this affective understanding, "appreciate" is not a clear verb. If an affect is desired, the ILO might better be stated as "the student views backpacking as an experience having deep personal meaning." As a cognition, the ILO could state that "the student understands why individuals take up backpacking as a recreational activity."

Priority of ILOs

Your list of ILOs may be short (5–10) or lengthy (more than 50). The list may include ILO statements with supplementary explanations (when needed), lists of concepts and assertions, and flowcharts or lists for skills. The list may be a conglomerate of crucial learnings and relatively trivial learnings. If the list is long, it may be wise to eliminate some less important items. Everything cannot be taught. Often we accomplish more (in depth) by attempting to cover less (in breadth). Now is the time to consider priorities.

By indicating ILOs of highest priority, the set of ILOs as a whole communicates its meaning more clearly. Guidance for later phases of course planning (instructional planning and evaluation) is provided by specifying which ILOs are of greatest importance to the course and thus should receive greatest emphasis. Priority should be assigned in terms of the course as a whole rather than on the basis of each category of ILO. Your course may be balanced in terms of category or have a cognitive, affective, or psychomotor emphasis. Whatever the emphasis, high-priority ILOs are those cognitions, affects, cognitive skills, and psychomotor-perceptual skills that a student cannot leave the course without learning.

The following guidelines should assist in selecting the ILOs of highest priority in your course:

1. The basic question to consider in selecting high-priority ILOs is: If only a limited number of ILOs can be achieved by the students in your course, which would they be? ILOs thus identified are high-priority ILOs.
2. Consider the goals expressed by your course rationale. Which learnings are absolutely essential to achieving those goals?
3. Consider your ILOs in light of your central question(s). Which ILOs must be achieved to enable a student to answer or deal with the central question(s)?
4. Consider your ILOs in light of your conceptual map and flow-chart. What ideas occupy central or high positions on your map? What relationships among which ideas are crucial to understanding the content?
5. Are some ILOs prerequisites for a number of other ILOs, so that they must be mastered early in the course?
6. What would a learner have to achieve for you to consider that learner as having successfully completed your course?

COURSE-PLANNING STEP 4.6. Identify ILOs in your course that are of highest priority based on a reexamination of (a) your course rationale, (b) your central questions, (c) your conceptual map, and (d) your flowchart(s). Place an asterisk next to each high-priority ILO on your list of categorized ILOs. Leave unmarked those ILOs that are important but not of *highest* priority. Now eliminate from your list any ILOs that you consider trivial.

Overall Balance of ILOs

The final step in refining ILOs is to examine them in their entirety, focusing on their balance as a whole. Each ILO should be clearly stated by this point.

Balance entails completeness and nonrepetitiveness of ILOs as well as consistency with the course rationale. The following questions may be helpful when considering course balance:

1. Do the ILOs fit the rationale? Reread the course rationale, and examine the set of ILOs. Are there learnings in conflict with the rationale. Are there additional learnings necessary to make the course fit the rationale more closely? Does the rationale now need revision?
2. Are there redundancies? This requires looking for ILOs that are essentially restatements of other ILOs. These can be literal repeats or ILOs stated so that they encompass other ILOs.
3. Are there gaps? This requires looking for ILOs that are not included. This may occur in the form of content or behaviors that are omitted.
4. Is there a predominant category? This requires looking at the four categories of ILOs. Are one or more categories missing? Does one category seem overloaded? For example, if someone is to define, describe, explain, and identify something, aren't there also some ideas that person should grasp? If someone is to value a procedure, should the individual understand or be able to do it?
5. Are high-level cognitive skills supported by appropriate cognitions? Conversely, are cognitions accompanied by learnings that make use of the ideas?

You have great freedom in determining the balance of the course. There may be valid reasons for gaps, redundancies, or the predominance of a particular category of ILOs. *These considerations are intended only to assist you in creating the balance you desire.*

COURSE-PLANNING STEP 4.7. Examine your ILOs as a whole, looking for overall balance. This requires eliminating redundancies and filling in gaps. Check the rationale for consistency and make any necessary revisions.

Summary

The combination of proper category, indication of relative priority, clearly described behavior and content, and supplementary explanations or elaborations when needed should give you a set of ILOs that is clear, coherent, and comprehensive. A person reading your intended learning outcomes should have little difficulty understanding what is supposed to be learned in your course. These ILOs will be used in instructional planning, which, among other things, consists in designing the units of your course. The ILOs should be appropriate to serve this function. That is, each ILO should be teachable and learnable rather than a goal that can be achieved only indirectly (that is, through other learnings). This chapter ends for the time being the curricular aspects of course planning. You have now clearly formulated the "what" and "why" of your course. What remains are instructional considerations (the "how") and evaluation ("Was it successful?"). Naturally, you will return to your ILOs and rationale as further planning lends new insights to your previous work.

Questions for Discussion: Curriculum Development

1. Compare your initial list of ideas with your present list of ILOs. How different are the two?
2. For each ILO, specify from where it originated: the original list, the central questions, the course outline, the rationale, classroom discussion, or the clarification process, etc.
3. If you didn't already know the material, would you like to take your course?
4. How are your high-priority ILOs distributed across categories? Is this as it should be? Why?
5. Do you think you are planning too many ILOs for your course? Does your course need to be pared down in scope to get the kind of depth you want?
6. Do you plan to give your course ILOs to your students?
7. Rate the clarity of the ILOs used to introduce each chapter of *Course Design*.

References

Bloom, B. S. (Ed.). *Taxonomy of Educational Objectives, Handbook I: Cognitive Domain*. New York: David McKay, 1956.

Bruner, J. S. *The Process of Education*. New York: Vintage, 1960.

Bruner, J. S. *Toward a Theory of Instruction*. Cambridge, MA: Harvard University Press, 1966.

Bruner, J. S., Goodnow, J. J., and Austin, G. A. *A Study of Thinking*. New York: John Wiley, 1956.

Gagné, R. M. *The Conditions of Learning* (3rd ed). New York: Holt, Rinehart & Winston, 1977.

Chapter 5

Forming Units of the Course

After completing this chapter the reader should be able to

1. Cluster a set of ILOs into coherent units after considering each of the five bases for clustering. This ability assumes an understanding of each of the five bases and how they can be used for clustering ILOs.
2. Design instructional foci for each of a course's units. This ability entails an understanding of four criteria: appropriateness for ILOs, appropriateness for learners' abilities, motivation, and feasibility.

To this point we have been concerned with developing a set of refined and carefully expressed intended learning outcomes and with explicating educational goals in a course rationale. The intended learning outcomes express what is to be learned. The educational goals and the whole rationale justify these ILOs.

With this chapter, we enter the instructional planning phase of course design. Instructional planning consists in planning a series of events around a particular activity, stimulus, or vehicle for communicating ideas. These events and the focus around which they are planned are designed to lead to the learning of something desirable (that is, the ILOs). Instructional planning can occur at various levels of specificity, ranging from individual lessons to groups of lessons to groups of groups of lessons. Planning around a focus and toward an objective can be done at a highly specific level (that is, lesson planning) and at a general level (that is, unit planning). This chapter deals with the task of forming units for the course, each unit specifying one or more "instructional foci" around which the instructional events will be organized and one or more ILOs toward which the events will be directed. The subsequent chapters continue the process of instructional planning by showing how to sequence and group the units into a unit outline and how to specify the instructional events that are to take place within each unit.

Forming the course's units can be approached in two distinct ways. We can cluster the ILOs into coherent groups, with each group then becoming a unit. Alternatively, we can design units around an instructional activity (for example, a field trip), stimulus (for example, a case study), vehicle for communicating ideas (for example, a sonnet), or around groups of activities, stimuli, and vehicles for communicating such as themes and problems. Each activity, stimulus, or vehicle for communicating that serves as a means of learning a set of ILOs we will call an *instructional focus*. Whether we form units around clustered ILOs or instructional foci, we are breaking up the course into "chunks"; each chunk represents a coherent portion of the course designed to achieve a specified set of ILOs. Since neither approach is appropriate for all courses, we present both approaches to forming units. Then you, as the course planner, can decide which approach (or combination of approaches) is most appropriate for your particular course.

Elementary teachers rarely plan courses. As we have said in Chapter 1, the *unit* is a more appropriate curriculum "chunk" for elementary planning. The next two chapters of *Course Design* deal with course organization and the arrangement of units in particular. If you are planning a unit instead of a course, you will have to make some adjustments so that the guidelines presented are appropriate for your level of planning. The principles of course organization will remain the same but their application will have to be modified. We have incorporated suggestions for these changes at the end of this chapter. Elementary teachers or others planning units should read through this section before doing any further work.

Forming internally coherent units is one major step in producing a coherent course design. This built-in coherence increases the likelihood that students will see the interrelationships of course elements and thus see how the elements fit together into a whole.

Clustering ILOs into Units

The clustering of ILOs into units is a process of creating units from the list of ILOs previously developed. But before presenting guidelines for clustering ILOs, we must deal with some preliminary questions.

Units

How big is a unit? No precise answer, such as "between 5 and 10 ILOs," can be given to this question. Nevertheless, considerations of coherence and scope may help you decide on the unit size for your course.

First, a unit should be a coherent whole. That is, the ILOs comprising the unit should make some sense together. Upon completion of a unit the student should know or be able to do some things that are related to each other. Each unit should be given a title. This serves as one check on the coherence of each unit.

Second, each unit should be manageable in scope. Students should be able to view each unit as a coherent set of learnings that relate to one another. Each unit should not be so large as to inhibit discussing it as a whole. For example, a unit on the Civil War is probably more manageable than a unit on American History, 1850–1900. Similarly, a unit on Central Tendency in Statistics is more manageable than a unit on Descriptive Statistics.

Should ILOs from various categories be together in a unit? This is a difficult question to answer unequivocally. It probably makes sense to mix various categories of ILOs (that is, cognitions, cognitive skills, affects, psychomotor-perceptual skills) together in a unit. This is particularly true when the ILOs support one another. But a unit may, at times, consist of just one type of ILOs. This can occur when basic ideas or skills need to be provided or a set of ideas or skills are so important that they must stand alone for emphasis.

Can an ILO be included in more than one unit? Certainly, particularly high-priority ILOs. How many units should you have? As many as you need to cover or include all the ILOs, with repeated ILOs if necessary for emphasis.

As in earlier course-planning steps, the guidelines presented here should assist you in making decisions but not make decisions for you. Which ILOs should be clustered to form a unit may sometimes appear obvious and at other times appear almost arbitrary. We recommend that you go through the guidelines and consider the options you have for clustering before deciding which ILOs will comprise each of your units.

Bases for Clustering ILOs

There are five major organizational bases for ILOs. ILOs can be organized according to (1) the way the world is (*world-related*), (2) the way ideas are organized (*concept-related*), (3) the way knowledge is generated (*inquiry-related*), (4) the way pupils learn (*learning-related*), and (5) the way learnings are to be utilized in life (*utilization-related*). These five main bases for organizing ILOs are used in this chapter to help you think about clustering ILOs into units. These same bases are used again in the next chapter to help you organize the units into an appropriate sequence.

The world-related basis for clustering groups ILOs in a manner consistent with the temporal, spatial, and physical properties of things as they exist in the world. Some world-related dimensions include: chronology (should ILOs be grouped because they occur or occurred simultaneously or because they all represent causes or effects?); physical complexity (should ILOs be grouped because they deal with objects, processes, or entities alike in their physical characteristics?); and location (should ILOs be grouped because they entail content that is arranged together spatially in the world?). The world-related basis is particularly applicable for ILOs dealing with events, objects, or processes that have identifiable properties.

Following are two examples of ILOs clustered on a world-related basis:

> *Unit: The Pond (location)*
> Identifies pond-dwelling insects.
> Identifies pond-dwelling fish.
> Compares types of plant life common in ponds.
> Understands the contribution of various forms of pond life to ecological balance.

> *Unit: Low Tide (chronology)*
> Understands what is the effect of the moon on tides.
> Understands how some fish are trapped at low tide.
> Remembers names of plant and animal life observable at low tide.

The concept-related basis for clustering is a consideration of the conceptual properties of ILOs. Some concept-related dimensions include: logical prerequisites (should ILOs be grouped because the ideas must be learned and understood before later ideas can be understood?); conceptual similarity or relatedness (should ILOs be grouped because the ideas involved are related in some respect?). Note that the concept-related basis is particularly applicable to cognitions.

When considering clustering ILOs on a concept-related basis, the conceptual maps developed in Chapter 2 should prove helpful. Examination of the conceptual map should enable you to identify related or similar concepts. Some maps may also help you identify ideas that are logically prerequisite to other ideas.

Following are two examples of ILOs clustered on a concept-related basis:

> *Unit: The Circle (prerequisites)*
> Understands the notion of diameter.
> Understands the notion of radius.
> Understands the notion of circumference.
> Remembers the value of pi.
> Can relate the diameter to the circumference of a circle.
> Can apply the formula for the area of a circle to various problems.

Unit: Respiratory Systems (conceptual similarity)
Understands the mechanics of how people breathe.
Understands the process by which fish extract oxygen from water.
Understands respiration in reptiles.
Understands how seagoing mammals breathe.

The inquiry-related basis for clustering is a consideration of how knowledge is produced. Using this basis for grouping ILOs, the question to consider is: Should ILOs be grouped together because they represent similar phases of inquiry (that is, the process of generating, discovering, or verifying knowledge)?

Following is an example of ILOs clustered on an inquiry-related basis:

Unit: Facts about Light that Require Explanation
Knows that light travels in straight lines.
Knows that light can be reflected.
Knows that light can be absorbed.
Knows that light can be transformed into heat.
Knows that light can be diffracted.
Knows that light can be refracted.

The learning-related basis for clustering is a consideration of how students will learn the ILOs. Some learning-related dimensions include: familiarity (should ILOs be grouped because the learners are familiar with them or should familiarity vary within the clusters?); interest (should ILOs be grouped because they are of equal interest to the students or should relatively more interesting ILOs be grouped with relatively less interesting ones?); difficulty (should ILOs be grouped because the ease or difficulty with which they can be learned is similar or should the groups have a mix of difficulty level?). Another dimension of the learning-related basis is empirical prerequisites. An empirical prerequisite as used in reference to ILOs is something a student must learn to do before learning a subsequent ILO; that is to say, skill B cannot be learned unless the student has already mastered skill A. This dimension is particularly appropriate in the areas of psychomotor and cognitive skills. Your flowchart(s) will be particularly relevant here. In general, the learning-related basis is appropriate for any course because how students learn is an important consideration in planning.

Following are two examples of ILOs clustered on a learning-related basis:

Unit: English Classes (ease of identification)
Can identify nouns.
Can identify the singular/plural distinction and formation.

Can identify irregular nouns.
Can identify verbs.
Can identify inflectional endings of verbs.
Can identify irregular verbs.

Unit: Beginning Skating (empirical prerequisite and difficulty level)
Ability to start.
Ability to balance standing still and gliding.
Ability to stride.
Ability to stop.
Ability to regain one's feet.
Ability to push off.
Ability to maintain posture.

The utilization-related basis for clustering is a consideration of how the ILOs are to be used in the future by the learner. If there are skills that are part of a procedure and hence will be performed together in the future, you may want them to be grouped into a unit. Here again your flowcharts may be useful. Certain facts or theories may be expected to be used together in solving personal or societal problems, so this is a consideration for clustering. The utilization-related basis for clustering is probably most appropriate in occupational, recreational, or problem-oriented courses because the future use of the ILOs is specific and even predictable, and this future use of the learnings is probably a prime, if not the only, reason for the course.

Following is an example of ILOs clustered on a utilization-related basis:

Unit: Water Pollution (societal problem)
Understands how industry contributes to pollution.
Understands how municipalities contribute to pollution.
Understands how private citizens contribute to pollution.

Clustering Guidelines

1. When clustering, do not hesitate to include a particular ILO in more than one unit. This may be necessary to emphasize a high-priority ILO or because more than one unit's topic suggests its inclusion.
2. Undoubtedly the five bases for clustering vary in their appropriateness for particular courses. There may be other bases for clustering ILOs. Moreover, any set of ILOs composing a course can be clustered in many ways. What is important here is flexibility;

you should at least consider the many alternatives available to you.

3. Consider your course rationale in making clustering decisions: think about what you have said about your approach to the subject matter, about your conception of the individual learner and the learning process, and about how you see that individual interacting with society. Course-planning decisions are interdependent; what you decided about the course's approach should influence present decisions.

4. Keep in mind that any one consideration for clustering is probably inadequate and that the ILOs comprising a unit are probably best clustered on several bases simultaneously. Don't hesitate to use a novel approach to unit organization.

COURSE-PLANNING STEP 5.1. Cluster the ILOs of your course into units. You may find it convenient to use code numbers from your list of ILOs so that you do not have to write them over (for example *CS1* refers to the first of your cognitive skills in your list from Chapter 4).

If you experience difficulty in completing Step 5.1 or if you find that the clustering of ILOs seems an inappropriate approach to forming units for your particular course, you may want to try forming units around instructional foci. This alternative approach to forming units is particularly appropriate for those courses in which nearly all the ILOs cut across all or most units. Naturally, if most ILOs apply to many units, clustering the ILOs into units presents serious problems. In such cases, some focal points other than ILOs would have to be designed to produce a set of coherent units. The section that follows presents such an approach. You should read this section whether or not you use this approach to forming units; eventually you will have to select instructional focal points in order to plan a teaching strategy for each of your units.

Forming Units Around Instructional Foci

Clustering ILOs into units is a useful approach in constructing units for most courses. Nevertheless, many planners (particularly those mainly concerned with affective ILOs) have difficulty thinking about units without first considering their teaching strategies.

Instead of forming units around clusters of ILOs, units can be designed around themes and problems; around instructional activities such as projects, debates, field trips, papers, and experiments; around stimuli for thinking such as case studies and photographs; or around vehicles for communicating what we know or feel, such as books or poems. Such themes, problems, activities, stimuli, and vehicles for communicating are *instructional foci;* they serve as focal points for learning and lend coherence to a set of ILOs.

Chapter 7 shows how an instructional focus forms the "heart" of a teaching strategy (that is, what teachers and students *do* with the instructional focus). But the point here is that instructional foci may be useful for you to think about as an approach to course organization.

Instructional Foci

The concept of an instructional focus for learning has been most clearly explicated by John Goodlad (1963). Notice that he uses the term "organizing center," which we will consider equivalent to our term, "instructional focus."

The organizing center is a focal point for teaching and learning. It is instructional flesh on curricular bones. The organizing center for learning occupies a segment of time and of space, being intended for identifiable learners in a specific instructional setting. It may consist of a picture to look at, a book to read, an idea to contemplate, an issue to resolve, a place to visit. The organizing center may be useful for a few minutes, hours, days, or even weeks. It may be intended for one person or for hundreds. (p. 94)

Instructional foci (or organizing centers) are not aims or ends in themselves but are instrumental in nature. For example, "understanding the wave properties of light" could not be considered an instructional focus, while "experiments with shallow, glass-bottomed tanks of water ('ripple tanks')" might well be an instructional focus through which the properties of waves might be observed and understood. In a similar manner, "appreciating the beauty of late Beethoven quartets" couldn't be an instructional focus, though it is a potential ILO; but "the March University concert" is a good candidate for an instructional focus.

Much attention has been given to "ends," in terms of specified ILOs. Now we turn to the "means" by which these ends are to be accomplished. Several words of caution are appropriate here. First, it is sometimes difficult to distinguish clearly between means and ends. For example, if one activity in a course is to "type several original business letters," this could clearly be expressed as an ILO, "the student has the ability to type grammatical and correct original business letters" or as an instructional focus, "original business letters." It could even be seen as an evaluative device to determine whether or not the above ILO has been accomplished. The temptation in such a situation is to shrug and plead indifference. After all, as long as the student really does type several original business letters, does it matter what we call it? The answer to this is that it isn't just "what we call it," but how we see, understand, and plan the educational process.

Instructional foci (as the term implies) serve as focal points for course-related experiences; ILOs provide direction for those learning experiences. Together they give the structuring of learning experiences coherence and rationality. Thus, while it may appear difficult to determine what is a means and what is an end, it is important to decide on means and ends and to consider the consequences of these decisions for the course as a whole.

In his discussion Goodlad (1963) specifies several criteria for good instructional foci. First, instructional foci should encourage students to practice the type of behavior desired. In our terms this would suggest that the instructional focus should put the student in a position to use the psychomotor or perceptual skills to be taught, to use cognitive skills in making genuine choices, and to come to an understanding of content. Next, the instructional focus should encourage the practice of several behaviors simultaneously. This is not only for the sake of economy and efficiency, but is also completely consistent with the formation of unit-sized course chunks. It is the function of the instructional focus to help students achieve a coherent set of ILOs within a particular unit.

Goodlad (1963) goes on to specify other criteria. The good instructional focus should support and complement learnings in different areas of instruction. It should be planned with both past and future learning outcomes considered and should be so designed that all levels of student accomplishment, from the highest to the lowest, are reached, and so that a variety of interest and learning styles are accommodated. A good instructional focus has an educational significance of its own. It has intrinsic merit and contributes to a worthwhile learning experience. Whenever possible, literature should be good literature, art and film of recognized worth, and texts of high quality. Finally, Goodlad suggests, a good instructional focus "leads beyond itself to other times, other places, other ideas" (p. 100).

One example of an instructional focus that might be used for a course is a field trip to a local historical museum. This might have been chosen to accomplish ILOs such as the following:

The student has a sense of history about the community.
The student recognizes the change in life-style accompanying technological change.
The student recognizes certain artifacts as characteristics of the Revolutionary period.

Many of the same ILOs might be appropriate to several other instructional foci, a certain book, for example, or a film. The course would have many more ILOs, and not all would be accomplished by or even related to the field trip to the local historical museum. For example:

> The student knows what the major causes of the American Revolution were.
>
> The student can remember tactics in the major battles of the Revolution.
>
> The student recalls the names of the major military leaders of the Revolution.

It is hard to see how a trip to a local historical museum could be instrumental in accomplishing the above outcomes.

In thinking about instructional foci like this field trip, we might think of unexpected but nonetheless valuable things that could be gained. Perhaps something unusual in the museum will catch the interest of a student strongly enough so that independent research is done on material related to the course. Such an unexpected spinoff is characteristic of good instructional foci. While these things cannot be written into the plan of a course (you certainly can't plan the unexpected!), no course should be so inflexibly formed that it can neither admit nor capitalize on surprises.

Another instructional focus might be a case study of prejudice in a northern suburb. Discussions of the case study might relate to ILOs concerned with the student respecting his or her own opinions, valuing the opinions of others, and having a high regard for logical and accurate discussion. An instructional focus of this sort, although addressed directly to a body of content (bias, justice, tolerance of others, equality under the law, etc.), can be an indirect means for accomplishing affective understandings.

Selecting Potential Instructional Foci

What instructional foci you select for each of your units and how you use them will be crucial for your course. Therefore, this step in course planning should receive a great deal of serious thought. First you will be asked to develop a set of potential instructional foci that are interesting, appropriate for your audience, and appropriate for your ILOs. If you already have formed units by clustering ILOs, then the discussion should be placed in the context of selecting instructional foci for units with specified ILOs. If you are still in the process of forming units, then you should consider this discussion in the context of the course as a whole.

In order to stimulate your thinking on instructional foci, the following general considerations may be useful:

1. a. How do you want your audience to perceive the unit or units?
   b. What instructional foci will provide for interaction with students that will be exciting? fun? challenging? comfortable?
2. a. What emotional climate is desired?
   b. What instructional foci will contribute to group cooperation? competition? self-fulfillment?
3. What energy levels should be developed?
   a. Do you want to provide for variety by shifting from an intense to a more relaxed setting?
   b. Should the pace be fast or slow, or should it vary?
   c. When during the course do you need an interest "grabber"? For example, energy typically drops about two-thirds of the way through a course. Is that the time to try to provide an "engaging experience"? How about something special in the beginning to get the students into the course and one at the end to leave them on an "up" tempo?

COURSE-PLANNING STEP 5.2. With these general considerations, together with your ILOs, jot down a list of potential foci for each of your units (if you already have formed units) or for your course as a whole (if you are presently in the process of forming units around instructional foci).

The process of sorting through your *potential* instructional foci and selecting the ones *most appropriate* for each unit is best done by considering your ILOs. Some instructional foci increase the probability for instructional events that foster the achievement of key ILOs. Others do not make such events probable but do make them possible. Still other instructional foci, however interesting, make such events improbable and perhaps impossible.

Selecting the Most Appropriate Foci

In deciding which instructional foci are most appropriate for your units, you should consider four major criteria: appropriateness for the ILOs, appropriateness for the learners' abilities, potential for motivation, and feasibility. The appropriateness for the ILOs will depend on the degree to which an instructional focus provides an opportunity for learners to practice the intended learnings (for ILOs that are skills) or for learners to interact with good examples of the ideas to be learned (for ILOs that are understandings). The appropriateness for the learners' abilities will concern the background understandings and skills necessary for competent use of an instructional focus. The capacity an instructional focus has for motivation will depend on how well it challenges the learners and stimulates their interests. The feasibility of an instructional focus will depend on the availability of resources, their ease of use, and the cost involved.

We cannot prescribe how to make your decisions about what instructional foci to select. Nevertheless, we suggest that you consider your ILOs and then rate each potential instructional focus as 1, 2, or 3 (high to low) on each criterion.

Several examples that illustrate the selection of the most appropriate instructional foci follow. Each of these examples illustrates a different design problem through an actual student-developed project. The first three illustrate the process of selecting instructional foci for as yet unformed units. Examples 5.4 and 5.5 illustrate the process of selecting instructional foci for units already formed. As such, these examples should be examined carefully by all planners after they have formed their units by whatever approach has proved most useful.

EXAMPLE 5.1.   In a course entitled "German, Level III"* the ILOs could not be clustered into units. Instead, the planner decided to organize units around themes. Each theme would serve as a vehicle for learning most of the course ILOs. Each unit in turn could be taught through a number of more specific instructional foci. The themes can be considered instructional foci (or categories of specific instructional foci) because they serve as focal points for teaching a set of ILOs. They introduce content into the course that is not represented in ILOs but is used only as a device for accomplishing ILOs. In other words, each theme represents a category of *instrumental content* (that is, content used as a vehicle for learning) rather than a category of *curricular content* (that is, content that is to be learned). For convenience we will call this sort of design element a *thematic instructional focus*.

Within each unit, methods and materials must be selected. Within-unit instructional foci are still necessary. Since Examples 5.4 and 5.5 illustrate the process of selecting instructional foci for units already formed, we will discuss here only the process of selecting thematic instructional foci (that is, units) for this course.

After some research, the planner was able to list potential themes for her course. See the results in Table 5.1.

EXAMPLE 5.2.   In forming units around instructional foci (IF) the important decision is often not which foci to use (if they are all equally appropriate for the ILOs and learners' abilities, and are equally stimulating and feasible) but how to organize them into coherent units. The

---

*We are indebted for this material to Raquel Thomison, Cornell University, 1977.

TABLE 5.1.   Chart for German, Level III

Total Score	Possible Unit Title	ILOS	Ability	Motivation	Feasibility	Comments
6	Politics	1	2	2	3	Complicated subject matter; topic could be discussed in unit on the DDR
4†	Religion	1	1+	1	2	Important unit on Christmas; appropriate materials might be difficult
6	Industry	1	2	2	2	Stimulating articles difficult to find
4†	Family	1	1	2	1	Partial repetition from Level II
3†	Women	1	1	1	1	Timely topic
3†	Youth	1	1	1+	1	Excellent for motivation
3†	School	1	1	1	1	Good opportunity to compare school experience
5	University	2	2	2	1	Less appropriate than topic on school
6	Science	3	1	2	2	Surveyed in German, Level II
4†	Occupations	1	1	2	1	Good materials available
6	Modern History	2	1	1	2	Too broad
6	German/Austrian Cooking	2	2	1	3	Difficult to find materials; topic included in other units
3†	Free Time	1	1	1+	1	Opportunities for cultural comparison

(continued)

TABLE 5.1.   (*Cont.*)

Total Score	Possible Unit Title	Criteria for Unit Topics*				Comments
		ILOS	Ability	Motiva- tion	Feas- ibility	
3†	Social Life	1	1	1+	1	Opportunities for cultural comparison
4†	Sprache	1	1	2	1	Unifies topics
3†	DDR (East Germany)	2	1	1+	1	Timely topic
5	Description of German/Aus- trian Cities	3	1	1	2	Highlights cov- ered in Level II; is a detailed ap- proach warranted?

*Scale: 1 = Good, 2 = Fair, 3 = Poor.
†Indicates a thematic instructional focus rated high enough to be used as a unit.

situation is typically faced when each focus requires only a brief amount of time.

For example, one planner* designed a course to make "readers aware of how authors consciously or unconsciously influence the readers' feelings, moral attitudes, and social values." This course attempted to help pupils "read with discrimination and care in order to understand just what it is a writer is portraying as 'good' or 'bad,' how those values relate to accepted societal values, and how the author's values affect the reader."

This planner decided on the following instructional foci:

1. Comic books
2. Folksongs
3. Advertisements
4. Newspaper articles, columns, and editorials
5. Nursery rhymes
6. Fairytales
7. Short stories
8. Children's stories
9. Magazine articles
10. Popular songs
11. Novels

*We are grateful to Margaret Berger for the following excerpts from her project at Cornell University, 1974.

12. Religious songs
13. Protest poetry
14. Plays
15. Ethnic poetry
16. English and American "accepted" poetry

Then she organized these foci into the following units:

Unit 1: *Obvious Propaganda Techniques*
    IF: advertisements

Unit 2: *Newspapers and Other Written Media*
    IFs: newspaper articles, columns, and editorials
        magazine articles

Unit 3: *Young People's Literature*
    IFs: comic books
        children's stories
        nursery rhymes
        fairytales

Unit 4: *Prose, Fiction*
    IFs: novels
        short stories

Unit 5: *Poetry*
    IFs: popular songs
        folksongs
        religious songs
        ethnic poetry
        protest poetry
        English and American "accepted" poetry

Unit 6: *Drama*
    IFs: plays

EXAMPLE 5.3. Often in designing units for a course, the decision we face is what *kind* of instructional focus will be the *primary* one around which to form our units. For example, one planner* developing a course on nineteenth-century British literature stated the following ILOs (among others):

1. Students will be able to recognize their own feelings, thoughts, and values as they encounter them in their reading of great works of fiction and nonfiction.

*We are indebted for his ideas on this course to Chris Connelly, Cornell University, 1974.

2. Students will be able to analyze and organize these familiar feelings, thoughts, and values as they encounter them in great works.
3. Students will be receptive to, and will comprehend, feelings, thoughts, and values that are unfamiliar to them as they encounter them in great works.

Clearly, this planner is attempting to bring together two sources of content, one from the literature and one from within the student. Since these ILOs could not be clustered into units, this planner considered various ways of forming units around instructional foci. For example, the planner could have organized units around themes such as the following:

1. The child in society
2. Women in society
3. The individual in society
4. Class consciousness
5. Humans and their thoughts
6. Writers and their art

Or the planner could have organized the units around genres:

1. Prose fiction: Dickens (*Oliver Twist*), Brontë (*Jane Eyre*), Carroll (*Alice in Wonderland*), Butler (*The Way of All Flesh*), Hardy (*Jude the Obscure*), Conrad (*The Secret Sharer*)
2. Poetry: The Romantics (Wordsworth, Byron, Keats), Tennyson, Browning
3. Nonfiction: Carlyle (portraits of his contemporaries), Arnold and Mills (essays), Keats (letters)
4. Secondary sources: texts, histories, biographies

Or units could have been organized around activities:

1. Hypothetical problem situations
2. Discussions
3. Lectures
4. Laboratory groups dramatizing passages
5. Tutoring sessions

Instead of choosing only one of these three designs, the planner could combine all three designs. For example, the planner could organize units around themes, then around genres within each unit, and then employ the five activities whenever appropriate. This is only one of several possible solutions to the problem. Which solution is the best depends on which aspect of the course (that is, themes, genres, activities) the planner wishes to emphasize.

These three examples show that there are many ways of forming units around instructional foci because there are many kinds of instructional foci. There is no single approach appropriate for all courses. All we can recommend is to consider as many alternatives as you can think of and analyze the strengths and weaknesses of each.

Examples 5.4 and 5.5 illustrate the selection of instructional foci for units already formed.

EXAMPLE 5.4.*

Unit: Ecosystems
1. The student grasps the concept of an ecosystem and its four subdivisions. (Grasping the concept here involves knowledge of what constitutes an ecosystem and what does not, as well as a knowledge of what phenomena are explained by ecosystem.)
2. The student understands the interrelationships of the component parts of ecosystem subdivisions. ("Understand" here includes the belief that these subdivisions are related, the knowledge of what counts as evidence for this belief, and an awareness that the subdivisions act as one system.)
3. The student is able to trace the flow of energy through a food chain.
4. The student is able to define habitat and niche and will know how each relates to the other. ("Know how" here involves recognition of what counts as evidence of the relationship between habitat and niche.)

Potential Instructional Foci
Basic Ecology, Buchsbaum
field trip to wetland and climax forest
terraria
SRA film series
outside reading, in-class reports
lecture with visuals

These potential foci were then placed on a chart (see Table 5.2) and rated on the criteria.

EXAMPLE 5.5.

Unit: Manipulations through Language
1. The student will know that language is a powerful manipulative tool. ("Know that" in this ILO refers to the student believing in

---

*The inclusion of ILOs is intended to give you a better feel for the sample unit. The ILOs are not meant to represent a complete unit.

TABLE 5.2.   Selecting Instructional Foci (IF): Ecosystems*

Potential IF	ILOS	Ability	Criteria† Motivation	Feasibility
Basic Ecology	1 (high)	2	2	1
field trip	1	2	1	3 (low)
terraria	2	1	1	2
SRA film	2	2	2	2
reading	2	1	3	1
lecture	1	1	3	1

*Using this chart as an aid in evaluating potential instructional foci, the following instructional foci have been selected for this unit: *Basic Ecology* as text; terraria.
†Scale: 1 = Good, 2 = Fair, 3 = Poor

the power of language and understanding why language is powerful.)

2. The student will be able to recognize words and phrases that often convey misleading meanings.
3. The student will be able to identify what impression an author wants to make on a reader.

Potential Instructional Foci
teacher presentation
newspapers and magazines
commercials (produced by students)
commercials (TV)

These potential foci were then charted (see Table 5.3) and rated on the criteria.

COURSE-PLANNING STEP 5.3.   From your list of potential instructional foci, select those that are (a) most appropriate for the ILOs, (b) most appropriate for the learners' abilities, (c) most likely to provide motivation, and (d) most feasible. When considering appropriateness for ILOs, pay particular attention to high-priority ILOs. If you are selecting instructional foci for units already formed, limit yourself to two foci per unit. If you are selecting instructional foci as an approach to forming units, then each instructional focus or coherent group of foci you choose will constitute a unit.

COURSE-PLANNING STEP 5.4.   If you are designing each of your units around an instructional focus, list the ILOs appropriate for each unit. That is, key ILOs to each of your units based on what each instructional focus or group of foci (that is, unit) is supposed to accomplish.

TABLE 5.3. Selecting Instructional Foci (IF): Language Manipulations*

		Criteria†		
Potential IF	ILOS	Ability	Motivation	Feasibility
Teacher presentation	2	2	3	1
Newspapers and magazines	2	1	2	1
Writing commercials	2	2	1–2	2
Viewing commercials	1	2	1–2	3

*Using this chart as an aid in evaluating potential instructional foci, the following instructional focus for this unit has been selected: newspapers and magazines.

†Scale: 1 = Good, 2 = Fair, 3 = Poor.

Titling the Units

Providing the title for a unit is very similar to the elementary school exercise of choosing the best heading for a paragraph or title for a story. In the context of course design, titling a unit serves as a check on the coherence of a unit. If a group of ILOs together with a small group of instructional foci cannot be titled, it may be wise to examine them for coherence and make any necessary changes.

COURSE-PLANNING STEP 5.5. Title each of the units of your course.

Organization and Sequence for Elementary Unit Planning

Most elementary units planned by teachers have neither the length nor the scope to make clustering ILOs a useful approach to organization. Elementary instruction typically employs a wider variety of instructional foci and learning activities than secondary instruction does. Compared to secondary and postsecondary teachers, elementary teachers must deal with shorter student attention spans, students who cannot reason formally, and, often, students with fewer areas of common knowlege in their backgrounds. This usually necessitates a more active instructional mode with different foci of shorter duration. We suggest that elementary teachers proceed through Chapters 5 and 6 as follows:

1. Review all the planning you have done so far. Return to your list of initial ideas. Gather and browse through any resources con-

taining activities, materials, and other instructional ideas related
to your unit. Compile *all* the instructional ideas that you find
appealing. Instructional ideas include a great many things. Some
examples are library research projects, teacher demonstrations,
reading and discussing newspapers, debate, simulations, experimentation, teacher presentation, writing assignments, and building scale models. In short, any of the many tasks elementary students typically engage in qualify here.

2. ILOs should now be "keyed" to these instructional ideas. That is,
decide which activities are likely to lead to which ILOs and indicate this.

3. Examine the list for coverage. Are all your high-priority ILOs included at least once? Add instructional ideas if necessary.

4. Eliminate some of the instructional ideas on your list. To do this,
use the criteria suggested for selecting instructional foci. Decisions
about appropriateness, feasibility, and motivation should, of
course, consider the age and the development of the students.
Priority of ILOs must be considered in making this selection; be
sure to specify any time constraints with which you must work.
You should now have a list of ideas that you intend to use in teaching your unit.

5. Chapter 6 discusses the sequence of course units. As we noted with
secondary teachers, elementary teachers have more alternative instructional sequences than they usually realize. You should read
Chapter 6 now and then make a sequence of the instructional
ideas you have developed. Many suggestions in Chapter 6 should
prove helpful; your instructional ideas will probably fall together
into groups and these groups can then be put into a sequence.

6. Chapter 7 deals with the development of general teaching strategies. You should find the chapter's guidelines helpful. We suggest
that you consider teaching strategies for each of your clusters of
instructional ideas.

Questions for Discussion: Forming Units

1. Which do you feel are your best instructional foci? Why? What
does this choice indicate about your own personal criteria for
choosing foci?

2. What does your choice of approach in forming units indicate
about your course?

3. Have you decided on the sequence of your units or is this decision
still open?

4. What approach to forming units was followed in *Course Design?* What are the book's "units"?
5. Does any instructional focus predominate in this book?

References

Goodlad, J. I. *Planning and Organizing for Teaching.* Washington, DC: National Educational Association, 1963.

Organizing the Course's Units

After completing this chapter, the reader should:

1. Know that there are alternative ways of sequencing content.
2. Be inclined to think about alternatives when faced with the task of sequencing content.
3. Be able to group and sequence a given set of units into a coherent outline.

In part, instructional planning consists of organizing instructional content into a coherent, feasible design for teaching. The previous chapter dealt with one part of this process, that is, forming unit-sized chunks of content for the course. The present chapter continues organizing the course by showing how to sequence and group these units into a course design that is coherent, not only within each unit, but also across units. The coherence of the course as a whole is the major concern of this chapter.

We discuss, first, the ways in which content can be organized for instructional purposes. More specifically, we consider the question, What are the alternative principles by which instructional content can be sequenced? These principles are then applied to the task of sequencing your course's units.

Alternative Sequencing Principles*

The sequencing principles presented here are essentially the same principles you met in the previous chapter as "bases for organizing ILOs." Therefore, the first part of this chapter reiterates and expands on familiar ideas in order to apply these ideas to the problems of sequencing units rather than to the clustering of ILOs.

*This section is adapted from Posner and Strike (1976).

The five major bases or principles for organizing units can be summarized by the five questions that follow. Each question represents a category of sequencing principles.

1. What relationships exist among people, objects, or events of the world and in what ways can units be sequenced so that their sequence is consistent with the *world?* Subcategories include relationships based on space, time, and physical attributes.
2. What are the *conceptual* properties of the knowledge to be taught and in what ways can units be sequenced so that their sequence is logically consistent with the organization of the ideas? Subcategories include relationships based on class relations, propositional relations, sophistication level, and logical prerequisites.
3. How does knowledge come about and in what ways can units be sequenced so that their sequence is consistent with this process of *inquiry?* Subcategories include relationships based on the logic and the empirics of inquiry.
4. How does the student learn and in what ways can the units be sequenced so that their sequence is consistent with the learning process? Subcategories include relationships based on empirical prerequisites, familiarity, difficulty, interest, internalization, and development.
5. How will the student utilize the knowledge and skills learned and in what ways can the units be sequenced so that their sequence is consistent with the *utilization* process? Subcategories include relationships based on procedural order and anticipated frequency of utilization.

Many decisions regarding the sequencing of units are not based on any of these five major categories of sequencing principles; instead, they are based on factors relating to the implementation of programs in specific situations. Such factors as materials and the facilities available, time schedules, weather and climate, location of the school, transportation needs, and teachers' interests or competencies are likely to be powerful determinants of sequencing. These factors have been referred to as "frame factors" (Dahllof & Lundgren, 1970) and may be considered a sixth basis for organization, *implementation-related*. Principles that are implementation-related, however critical they may be in organizing programs, are dependent not on relationships among units of content (the focus of this chapter) but on the administrative, physical, personnel, societal, and time frames of the particular teaching situation. As such, this type of situation-dependent sequencing principle has not been included in the present scheme.

Sequencing Principles: Types and Subtypes

The five major types of sequencing principles are discussed here in greater detail. In addition, several subtypes are described for each major type. (The scheme is presumed to be comprehensive for major types but not for subtypes.) This categorization can be considered a sort of "shopping list" from which to choose sequencing principles for your course. Although the principles are presented in relatively "pure" form, consider how you might combine several of them to create the most feasible and rational approach possible.

1. *World-related sequences* are those sequences in which there is consistency between the ordering of units, on the one hand, and empirical relationships between events, people, and objects as they exist or occur in the world, on the other hand. World-related subtypes include spatial relations, temporal relations, and physical attributes, to name just a few. An exemplar of this type is the typical sequencing of history content based on the chronological sequence of events (that is, the subtype Time).

a. *Space.* Sequences based on spatial relations are those in which the units are ordered in accord with the physical arrangement or position of the phenomena of interest. Sequencing principles of this subtype include closest-to-farthest, bottom-to-top, east-to-west, and so forth. *Examples:* Teach the positions of the offensive line, the halfbacks, and the quarterback in that order. Teach the parts of a plant from the root to the stem to the leaves and flower, in that order. Teach about the states according to geographical location.

b. *Time.* Often the content (most typically history content) is sequenced chronologically from the earliest to the most recent events. *Examples:* Teach the major ideas of Marx before teaching about the nature of the Russian Revolution. Teach the names of the states in order of admission to the Union.

c. *Physical attributes.* World-related sequences may be based on physical characteristics of the phenomena of interest such as size, age, shape, number of sides (for example, in geometry), brightness (for example, in astronomy), empirical complexity (for example, in comparative anatomy), and countless other physical (and chemical) characteristics. This subtype is most commonly employed in the natural sciences because these disciplines are concerned with properties of things in the natural world. *Examples:* Teach the names of the states in size order (size). Teach the anatomy of an amphibian, then a shark, then a cat (empirical complexity). Teach the structure of a primitive society before teaching about a complex industrial society (empirical complexity).

2. *Concept-related sequences* are assumed to reflect the organization

of the conceptual world. That is, a sequence in which units (each unit organized around a major idea) are structured in a manner consistent with the way the ideas themselves relate to one another is termed a concept-related sequence. The conceptual maps developed in Chapter 2 are particularly useful in guiding concept-related sequences. A traditional course embodying concept-related sequences is geometry when taught deductively (see the subtype 2*b*, Propositional Relations). Many courses developed in the 1960s placed a high priority on the organization of ideas (for example, BSCS biology, ESCP earth science, PSSC physics, CHEM Study chemistry). These courses are described by the term "the structure of disciplines" (Elam, 1964; Ford & Pugno, 1964; Goodlad, 1966; Kliebard, 1965; Schwab, 1962). This term describes an approach in which the "fundamental" ideas of a discipline (that is, those ideas that subsume many others) are used as the central themes for purposes of grouping and sequencing content (Bruner, 1960). One argument for this approach is that since the "knowledge explosion," the student can no longer learn everything. Therefore, analysis of each discipline is needed to determine those fundamental ideas that form the structure of the discipline (Bruner, 1960). By learning this structure, the student can learn the essence of the discipline in the most economical manner, without having to learn every one of the many facts subsumed by each "basic" idea.

a. Class relations. A class concept is a concept that groups a set of things or events together as instances of the same kind of thing because they share common properties. Sequences embodying this subtype include teaching the characteristics of the class before teaching about the members of the class (Ausubel, Novak, & Hanesian, 1978), or vice versa (Bruner, Goodnow, & Austin, 1956). In either case, the order of teaching the members of the class is less important than teaching them in conjunction with or separately from the class concept. *Examples:* Teach about mammals before teaching about specific animals in that group. Define "discrimination" before examining racial and sex discrimination. Investigate various forms of democratic governments through case study before attempting to define "democracy." Compare sound and light before teaching about wave motion.

b. Propositional relations. A proposition is a statement that asserts something. Sequences of this sort include teaching evidence prior to the proposition that the evidence supports or teaching a theory prior to the facts that the theory explains. *Examples:* Teach an overview of the theory of natural selection before studying the adaptation of Darwin's finches (theory-instance). Teach the principle of "equal protection under law" before studying the 1954 Supreme Court decision on civil rights. Teach the volume of a gas at several temperatures and pressures before teaching Boyle's Law (evidence-conclusion). Teach about chemical compounds before teaching about biological organisms (reduction).

c. *Sophistication*. Ideas can differ in their level of precision ("acceleration" is less precise than v/t), conceptual complexity (the number of ideas subsumed by another idea), abstractness (the distance from particular things or facts; usually the opposite of concrete), and level of refinement (adding qualifications to an idea refines it). Sophistication embodies all these aspects. The concept of sophistication here is similar to Bruner's (1960) in his discussion of the "spiral" curriculum that returns periodically to ideas at higher and higher levels of sophistication. *Examples:* Teach real numbers before teaching about imaginary numbers (abstractness). Teach the idea of stimulus before the idea of conditioning (conceptual complexity). Teach Newton's laws before Einstein's refinement of those laws.

d. *Logical prerequisite*. An idea is a logical prerequisite to another concept or proposition when it is logically necessary to understand the first idea in order to understand the second. (See Phillips & Kelly, 1973, for the distinction between logical and empirical prerequisites.) *Examples:* Teach what "velocity" means before teaching that "acceleration" is the change in velocity. Teach the concept of set before the concept of number.

3. *Inquiry-related sequences* are those that derive from the nature of the process of generating, discovering, or verifying knowledge. Such sequences reflect the nature of the logic or methodology of a given area of thought (Parker & Rubin, 1966; Schwab, 1964). Dewey's (1916, chaps. 11, 12) attempt to structure teaching according to his analysis of the scientific method is a major example of an inquiry-related approach to sequence.

a. *Logic of inquiry*. Logic may be narrowly defined as the science of valid argument, or more broadly defined as the analysis of the norms of adequate inquiry. Sequencing principles rooted in logic reflect views of valid inference. For example, two different logics (epistemologies) yield different sequencing principles concerning discovery learning. A view that considers discovery to be a matter of generalizing over numerous instances (that is, induction) provides instances of a generalization prior to attempting to have the student discover the generalizations (Glaser, 1966). A view that considers discovery to be a matter of testing bold conjectures seeks to elicit hypotheses and then turns to a process of evidence collection (Bruner, 1960; Popper, 1959). (See Shulman, 1970 for a comparison of these two approaches to discovery learning.) *Examples:* Explain how Galileo arrived at the hypothesis that the change in velocity per unit of time for a freely falling object is a constant; then have the students find that the acceleration of any object allowed to fall freely is 9.8 m/sec, so long as air resistance is not a factor (hypothesis generation-evidence collection). Discover ways to light a bulb with a battery, then generalize a rule (induction).

b. Empirics of inquiry. Some features of proper inquiry are rooted in descriptions of how successful scientists actually proceed or in the social or psychological conditions of fruitful inquiry. Let us suppose, for example, that successful scientists were found to study a problem area before working on specific problems. This might lead to sequencing content in such a way that it emphasizes the need for a general survey of an area prior to the consideration of special problems. *Examples:* Teach what other researchers have discovered about reinforcement schedules before teaching students to frame hypotheses about optimum reinforcement schedules. Teach how to write grant proposals before teaching how to collect data.

4. *Learning-related sequences* draw primarily on knowledge about the psychology of learning as a basis for curriculum development and instructional planning. Most psychologists, although they might disagree about the particular instructional approach to be used, argue that the nature of the subject matter is not as relevant to course organization as are empirical claims about the way people learn (see, for example, Gagné, 1970; Ausubel, 1964). Exemplar sequences of this type can be found in AAAS' *Science—A Process Approach*, which is sequenced on the basis of empirical prerequisite relationships, and ESS science, which is sequenced on the basis of interest.

a. Empirical prerequisite. If it can be determined empirically that the learning of one skill facilitates the learning of a subsequent skill, the first skill can be termed an empirical prerequisite of the second (Gagné, 1970).* *Examples:* Teach discrimination between initial consonants; then teach the use of word-attack skills; then teach reading. In basketball, teach passing skills before teaching the fast break. In English, teach alphabetizing words before dictionary skills.

b. Familiarity. An individual's past experiences are often the basis of sequencing. Familiarity refers to the frequency with which an individual has encountered an idea, object, or event, that is, how commonplace it is to the individual. Seldom-seen phenomena or phenomena that an individual has heard about only occasionally are considered remote from that person's experiential past. Sequences of this subtype order units from the most familiar to the most remote (Dewey, 1938). *Examples:* Teach about American schools before teaching about Swedish schools. Teach the various occupations in the local community before teaching about careers in other communities and in other nations.

c. Difficulty. Factors affecting difficulty as conceived here include the following: how fine a discrimination is required, how fast a procedure must be carried out, and the mental capacity required for

---

*Refer to Posner and Strike (1976) and Phillips and Kelly (1975) for the distinction between logical and empirical prerequisites.

learning (for example, memorizing five names is typically more difficult than memorizing two names). Sequences of this subtype would teach the less difficult content before the more difficult (see Suppes, 1967). *Examples:* Teach long vowel sounds before short ones. Teach weaving slowly, then teach the pupil to speed up. Teach the spelling of short words before longer words. Teach rhymes before blank verse.

   d. Interest. Instructional foci that stimulate or arouse interest are commonly those with which the student has had some limited experience (that is, not totally unknown to the individual) but which remain a challenge, retain the potential for surprise, or can arouse curiosity. The most commonly prescribed sequence of this subtype is to begin with those elements that are more likely to evoke student interest. The "activity" and the "children's interest core curriculum" (Smith, Stanley, & Shores, 1957) serve as illustrations of this subtype. *Examples:* Teach students how to pick a lock before teaching them how a lock works (Mager & Beach, 1967). Teach students how to dig out a local cellar hole before teaching archeology.

   e. Development. The work of Piaget and Kohlberg has served as a focus for much current dialogue on the sequencing and structure of subject matter (see, for example, Sullivan, 1967). Much of this dialogue centers on the importance of organizing instruction in a way that reflects the manner in which people develop psychologically. Developmental psychologists such as Piaget and Kohlberg contend that ILOs are best learned when the learner is developmentally "ready" to learn them. That is, "the ideal order of studies is one in which each experience is introduced at the most propitious time in the person's development" (Phenix, 1964). *Examples:* Teach students to base their concepts of morality on authority, then on democratically accepted law, and finally on individual principles of conscience (Kohlberg, 1963).

   f. Internalization. When the educational intent of a sequence is to have the student internalize a belief or value, units can be ordered in a manner that reflects an increasing degree of internalization (Krathwohl, Bloom, & Masia, 1964). *Examples:* Teach students to listen willingly to Marxian ideas, then teach them to interpret events in terms of a Marxian ideology, then teach them to view the world based on a Marxian value system. Teach students to recognize certain behaviors in others, then in themselves.

   5. Utilization-related sequences. Knowledge and skills can be utilized in social, personal, and career contexts. These three contexts can serve as bases for organizing units. Organizing units around personal and social needs has been advocated by some leading proponents of the "core curriculum" (Giles, McCutchen, & Zechiel, 1942). After needs are identified by "experts" (for example, psychologists, sociologists, anthropologists), units are organized around them. The "adolescent-needs core," the "social-functions core," the "social-problems core" (Smith, Stanley, & Shores, 1957), and the "life activities curriculum" (Saylor & Alexander, 1966) are representative of this approach. Another utilization-related approach to organizing units employs vocational and career-based topics. Saylor and Alexander describe how

> . . . units of study are organized on the basis of the knowledge and skills needed to perform an occupation or to carry out the duties required in a job. The mode of organization is determined by an analysis of what the workers do in a particular job and what responsibilities they fulfill as a part of the job. (1966, pp. 179–180)

The personal, social, and career contexts are appropriate primarily as categories of clustering principles, for clustering ILOs into units, and for grouping units. Within each utilization context, units can be sequenced in a way that reflects procedures for solving problems or fulfilling responsibilities, or according to the utilization potential for a given content element.

   a. *Procedure.* In training programs, when a procedure or process is being taught and the units represent steps in the process, it is often appropriate for the sequence to reflect the order in which steps will be followed in carrying out the procedure. Your flowcharts for skill ILOs might be particularly useful here. One important type of procedure that is often taught is that used in confronting personal or societal problems (for example, career decision making or air pollution) (Smith, Stanley, & Shores, 1957). When units are developed to enable the pupil to solve these types of life-related problems, the units may be sequenced in an order consistent with the individual's utilization of knowledge for this purpose. *Examples:* Teach the effects of air and water pollution (that is, establish a phenomenon as a "problem"), then teach the causes (that is, analyze the problem), and then teach how to eliminate or correct the factors that cause pollution (that is, suggest solutions). In landscape architecture, teach students how to analyze a site; then how to choose landscape structures and construction materials; then how to fit trees, shrubs, and flowers to the plan; then how to design the public and living areas.

   b. *Anticipated frequency of utilization.* Some course designs begin with the most important content, where "most important" means that which the student is likely to encounter most often. That is, the likelihood of encounters the student will have with various phenomena is predicted, and the order of the phenomena taught is based on the anticipated frequency of utilization in the student's future experiences. *Examples:* Teach compound interest before stock transactions. Teach how to change a TV tube before teaching how to change a resistor (Mager & Beach, 1967)

Use of the Categorization Scheme

One use of the categorization scheme is to provide a "shopping list" of sequencing principles. Awareness of this categorization system increases the probability that you will sequence units in a particular way because the chosen sequence is the most appropriate for your purposes, as stated in your rationale, not because you have never thought of any alternative sequences. That is, the use of the scheme will presumably lead to greater flexibility as you organize the units of your course.

Questions for Discussion: Principles of Unit Organization

1. In what subject-matter areas is unit organization most important? Why?
2. Are there courses of study that will include divergent, practically unrelated units in which organization will serve little or no purpose?
3. What are the criteria for choosing one principle of unit organization over another? How do these reflect educational philosophy?
4. Think of one of the best courses you have taken. Do you recall how the units were organized? Did that make a contribution to the quality of that course?
5. Think of one of the worst courses you have taken. Do you recall how the units were organized? Did that affect the quality of the course?
6. What would be the effect if, due to unexpected questions in class, the instructor teaching your course were to teach a unit out of sequence? Would this significantly weaken your course?
7. To what extent should the student be consciously aware of the unit organization?
8. Do you see any possible dangers in leaving the student uninformed about the organization of a course?
9. Can you think of other principles for organizing units other than those mentioned in this chapter?
10. What principle(s) were followed in the organization of chapters in *Course Design*?

Organizing the Units

Often courses are organized in a "traditional" manner; for example, history content is traditionally sequenced chronologically, with each unit representing a historical period. The preponderance of traditionally organized courses probably reflects, in part, the failure of planners to consider alternative course organizations adequately. For example, a history course could be organized around such ideas as industrialization, nationalism, and revolution rather than being organized chronologically.

Each organization can result in distinct kinds of learnings being achieved. Pupils in a history course organized chronologically would presumably gain a good sense of what events came before what other events; pupils in a conceptually organized course would likely learn the ideas the course was organized around. (Chapter 8 discusses these side effects more thoroughly.) Course organization can be an important factor in implementing a course's rationale. For this reason, a course's organization should be planned so that it is consistent with the rationale.

The overriding goal of this section is to organize the course's units in the most teachable and reasonable manner possible, as well as in the manner most consistent with the course's rationale. This goal will be accomplished by considering alternative patterns of organization.

Organized units are units in the order in which they will be presented to students taking the course. This organization is expressed in the form of a unit outline. There are three levels of unit organization: (1) the grouping of units, (2) the sequencing of groups, and (3) the sequencing of units within groups.

Grouping units consists in clustering units together in a meaningful fashion. This is analogous to clustering ILOs into units except that it is done on a more macro-level, that is, units themselves are clustered. Sequencing groups consists in ordering the grouped units in the way they will be taught. Sequencing units means ordering the units within a group in the way they will be taught. The lists that follow should help clarify what we mean by levels of grouping and sequencing of units. In these lists, the *ILOs* for a course in general math have been *clustered* into the following *units:*

> the set of whole numbers
> measurement
> the system of decimal fractions
> the metric system
> subtraction and division of whole numbers
> finite decimal operations
> addition and multiplication of whole numbers
> set theory
> whole numbers—bases other than ten
> the number line
> real numbers

These *units* could be *grouped* as follows:

> *Measuring*
> > the metric system
> > measurement

Whole numbers
  subtraction and division of whole numbers
  the set of whole numbers
  addition and multiplication of whole numbers

Decimals
  finite decimal operations
  real numbers
  the system of decimal fractions

Sets
  set theory
  the number line
  whole numbers—bases other than ten

The *groups* could then be *sequenced* as follows:

  whole numbers
  sets
  decimals
  measuring

Within these *groups* the *unit sequence* may be as follows:

Whole numbers
  the set of whole numbers
  addition and multiplication of whole numbers
  subtraction and division of whole numbers

Sets
  set theory
  whole numbers—bases other then ten
  the number line

Decimals
  the system of decimal fractions
  finite decimal operations
  real numbers

Measuring
  measurement
  the metric system

The example illustrates an organized course in which ILOs have been
clustered into units, the units have been organized into groups, the
groups are sequenced, and the units within each group are sequenced.
There are really two major decisions to make. One is deciding at what

levels you wish to organize your course; the other is the choice of actual organizational principles for those chosen levels. We will not attempt to prescribe which decision you should make first. For some planners, depending on the course, choosing levels of organization may be the appropriate first decision. In other instances, the planner must begin planning at one level, and wait to see if other organizational principles suggest themselves as the planning proceeds.

Alternative Organizations: Some Examples

To illustrate what is meant by alternative approaches to organization in the context of course design, let us examine some examples of unit outlines for various courses that have each been organized two different ways. You will probably receive maximum benefit from the discussion following the examples by closely examining the examples and then comparing them carefully.

EXAMPLE 6.1.

American History I
1. Exploration of North America
2. Early Settlement of North America
3. Europe and the New World
4. British Dominance of Eastern North America
5. Colonial Life
6. Relationship between Colonies and Great Britain
7. American Revolution
8. Foundations of American Government
9. Westward Expansion of North America

American History II

Settlement of North America
1. Exploration of North America
2. Early Settlement of North America
3. Westward Expansion of North America

Colonial Society
4. Colonial Life
5. Foundations of American Government

Issues in Colonial North America
6. Europe and the New World
7. British Dominance of Eastern North America
8. Relationship of Colonies to Great Britain
9. American Revolution

The nine units of American History I are organized in chronological sequence. That is, the events in unit 1 temporally precede those in unit 2, the events in unit 2 precede those in unit 3, and so on. American History II is an example of a conceptual organization. That is, the units are grouped around three historical ideas: settlement, society, and issues. The units within the groups can be considered chronologically sequenced. An American history course that has as a goal providing students with an appreciation or understanding of causal factors in history or a sense of the timing of various events would probably best be sequenced chronologically. Course emphasis, on the other hand, could be on underlying issues, major themes in history, or the ability to think about history in a conceptual way, in which case a conceptual sequence would be most suitable.

EXAMPLE 6.2.

Geology I

Observable Features of the Earth
 1. Gross Features of the Earth
 2. Rivers and Valleys
 3. Atmosphere, Weather, Climate
 4. Minerals and Rocks
 5. Snow and Ice
 6. Elements and Compounds

Forces Acting on the Earth's Form
 7. Rock Weathering and Soil
 8. Ground Water
 9. Valley Glaciers
10. Continental Glaciers
11. Wind as an Agent of Gradation
12. Gradation by Mass Movement of Surface Materials

Geology II

Units of Earth's Geologic System
 1. Elements and Compounds
 2. Minerals and Rocks
 3. Atmosphere, Weather, Climate
 4. Snow and Ice

Forces Shaping the Earth
 5. Rock Weathering and Soil
 6. Valley Glaciers
 7. Continental Glaciers
 8. Wind as an Agent of Gradation
 9. Gradation by Mass Movement of Surface Materials

Physical Features of the Earth
10. Gross Features of the Earth
11. Ground Water
12. Rivers and Valleys

Geology I contains units sequenced within groups according to the assumed familiarity of the content of the learners. The units progress roughly from those most familiar to the learner to those least familiar. Note that sequencing on the basis of familiarity requires information about the audience because different audiences may find different topics more or less familiar. The groups are formed on the basis of common properties: features and forces. Geology II contains units grouped in a conceptual organization. The units are formed around three geological ideas: basic units, forces, and physical features. The groups are, in turn, logically sequenced from raw materials, to forces acting on them, to the resulting geological features. The two sequences reflect very different though not incompatible concerns on the part of the course designer. Geology I is sequenced in a manner designed to facilitate learning based on the assumption that the content is difficult because of the students' unfamiliarity with it. Geology II emphasizes a concern for the students being able to grasp geological ideas and to relate physical features to their shaping forces. The difference between Geology I and II is one of emphasis.

EXAMPLE 6.3.
  The Media I

  Media Functions
    1. Role of the Media in Shaping Society
    2. Current Activities of Broadcast and Print Media
    3. Differences Between Various Media
    4. Advertising

  Historical Context
    5. Development of U.S. Media
    6. International Media Systems
    7. The Future of the Media

  Influences on the Media
    8. External Influences on the Media
    9. Legal Constraints on the Media

  Accessibility
  10. Public Access to the Media

The Media II
1. Advertising
2. Public Access to the Media
3. Role of the Media in Shaping Society
4. Current Activities of Broadcast and Print Media
5. The Future of the Media
6. External Influences on the Media
7. International Media Systems
8. Differences Between Various Media
9. Development of U.S. Media
10. Legal Constraints on the Media

The Media I and II represent part of a high-school senior English course. The Media I has a conceptual organization of units. That is, the units are grouped around the concepts of function, historical context, influence, and accessibility. The units in The Media II are ordered on the basis of interest. That is, the sequence progresses from those units thought to be of greatest interest to the learner to those units thought to be of lesser interest. The Media II reflects a greater concern, on the part of the planner, with the motivation of learners. That is, an emphasis on understanding conceptual relations (stressed in The Media I) is sacrificed for an emphasis that is likely to get the students interested in the course.

EXERCISE 6.1.   Now try suggesting alternative organizations. For each set of units below, decide on two possible types of organizations that could be employed and organize the units in each of the two selected patterns. You will probably find that additional units must be added to effect your chosen patterns. Feel free to add these units. The units presented in the exercises are listed in random order. Your task is to create a sensible pattern or flow of units.

Exercise A: Basic Ecology
Biomes of the World
The Community
Ecological Succession
Periodic Changes in Communities
The Living Environment
What is Ecology?
The Distribution of Plants and Animals
Climatic Gradients in Plants and Animals
The Physical Environment

Exercise B: Introduction to Sociology
Culture
Groups

Social Organization
Collective Behavior
Socialization
Social Stratification
Major Social Institutions
Urbanism and Industrialism

Exercise C: American History I
The Jacksonian Era
The Road to Revolution
The Origin of the Thirteen Colonies
The Confederation and the Constitution
The War of 1812
The Winning of Independence
The Development of the Thirteen Colonies
People Moving West
Jefferson in Power

To this point the outlines presented have been examples of relatively pure types. A "pure" type refers to the use of just one basis or principle of organization at a particular level. Often it is impossible or undesirable to produce a pattern that represents a pure type of organization. For example, we might want our course organization to reflect the way the world is, the way people learn, and the way they will utilize learnings in life. In such cases we attempt to produce a unit organization that reflects an optimal blend of principles. A "blend" refers to an organization of content that embodies more than one principle or basis.

EXAMPLE 6.4.

Economics and History I
1. Basic Economic Concepts
2. The Depression (an in-depth view)
3. The New Deal (policies and politics)
4. The Development of the U.S. Economy
5. The Economy Today
6. Economic Futurism (the next 50 years)

Economics and History II
1. The Economy Today
2. Basic Economic Concepts
3. The Development of the U.S. Economy
4. The Depression (an in-depth view)
5. The New Deal (policies and politics)
6. Economic Futurism (the next 50 years)

Economics and History is an advanced high-school course. Economics and History I begins with basic ideas; takes a micro-look at a period of economic upheaval in the United States; then takes a macro-look at past, present, and future economic conditions. The organization of units represents a blend of logical prerequisites (that is, basic economic ideas), level of abstraction (since a "micro-look" at the Depression is more concrete than a "macro-look" at the New Deal), and chronology (that is, past, present, and future). Economics and History II begins with the present, moves to basic ideas, then to a macro-to-micro view, and finally ends with a look at the future. The organization of units represents a blend of learning theory (since the unit starts with something familiar, that is, the present), conceptual structure (that is, the basic ideas), and chronology (that is, past to future). The major difference between these two units is that Economics and History II is sequenced so as to interest and presumably motivate students. Economics and History I reflects the planner's concern for providing basic economic ideas at the very outset of the course.

EXAMPLE 6.5.

Juvenile Delinquent Behavior I
1. The Prevalence of Juvenile Delinquency
2. Types of Juvenile Delinquent Acts
3. Types of Juvenile Delinquents
4. Primary Causes of Juvenile Delinquency
5. The Prediction of Delinquency
6. The Prevention of Delinquency
7. The Treatment of Delinquency

Juvenile Delinquent Behavior II
1. Primary Causes of Juvenile Delinquency
2. The Prediction of Delinquency
3. Types of Juvenile Delinquents
4. Types of Juvenile Delinquent Acts
5. The Prevalence of Juvenile Delinquency
6. The Treatment of Delinquency
7. The Prevention of Delinquency

Juvenile Delinquent Behavior I begins with an overview describing the prevalence of delinquency. Ideas are then presented (that is, types of acts, types of delinquents, primary causes), and methods of prediction, prevention, and treatment are included. Thus Juvenile Delinquent Behavior I represents a blending of learning-, concept-, and utilization-related bases. Juvenile Delinquent Behavior II intersperses methods of prevention, prediction, and treatment of delinquency with a logical development of ideas (that is, causes, types of delinquents, types of acts, prevalence). Thus Juvenile Delinquent Behavior II represents a blend of utilization- and concept-related sequencing principles. These two organizations are similar in emphasis. Juvenile Delinquent Behavior II integrates theory and practice to a greater extent than Juvenile Delinquent Behavior I. Delinquency II is directed more toward people who might actually counsel youth, whereas Delinquency I emphasizes an understanding of theory and of treatment instead of an understanding of how theory and practice are related.

This discussion of blending should be viewed as a representative rather than a comprehensive cataloging of options. Once understood, these alternatives should serve merely as a basis for thinking about unit organization flexibly, not as a structure into which thinking must be forced.

EXERCISE 6.2. Organize the set of units below into a pattern that embodies two or more organizational principles or bases. Again, feel free to add any units you may need.

> *Introductory Business Math*
> Interest and Compound Interest
> Stocks and Bonds
> Fundamental Mathematical Processes
> Payrolls and Taxes
> Fractions: Decimal and Common
> Financial Statements
> Percentage in Business

The organizational alternatives in both pure and blended forms should provide you with a number of options when organizing units. You should keep in mind the goals of teachability, reasonability, and consistency with the course rationale.

Again, flexibility is of primary importance when organizing your units. Consider the various alternatives available carefully before deciding on an organization.

Also try to approach course organization imaginatively. For example, one course planner used an approach that included "floating units," those units that can be inserted at any time in the course. A floating unit provides a breather at various times during the duration of a course, although course-related learnings are involved.

The makeup of each unit (that is, the particular cluster of ILOs) determines to some extent where that unit falls in a course. You may, at this time, want to reform some of your units in order to organize the course in a way that appears most appropriate to you.

COURSE-PLANNING STEP 6.1. Organize the units of your course into a unit outline. This step involves a combination of grouping and sequencing your units as explained by the various options. If in the process of organizing your units you find that the units themselves need to be reformed, don't hesitate to do this. Also, take another look at your rationale, making sure it is consistent with the unit outline. Now is a good time to revise your list of ILOs, adding new ones as needed or eliminating some if you find that they do not fit into any of your units.

Remember, course design is not a linear process. You will constantly need to go back to previous work, revising, adding, and deleting as you progress.

Questions for Discussion: The Unit Outline

1. In the process of organizing your unit outline, were any new ILOs suggested? If so, specify them.
2. What if a student missed a unit in your course? What would you accept as a minimal makeup?
3. Suppose that considerations of time forced you to abbreviate your course by one-fifth. How would you do this? Would you shorten units, delete one or more units, combine units, or none of these?
4. Suppose you were able to add 20 percent more instructional time to your course. What would you do? Would you expand some units (which?), add new units, split some units into two, or would you do something else?
5. Is there a mid-point "break" in your course? Do you have a "review" unit any place in your unit outline?
6. Sometimes a unit may serve more than one purpose. Could any of your units be retitled to indicate their other purpose? Which ones?
7. A student has enjoyed and profited from this course and asks you to suggest an elective to take next term. What would be the name of a course that could well follow yours?
8. How are your high-priority ILOs distributed across your units? If they are distributed unevenly, does this accurately reflect the relative priority for each unit? Are any units crucial? Are any units trivial or of little consequence?
9. A student looks at this outline and becomes interested and enthusiastic about taking the course. What kind of a person is this student? Is this the student you had in mind when you were first thinking about the course?

10. You may have rejected several alternative organizations. What grounds can you give for rejecting them?

Answers to Exercises

6.1

The organizations or "answers" given here represent possible orderings of the units provided in the exercise. "Correctness" of your answer rests on whether or not your organization is justifiable as being both teachable and reasonable.

A.
1. What is Ecology?
2. The Physical Environment
3. The Living Environment
4. The Community
5. Periodic Changes in Communities
6. Ecological Succession
7. The Distribution of Plants and Animals
8. Climatic Gradients in Plants and Animals
9. Biomes of the World

This is a concept-related sequence. Each chapter or unit is logically prerequisite to each succeeding chapter. The ideas presented in one unit are necessary to understand ideas presented in later units. Another possible ordering of units is illustrated below. This organization is also concept-related, but the units are grouped into categories.

A (alternative):

Introduction
1. What Is Ecology?

Adaptation of Living Things
2. The Distribution of Plants and Animals
3. Climatic Gradients in Plants and Animals
4. Biomes of the World

An Ecosystem
5. The Physical Environment
6. The Living Environment
7. The Community

Changes in Ecosystems
8. Periodic Changes in Communities
9. Ecological Succession

B:
1. Groups
2. Social Organization
3. Collective Behavior
4. Socialization
5. Social Stratification
6. Major Social Institutions
7. Urbanism and Industrialism
8. Culture

This ordering of units is illustrative of a sequence based on conceptual sophistication. The units progress from least to most sphisticated.

C:
1. The Origin of the Thirteen Colonies
2. The Development of the Thirteen Colonies
3. The Road to Revolution
4. The Winning of Independence
5. The Confederation and the Constitution
6. Jefferson in Power
7. The War of 1812
8. The Jacksonian Era
9. People Moving West

The units of this sequence are presented in chronological order.

6.2.

1. Fundamental Mathematical Processes
2. Fractions: Decimal and Common
3. Percentage in Business
4. Interest and Compound Interest
5. Payrolls and Taxes
6. Financial Statements
7. Stocks and Bonds

This sequence is a blend of two major types. Units 1, 2, and 3 are logically prerequisite to each other and logically prerequisite to the other units. That is, fundamental mathematical processes are needed in order to learn fractions. Likewise, the operations of the first three units are needed in order to calculate interest. Units 4 through 7 are sequenced on the basis of how frequently they are used. That is, problems and situations involving interest arise more frequently than problems or situations involving financial statements.

References

Ausubel, D. P. "Some Psychological Aspects of the Structure of Knowledge." In *Education and the Structure of Knowledge*, pp. 220–262. S. Elam (ed.), Chicago: Rand McNally, 1964.

Ausubel, D. P., Novak J. D., and Hanesian, H. *Educational Psychology: A Cognitive View*. New York: Holt, Rinehart & Winston, 1978.

Bruner, J. S. *The Process of Education*. New York: Vintage Books, 1960.

Bruner, J. S. *Toward a Theory of Instruction*. New York: Norton, 1976.

Bruner, J. S., Goodnow, J. J., and Austin, G. A. *A Study of Thinking*. New York: John Wiley, 1956.

Dahllof, U., and Lundgren, U. *Macro and Micro Approaches Combined for Curriculum Process Analysis: A Swedish Educational Field Project*. Paper presented at the annual convention of the American Educational Research Association, Minneapolis, MN, 1970.

Dewey, J. *Democracy and Education*. New York: Macmillan, 1916.

Dewey, J. *Experience and Education*. New York: Macmillan, 1938.

Elam, S. (Ed.). *Education and the Structure of Knowledge*. Chicago: Rand McNally, 1964.

Ford, G. W., and Pugno, L. (Eds.). *The Structure of Knowledge and the Curriculum*. Chicago: Rand McNally, 1964.

Gagné, R. M. *The Conditions of Learning* (2d ed.). New York: Holt, Rinehart & Winston, 1970.

Giles, H. H., McCutchen, S. P., and Zechiel, A. N. *Exploring the Curriculum*. New York: Harper & Row, 1942.

Glaser, R. "Variables in Discovery Learning." In L. S. Schulman and E. R. Keislar, (eds.), *Learning by Discovery: A Critical Appraisal*, pp. 13–26. Chicago: Rand McNally, 1966.

Goodlad, J. I. *School Curriculum and the Individual*. Waltham, MA: Blaisdell, 1966.

Kliebard, H. M. "Structure of the Disiplines as an Educational Slogan." *Teachers College Record* 66 (April 1965): 598–603.

Kohlberg, L. "The Development of Children's Orientation Toward a Moral Order: I. Sequence in the Development of Moral Thought." *Vita Humana* 6 (1963): 11–33.

Krathwohl, D. R., Bloom, B. S., and Masia, B. B. *Taxonomy of Educational Objectives. Handbook II: Affective Domain*. New York: David McKay, 1964.

Mager, R. F., and Beach, K. M. *Developing Vocational Instruction*. Palo Alto, CA: Fearon, 1967.

Parker, J. C. and Rubin, L. J. *Process as Content*. Chicago: Rand McNally, 1966.

Phenix, P. H. *Realms of Meaning*. New York: McGraw-Hill, 1964

Phillips, D. C., and Kelly, M. E. "Hierarchical Theories of Development in Education and Psychology." *Harvard Educational Review* 45 (1975):351–375.

Popper, K. R. *The Logic of Scientific Discovery*. London: Hutchins, 1959.

Posner, G. J., and Strike, K. A. "A Categorization Scheme for Principles of Sequencing Content." *Review of Educational Research* 46 (1976): 665–690.

Saylor, J. G., and Alexander, W. M. *Curriculum Planning for Modern Schools.* New York: Holt, Rinehart & Winston, 1966.

Schwab, J. J. "The Concept of the Structure of a Discipline." *Educational Record* 43 (1962) 197–209.

Schwab, J. J. "Structure of the Disciplines: Meanings and Significances." In G. W. Ford and L. Pugno (eds.), *The Structure of Knowledge and the Curriculum*, pp. 1–30. Chicago: Rand McNally, 1964.

Shulman, L. S. "Psychology and Mathematics Education." In Edward G. Begle (ed.), *Mathematics Education. The Sixty-Ninth Yearbook of the National Society for the Study of Education.* Chicago: University of Chicago Press, 1970.

Smith, B. O., Stanley, W. O., and Shores, J. H. *Fundamentals of Curriculum Development* (rev. ed.). New York: Harcourt Brace, Jovanovich, 1957.

Strauss, S. "Learning Theories of Gagné and Piaget: Implications for Curriculum Development." *Teacher's College Record* 74(1972): 81–102.

Sullivan, E. V. *Piaget and the School Curriculum: A Critical Appraisal* (Bulletin No. 2). Toronto: Ontario Institute for Studies in Education, 1967.

Suppes, P. "Some Theoretical Models for Mathematics Learning." *Journal of Research and Development in Education* I (1967): 5–22.

Chapter 7

Developing General Teaching Strategies

After completing this chapter, the reader should be able to:

1. Integrate appropriate instructional principles and strategies with ILOs and instructional foci in order to develop general teaching strategies for course units.
2. Compose a rationale for each unit in a course. Each unit rationale should describe (a) what the unit is about, (b) what it builds on, and (c) what it leads to.

Instruction, in our framework, is made up of all the purposeful activities of a teacher aimed at producing, stimulating, or facilitating learning in students. Instruction deals with how—what methods, materials, strategies, tasks, incentives, and the like can be employed to encourage learning.

Learning is an active process and, therefore, requires that students engage in some activity. The activity need not be overt and physical, it can be listening, reading, and thinking. This chapter presents guidelines for the development of teaching strategies that engage students in appropriate learning activities.

Before describing features of these teaching strategies, some perspective on instructional planning is necessary. Instructional planning entails more than devising teaching strategies. Effective instructional planning also requires the design of optimal learning environments. Such environments include (but are not limited to) provisions for the following:

1. Goals—learners know where they are going.
2. Feedback.
3. Motivation.
4. Risk taking—learners feel that it is safe to try.

Stop to think about some of your significant educational experiences. It is likely that you or your teacher began with some sort of goal or purpose. That goal may have been like a destination you were trying to reach, such as achieving a certain degree of skill in debating, playing the piano, or playing tennis. Or, your goal may have been developing an understanding of a particular topic, or an idea, such as the Gross National Product. While still a novice, you probably had only a vague idea of the goal and one thing you achieved was a clearer idea of what there was to be learned in a particular area. In fact, your initial goal might be described more as a direction than as a destination. Students can begin to learn and teachers can begin to teach once they have some initial direction. As they progress, they will undoubtedly modify and clarify their goals. In addition, they will probably arrive at some initially unanticipated points. Their accomplishments will often result in a readjustment of their plans and a resetting of their goals.

Most successful educational experiences also require feedback. Feedback means getting information about progress toward the goal. Good instruction includes such feedback. In addition to guiding students personally and directly, teachers can set up situations that inherently provide students with feedback. Playing tennis against an opponent, clocking speed on a stopwatch, answering textbook questions while reading difficult material, engaging in a conversation about a new topic, and solving problems while studying new material all provide feedback for students. Feedback does not mean that the teacher judges the student's performance. Instead, feedback helps students in monitoring their own progress and in deciding for themselves how best to expend their energies.

For a host of reasons, people typically learn well what they want to learn. Although students can do passably well at some skill they have no interest in acquiring, or get a good grade in a boring course, significant learning is not as likely when students are unmotivated.

Motivation is a complex topic. Many factors contribute to the motivation of students and all students are different. Interest, curiosity, competition, social reasons, parental pressure, the need to achieve, health, money, power, and fear are a few motivating factors. These act in complex combinations as well as alone.

Although there is much debate about the topic, motivation is best thought of as internal. That is, teachers don't motivate students, strictly speaking. But whether the things teachers do result in student motivation or not, is always a question. Therefore, the teachers' responsibility is to design environments that are likely to engage students in such a way that the students are motivated to learn.

Finally, significant learning often occurs in a setting where it is safe to try and fail. Learning always has beginning stages. Skill and understanding, depending on their complexity, can require a great deal of time and effort before any level of competence or mastery is attained. Learning, particularly in a group setting, can be a very threatening, high-risk venture. Yet, students learn better when they take reasonable chances and do not restrict their output; they make errors and learn from their mistakes. Instruction is improved by creating a setting in which students will take reasonable risks, where there is no danger of ridicule, and where errors are to be learned from, not to be ashamed of.

We raise these initial points in order to place instruction and instructional planning into a perspective. More is involved than creating strategies directly aimed at achieving intended learnings. Teachers must also plan for an effective and humane instructional climate.

In this chapter you will learn how to design general teaching strategies (that is, the instructional events) for each of your course's units. These general teaching strategies are described in your course design at a level more general than daily lesson plans but more specific than a list of resource materials to be used. A teaching strategy is based on an instructional focus (see Chapter 5). An instructional focus (for example, a poem) identifies the "heart" of the strategy but does not describe the pattern of interaction between the students and the teacher. This interaction (that is, who does or says what with or to whom) is described in the instructional strategy.

Even the most elegantly organized course, designed for the achievement of the most worthwhile learning, can fail if the teaching strategies employed are inappropriate or insufficient for the desired learnings. A good deal of attention and effort has already been given to the categorization of intended learning outcomes. One of the reasons cited for this work was the fact that different kinds of learnings require different kinds of instructional strategies.

Instruction and the design of instruction are not as straightforward as teachers often assume. Recent work in cognitive science is showing that a crucial determinant of learning outcomes is the kind of tasks in which students actually engage, and the kind of thought processes these tasks require, rather than the tasks teachers assign or the material teachers present (Doyle, 1983).

Planning instruction with an eye toward academic tasks means thinking about the actual work or products the students will formulate (for example, book reports, essays, comments during discussion, arithmetic work sheets), the operations used in this formulation (for example, memorization, following the correct steps, reading and synthesizing), and the resources students are provided for their work (for example, directions, books and other materials, knowledge they are presumed to have). In addition, recent research indicates that the thinking students do is often not the thinking we intend that they do. Therefore, the intended learnings must be communicated clearly to students and they must be held accountable for the desired outcomes. Student accountability is conveyed not only through tests and other formal methods of evaluation but also through the questions teachers ask, the feedback teachers give, and all the other cues teachers provide which indicate desired learnings.

For example, a teacher may want to present material about the relationship of gas volume to pressure and temperature. If the intended learning involves comprehension of this relationship, students will have to understand how pressure and temperature affect molecular behavior. They will need to know or learn a model that allows them to picture molecules and understand the effects of changing energy states on molecules. Students should be engaged in tasks requiring inferences about the effects changing these variables has on molecular structure. Experiments that allow students to "play" with these relationships and begin to develop their own formulae expressing the relationships are desirable academic tasks. Too frequently, however, our tasks and accountability system emphasize solving problems which require the simple application of a formula (for example, $PV = nRT$). Students learn how to substitute numbers into a formula rather than gain the higher level of understanding originally intended. It is this disparity between what we intend learners to think about during instruction and what they actually do think about that we must guard against. Teacher questions, such as what happens to tire pressure when traveling at high speeds, or how does a racquetball feel after being hit for awhile, would help students realize that they are accountable for more than applying a formula.

The elements of *Course Design* are based on a clear set of ILOs. It is very important that teaching strategies, classroom interaction, and evaluation be consistent with your intentions. When planning and implementing instruction, you must provide for ways to ensure that student thinking is indeed what you want it to be. This chapter begins by describing the kinds of instructional events that should take place (that is, the strategies that should be used) for effectively teaching cognitions, cognitive skills, psychomotor-perceptual skills, and affects. Accompanying each strategy is the principle of instruction that justifies and further explains the strategy.

The descriptions of effective instructional strategies and the accompanying instructional principles can be used in two ways: as a source of ideas for developing general teaching strategies and as a check on the validity of general teaching strategies already designed. You might have great ideas for instructional foci for your course but be unable to develop general teaching strategies specifically designed to accomplish each of your units' ILOs. In such a case, the instructional principles and strategies may supply you with ideas about how to use those instructional foci as a basis for accomplishing your desired learnings. On the other hand, you may have a good idea of how to proceed with instruction, but you may need some readily available resource for checking your teaching strategies against a fairly comprehensive set of criteria.

In either case, the instructional principles and strategies that follow should provide a convenient resource for planning instruction. They are not intended to replace a text in educational psychology; they are highly condensed and cite no supporting evidence for the claims made. They are intended only as a tentative starting point and should not be taken as established truths about instruction. They are all instances of a fundamental learning principle—students learn as a result of their active involvement with ideas and skills. The goal of instruction is to have students engage in the kind of thinking that is appropriate for the intended learning outcomes.

Cognitions

The following principles and strategies are presented as suggestions for the teaching of ideas that are classes or categories of objects or events, here termed "concepts." (Items 1 through 4 are adapted from Klausmeier and Ripple, 1971.)

Principles	*Strategies*
1. "Attending to likenesses and differences among things, qualities, and events is essential to subsequent classification" (p. 422).	1. "Emphasize the attributes of the concept" (p. 442). When teaching the concept of mammal, the pictures and verbal descriptions presented should have a minimum of irrelevant and distracting attributes, and the teacher should point out only the defining attributes.
2. Learning the proper label (that is, words or symbols) for a concept enables the learner initially to acquire the concept from the observed instances.	2. "Establish the correct terminology for concepts" (p. 422). When teaching the concepts of rocks and minerals, do not allow students to call either one "stones" or to interchange the two terms.
3. Understanding the definition of concepts to be learned facilitates concept learning.	3. "Indicate the nature of the concept to be learned" (p. 422). When teaching the concept of "menopause," explain that it is the time of permanent cessation of menstruation usually occurring around ages 45 to 50.

Principles	*Strategies*
4. "Understanding the concept is facilitated through encounters with positive and negative instances of the concept" (p. 443).	4. Give a good example of the concept and also nonexamples. When teaching the concept of "expository prose," make a simultaneous presentation of various examples of expository prose. Then present a few examples of nonexpository prose and explain why they are negative instances.
5. Practicing a concept with same-context examples reduces initial confusion, while subsequent practice with varied-context examples results in deeper understanding and transfer.	5. Begin with same-context, prototypic examples, then provide varied-context ones. When teaching the concept of "instruction," begin with examples of school-based instruction; then provide examples of informal instruction given by a master to an apprentice and by a parent to a child.
6. Thinking of additional instances of the concept extends the individual's concept.	6. Ask students to find instances of the concepts. When teaching the concept of a "value system," have students interview people to find out what makes them happy.
7. Thinking about a new concept as a member of a currently understood class or analogous to a currently understood concept helps make the concept meaningful to the learner.	7. Encourage the students to relate the concept to other concepts and to use it in interpreting their world. When teaching the concept of "roles," ask students how roles people play in life are like the roles actors play in the theater. Then have students analyze the various roles they play, their parents play, and their teachers play.
8. Thinking about the usefulness of a new concept in solving problems or in explaining facts helps the learner evaluate the adequacy of the con-	8. Ask students to use the concept by relating to real-life problems or situations. When teaching the concept of "roles," ask students how a person's roles relate

Principles	*Strategies*
cept in interpreting the world.	to each person's position and expectations. Then ask students to explain why conflicts often arise.

Some cognitions are ideas that are assertions, rather than categories or classes of objects or events. In teaching ideas that are assertions one may aim at memory of the assertions, comprehension of the assertions, or justified belief in the truth of the assertions.

Memory

If it is important for students to remember statements of fact, principle, generalization, theory, and other such ideas (that is, Bloom's taxonomy, level 1.0, often referred to as verbal or factual information), then the following principles and strategies may serve as helpful suggestions in instructional planning (adapted from Klausmeier and Ripple, 1971):

Principles	*Strategies*
1. An intention to learn well and to remember often aids memory.	1. Urge students to remember what they study at the beginning of the lesson rather than after they are finished.
2. Perceiving how the components of the task are related facilitates memory.	2. "Help the learner to identify meaningful relations" (p. 381). When teaching political facts about Peter the Great, relate these facts to the art, music, and literature of Russia during that time.
3. Mnemonic devices are especially useful in learning information that is difficult to make meaningful.	3. Help students use songs (for example, the alphabet song) and rhymes (for example, *i* before *e* except after *c*), form contrived sentences (for example, "Every Good Boy Does Fine" for tuning a ukelele), and use the etymology of obscure words to aid memory. Also, encourage students to identify their own mnemonic devices.

Principles	*Strategies*
4. Practice in using information (not just repetition) helps the learner remember it.	4. Provide for systematic use and review of material. "Distributed" (that is, periodic) rather than "massed" (that is, all at once) practice is preferable. When teaching formulas for the volume of various geometric solids (for example, cylinders, cubes, pyramids, etc.), have students use the formulas to calculate the amount of water held by each. Doing these calculations fifteen minutes a day for a week and then a quick review once a week is better than two hours of calculations on one day.
5. "Evaluating the adequacy and accuracy of one's information is essential for attaining independence in learning factual information" (p. 381).	5. "Encourage independent evaluation" (p. 381). Teach students to use reference books to check their information.

Comprehension

We are all familiar with memorizing statements without comprehending what the words mean. "I plegaleegints to the flag. . . . " If learners are to comprehend the meaning of statements, the following principles and strategies may serve as helpful suggestions in planning instruction:

Principles	*Strategies*
1. Words are symbols that vary in their meaningfulness for different individuals.	1. Explain (paraphrase) the statement(s) using words familiar to the learner. When teaching the theory that ontogeny recapitulates phylogeny, explain that the theory describes an organism's development as running parallel to the evolutionary stages of that organism.

Principles	*Strategies*
2. Individuals vary in their ability to comprehend information in a verbal mode as opposed to other modes of communication.	2. Translate into another mode of communication, for example, a graph or a picture. When teaching students the relative amounts that the federal government spends on defense, education, etc., draw a pie and label each slice according to the dollars spent for each purpose.
3. Individuals vary in their ability to identify concrete referents for particular words.	3. Point out or demonstrate concrete instances of the proposition.

Justified Belief

If the learners are supposed to believe in the truth of an assertion based upon evidence, then the following suggestions may be helpful:

Principles	*Strategies*
1. A belief is often based on firsthand experience with evidence.	1. Allow learners to experience firsthand evidence that determines the truth or falsity of the assertion. When teaching students the fact that an objective reporting of an event is difficult, stage a crisis in the classroom (for example, a physical confrontation), ask students to describe what they saw, and compare observations.
2. Beliefs are often based on consistency between new ideas and other things the learner believes to be true (that is, the existing belief structure).	2. Explain how the assertion fits in with other things that the learner believes. Explain Ohm's Law in electricity using an analogy of water circulating through pipes.
3. Beliefs are often based on understanding the implications of an idea.	3. Explain or allow learners to see the implications of the assertion. When teaching the theory of natural selection, ask students to describe what human

Principles	*Strategies*
	beings might be like 3000 years from today.
4. The more a learner understands the evidence both for and against an assertion, the better he or she will be able to justify the proposition in the face of an argument.	4. Present learners with evidence for and against the assertion and help them to evaluate the evidence. Hold a debate on whether the "gag rule" limits freedom of the press while preserving the individual's right to a fair trial.
5. The more the learner sees how the evidence was derived, the better he or she will understand it.	5. Help learners to see where the evidence comes from. When teaching the continental drift theory, have students try to fit the continents together as in a jigsaw puzzle.

The following principles and strategies relate to the conceptions or theories which students use to interpret their world.

Principles	*Strategies*
1. An awareness by students of their own fundamental assumptions about the world and those of the theories or conceptions they are supposed to acquire facilitates conceptual change.	1. Point out the fundamental assumptions of the new conception and ask students the extent to which the assumptions reflect their own assumptions about the world. Point out that Freud's theories assumed the existence of unconscious mental activity that one hides from oneself. Ask students if they believe people typically exercise "self-censorship."
2. A conceptual change will not be seen as necessary unless the students consider their current conceptions faulty.	2. Develop lectures, labs, demonstrations, problems, and homework assignments designed to create "cognitive conflict" in students, that is, where their current conceptions appear to be running into trouble in explaining facts. If students appear to conceive of light strictly

Principles	*Strategies*
	as a particle phenomenon, ask them to devise an explanation for refraction, interference, and diffraction phenomena.
3. The more intelligible and initially plausible a new conception appears, the more likely it is that students will consider it seriously as an alternative to their own conception.	3. Use exemplars, models, and analogies to make a conception intelligible and initially plausible. Explain that an electric circuit is something like an hydraulic (that is, plumbing) system.

Cognitive Skills

Cognitive skills are learned when they can be performed correctly, not when the learner can describe the steps. As skills, they require practice if they are to be learned. In order to help the learner practice a skill, the teacher needs to give the learner a task to perform in which the skill is employed. The teacher must also provide feedback regarding the learner's success in performing the skill. The following principles and strategies elaborate this process. (Items 1 through 9 are adapted from Gagné, 1970.)

Principles	*Strategies*
1. In order to learn a skill, the learner must first attend to the task.	1. Gain and control the learner's attention. Begin a lesson with a challenge, arouse students' curiosity, or surprise them or make them laugh by using an attention-getter that is relevant to the learning task.
2. Modeling one's behavior or the product of one's behavior serves as a guide to learning.	2. Provide a model for the learner's performance. When teaching students to solve quadratic equations, demonstrate the solution of a typical one, explaining all steps verbally while doing them on the board.
3. The learning of a cognitive skill presumes that the prerequisite cognitions and	3. Stimulate recall of relevant prerequisites (concepts propositions, skills). When teaching

Principles	*Strategies*
skills are available in memory. The more available the prerequisites are, the more easily the skill will be learned.	students to determine the number of neutrons in an atom, given only its atomic number and atomic weight, ask "What does the atomic number represent?" Then ask "What does the atomic weight represent?"
4. The performance of most cognitive skills begins with particular stimuli.	4. Present the stimuli inherent to the learning task. When teaching students to prepare "briefs" on legal cases, begin with a full description of the case.
5. In learning complex skills, cues may help the learner complete the task and thus learn to perform the proper sequence of steps.	5. Furnish external prompts. When teaching students to plan a meal, allow them to use a flowchart until they learn the steps.
6. The direction of thinking may be guided by instructions from the learner's environment.	6. Guide the direction of the learner's thinking. When teaching students to construct logical arguments, challenge the validity of an invalid argument by asking them to construct a syllogism for their argument and assess its validity.
7. Learning skills requires practice.	7. Provide practice of the skill. Homework often serves this purpose. Once students learn to graph the equation $y = x^2$ using strategies 1–6 (above) in class, the teacher may assign a set of similar problems to be done at home.
8. Feedback enables the learner to adjust his or her performance so that it can be corrected.	8. Provide feedback. Use daily weather maps to give students practice in predicting the weather for the following days. Then ask each student to

Principles

Strategies

keep track of their accuracy
and see if they can improve it.

9. Once a cognitive skill is acquired, it needs to be put to use. Generalizing the skill to new tasks is something that needs to be directly taught primarily through the use of a *variety* of settings and examples.

9. Provide for the transfer of learning to novel situations (for example, provide additional examples). When teaching students to estimate the stage of maturity of a river by observing its features, take field trips to actual rivers representing a variety of stages and ask each student to note the salient features and determine the rivers' relative age.

10. Problem solving is facilitated by representing the problem in a variety of modes and translating the problem from one mode to another.

10. Think about a problem using various representational modes. When teaching equivalent fractions, help students translate the problem into set-theoretic, spatial, and algorithmic forms (see Greeno, 1976).

11. Establishing the appropriate "problem space" is necessary for problem solving.

11. Help the student decide what the problem is about and what will count as an answer before attempting to answer it. When teaching dynamics in physics, have students list the given and the desired quantities, then show them how to classify the problem as an energy, force, or momentum problem before plugging numbers into formulas.

Psychomotor-Perceptual Skills

Whether teaching typing, physical education, agricultural science, industrial arts, cosmetology, driver education, science laboratory techniques, and other subjects that include psychomotor skills, the following principles and strategies may serve as an aid in planning instruction (adapted from Klausmeier & Ripple, 1971):

Principles	*Strategies*
1. "Attending to the characteristics of the skill and assessing one's own related abilities facilitates the learning of the skill" (p. 503).	1. "Analyze the skill in terms of the learner's abilities and development level" (p. 503). When teaching swimming, find out whether or not students can breathe properly in water before teaching them strokes.
2. "Observing and imitating a model facilitates initial learning of skilled movements" (p. 503).	2. "Demonstrate the correct response" (p. 503). When teaching the proper use of a table saw, begin with a demonstration.
3. "Verbalizing a set of instructions, or a plan, for carrying out a sequence of actions enhances the early phase of skill learning" (p. 503).	3. "Guide initial responses verbally and physically" (p. 503). When teaching students to play the guitar, remind them to relax their right hand. Then place their left in the proper position for a G chord.
4. Practicing under varying conditions facilitates the learning of skills through eliminating errors and strengthening and refining correct responses and form (p. 503).	4. "Arrange for appropriate practice" (p. 503) with respect to:
a. Some skills are "closely knit" (for example, diving); others are "loosely organized" (for example, football consists of an aggregate of component skills). Closely knit skills are best practiced as a whole, whereas with loosely organized skills, "each component skill must receive concentrated attention" (p. 509).	a. "Part-whole arrangement" (p. 509). When teaching the Morse Code, introduce all 36 code symbols at the first session.

Principles	*Strategies*
b. "The more closely the conditions of practice approach the conditions under which the skill will actually be used, the more effective the practice is" (p. 510).	b. "Context for practice" (p. 510). When teaching typing, begin with ordinary prose rather than with nonsense syllables.
c. Distributed practice is best "when the practice sessions are long enough to bring about improvement and when the time between sessions is long enough to overcome fatigue but not so long that forgetting occurs" (p. 512).	c. "Distribution of practice" (p. 512). When teaching guitar, require 30 minutes' practice each day rather than one hour on alternate days.
5. "Securing feedback facilitates skill learning through providing knowledge of results" (p. 503).	5. "Provide informational feedback and correct inadequate responses" (p. 503). After a student sings a middle *C*, play it on the piano for him to hear.
6. "Evaluating one's own performance makes possible the continued improvement of skills" (p. 503).	6. "Encourage independent evaluation" (p. 503). When teaching parallel parking, ask the student driver whether or not he or she is the proper distance from the curb and if not, what can be done about it.

Commonalities

Although it may appear that the teaching of cognitions, cognitive skills, and psychomotor-perceptual skills requires distinctly different strategies, the teaching of each also has some commonalities. Whether students are learning concepts or propositions, or cognitive or psychomotor skills, many educational psychologists agree that the following principles and strategies almost always are valid:

Principles	*Strategies*
1. In order to learn something, the learner must first attend to the task.	1. Gain and control the learner's attention.

Principles	*Strategies*
2. Relating a new task to what the learner already has experienced or is experiencing facilitates learning.	2. Determine what the learner already knows and teach accordingly.
3. Appropriately scheduled practice in increasingly varied contexts increases retention, transfer, and understanding.	3. Provide appropriate opportunities for practice.
4. Feedback or knowledge of results enables the learner to adjust his or her thinking or behavior.	4. Provide feed back during and after learning whenever possible.

Affects

The principles and strategies for teaching cognitions, cognitive skills, and psychomotor skills represent good instructional practice as we presently understand it. Nevertheless, use of the strategies in no way *ensures* that students will learn concepts, propositions, or skills. Their use merely increases the *probability* that the desired learning will take place. The teaching of affects is a difficult area for which to provide such principles and strategies. As well as having a cognitive element, affects usually require emotional involvement and often some degree of personal commitment. The range of how people cognitively react to a situation is great, but it is probably much less variable than their emotional reaction. Combine this with the fact that educators disagree as to what affects are (let alone agree on acceptable instructional practice), and you will understand the difficulty of suggesting a set of principles and strategies for affective learning. For these reasons, suggestions for the teaching of affects are not presented as a set of principles and strategies. Instead, we cite some samples of general instructional practices currently used or advocated for teaching affects.

Some General Ideas about Teaching Affects

1. Involvement in the learning experience is crucial to affective teaching and learning. Emotional involvement differs in some ways from intellectual or cognitive involvement; it involves strong feelings, some degree of risk, and a relating of the experience to the learner's personal life. If the learner is expected to attach positive value (for example, like, enjoy, value, respect) to a thing or

person, the learning experience must allow for positive emotion. The obverse is true for an ILO aimed at negative values or feelings.

2. An atmosphere of freedom and trust facilitates the willingness of the learner to take risks. Learnings that require self-understanding, self-knowledge, or beliefs and values involve varying degrees of personal risk. For example, learning whether or not to sample new recipes is much less profound and involves much less risk for the learner than learning whether or not he or she is prejudiced. When personal risk is high, the learner must trust and feel comfortable with the environment.

3. The depth or level at which the affective strategies can be used depend largely on the group (their age, maturity, size, trust, and respect for one another) and how comfortable the teacher is in leading these exercises.

4. Affective intended learnings usually have specific referents for the learner, such as respect for others' opinions, valuing clear writing, and being aware of one's attitude toward minority groups. The techniques we present are intended to give some idea of what teachers can do to involve learners emotionally. The referent or subject matter depends on the particular course, the learners, the teachers, and the milieu.

5. Many affects are best learned through modeling; that is, the teacher (or even certain fellow classmates) act in ways that embody the affect and learners attempt to imitate or model themselves after these so-called "significant others." Clearly, modeling accounts for much of our significant informal educational experiences. Parents, for example, have long realized that their children ignore suggestions to do as the parents say, not as they do.

Affective Teaching Techniques

What follows are suggestions for teaching affects. These suggestions are not in the form of principles and strategies; they are not intended to serve the same purpose. Rather, they represent a compilation of techniques that have been found to facilitate affective learning. These techniques include ways to structure learning situations and kinds of activities that may be used. The techniques are illustrative of the type of classroom situation or activity appropriate for teaching affects.

The techniques are organized into five categories. Each category represents a useful framework for thinking about these and other affective teaching techniques. In planning to teach an affective ILO, a teacher would probably want to use techniques from a number of categories rather than from only one type of category.

Feedback situations. There are ways in which to structure interpersonal interactions that facilitate the giving or receiving of feedback. Feedback is a response or return of information from one person to another. The response may be to an act performed by a person or simply to the person's presence. The response may be descriptive of what was seen, sensed, felt, and thought, or the response may be judgmental, that is, placing a value on the object or actor. Feedback is best accomplished in small group situations in which people are with the same group members for several meetings. Each time the group meets, exercises, and activities should aim at building trust. Two- and three-person groups, referred to in much of the affective literature as *dyads* or *triads*, are often employed to help establish this feeling of trust.

Simulations. Techniques can be used to help students explore thoughts, feelings, and fantasies about themselves, others, or even places and things. The teacher often sets up the situation that people will explore either individually or as a group. This technique makes the experiencing or expressing of certain feelings or values easier, as the risks associated with simulation are typically less than those associated with reality.

Attending to the present. Relatively straightforward techniques can be used to help students pay attention to present physical and emotional sensations and to feelings and values. They are an aid in helping students explore feelings and discovering how and when they block out the present. The technique may be as simple as having students begin sentences with the word "now."

Role playing. Techniques can be used that involve students playing the role of another person or object. Role playing is related to fantasy explorations except that role playing is more active; typically students act out a role in front of others. These techniques allow students to try out behaviors, feelings, and values not usually a part of their repertoire. In this way they can add to their own behavior repertoire, as well as identify more easily with the behaviors and the feelings of others. Becoming an object or playing the role of another person, describing these experiences, and generally using theater games are all role-playing techniques.

Communication. This category is a broad one, encompassing a great deal of the interpersonal interactions of the students. It includes kinds of communication often ignored by students, such as facial expressions, body language, and other nonverbal forms of communication. This category also includes situations in which the content of communication is specified. Describing "things I like to do" is such a situation.

These categories are neither exhaustive nor mutually exclusive. They illustrate the range of considerations necessary when planning for affective learning. The reader will find many ideas and examples of the situations and exercises described above in Borton (1970), Brown (1971,

1975), Duck (1981), Gordon (1966), Hawley and Hawley (1972), Morris (1978), Raths, Harmin, and Simon (1966), Schmuck and Schmuck (1974), Stevens (1971), Weil, Joyce, and Kluwin (1978), and Weinberg (1972).

Table 7.1 summarizes the instructional principles and strategies pre-

TABLE 7.1. A Checklist for Planning Teaching Strategies

Categories of ILOs	*Strategies*
Cognitions	
Ideas that categorize or group objects or events	1. Attributes of concept 2. Correct terminology 3. Nature of concept 4. Good examples and nonexamples 5. Same-context than varying-context examples 6. Finding additional instances 7. Relating concept to other concepts 8. Relating to real world
Ideas that are assertions Memory	1. Intention to remember 2. Meaningful relationships 3. Mnemonic devices 4. Providing practice 5. Evaluating accuracy and adequacy
Comprehension	1. Paraphrasing statement 2. Using nonverbal mode 3. Using concrete instances
Justified belief	1. Firsthand experience 2. How the idea fits with other beliefs 3. Implications of the idea 4. Evidence for and against the assertion 5. Where evidence comes from
Ideas that are theories or conceptions	1. Awareness of fundamental assumptions 2. Creating cognitive conflict 3. Exemplars, models, and analogies

(*continued*)

TABLE 7.1.   *(Cont.)*

Categories of ILOs	Strategies
Cognitive Skills	1. Attention 2. Model of performance 3. Recall of prerequisites 4. Presenting stimuli 5. External prompts 6. Guiding thinking 7. Providing practice 8. Providing feedback 9. Transfer 10. Variety of representational modes 11. Establishing problem space
Psychomotor-perceptual skills	1. Analysis of skill 2. Demonstrating correct response 3. Guiding initial responses 4. Providing practice 5. Providing feedback 6. Encouraging self-evaluation
Affects	1. Involvement 2. Trust and freedom 3. Group composition and teacher comfort 4. Supplying referent 5. Modeling

sented in this chapter. This summary can be used as a convenient check-list when developing general teaching strategies. The checklist represents a highly abbreviated version of an already condensed body of ideas. Therefore, it should not be surprising to find the checklist almost un-intelligible without first studying the previous discussion.

The foregoing suggestions for instructional planning were an attempt to give you some substantive grounds on which to base the general teaching strategies for each of your course's units. This process of specifying the instructional events that are to take place within each unit is obviously a complex and difficult part of course planning. It involves keeping several things in mind at the same time: ILOs, instructional foci, and relationships between units in the course, together with some of the instructional principles and strategies just presented. It is possibly the most strenuous and creative part of course planning because it requires keeping so many things in mind. You could begin by selecting the most appropriate instructional foci for your ILOs, while keeping the strategies and principles in mind. Or, if you already have decided on your instructional foci, you could use the principles and strategies to mold the instructional foci into teaching strategies that have the potential to accomplish your ILOs.

For example, you might know that you want to go on a field trip (that is, your instructional focus). But you would still need to decide what kinds of preparation and follow-up would be necessary and who would do what during the field trip.

Some Examples

The examples that follow illustrate the process of elaborating instructional foci into fully-developed general teaching strategies based on the unit's ILOs and the principles and strategies presented and summarized in Table 7.1. A rationale for each unit describing what the unit is about, what it builds on, and what it leads to is also included. Immediately following each example is a "Note" explaining how the instructional principles and strategies were employed in the development of the general teaching strategies.

EXAMPLE 7.1: UNIT II, ECOSYSTEMS. *Rationale:* Unit II deals with the processes and relationships existing in the environment. A respect and appreciation (course goals) for the complexity of nature is fostered through the construction of terraria, which are miniature ecosystems. Unit I, Our Environment, gives the student a sense of the many elements in the environment. Unit II, Ecosystems, looks at how these elements are interrelated. Succeeding units will examine these relationships and processes in greater detail, concluding with the role of human beings in the environment.

ILOs:
1. The student will grasp the concept of an ecosystem and its four subdivisions. Grasping the concept here involves knowledge of what constitutes an ecosystem and what does not, as well as a knowledge of what phenomena are explained by ecosystem. (Cognition)
2. The student will understand how the component parts of ecosystem subdivisions are interrelated. "Understand" here includes the belief that these subdivisions are related, knowing what counts as evidence for this belief, and being aware of the subdivisions acting as one system. (Cognition)
3. The student will be able to trace the flow of energy through a food chain. (Cognitive skill)

4. The student will know what the concepts "habitat" and "niche" are and will know how each relates to the other. "Know how" here involves recognition of what counts as evidence of the relationship between habitat and niche. (Cognition/Cognitive skill)

Instructional foci: terraria, *Basic Ecology*

General teaching strategies: The students' reading of *Basic Ecology* and the discussion of this reading, together with examples, provide their introduction to relevant ideas and terminology. Students will experience these ideas and will practice related skills by constructing terraria. After initial discussions about what they must consider in constructing terraria, students will have to rely on other resources for more detailed information. Working in small groups and being questioned by the teacher about what they are doing will give them an opportunity to explain the various aspects of ecosystems. The environment is a subject often involving strong feelings and values. Discussions of these feelings and values and the attachment of the students to their terraria should assist the students in developing an appreciation of the environment.

NOTE: The Unit II rationale points out the unit's principal concern is with the relationships among the elements in the environment. The ILOs are predominantly cognitions. A cognitive skill is also included. The instructional foci for the unit are a text (*Basic Ecology*) and a project (constructing terraria).

The instructional principles and strategies regarding cognitions indicate that instruction should establish correct terminology for the concepts, emphasize the attributes of the concept, and provide for use of the concept. The principles and strategies emphasize experience with firsthand evidence, seeing an assertion's implications, and considering what evidence might conflict with an assertion.

Reading and discussing *Basic Ecology* provide for opportunities to learn correct terminology, to learn attributes, and to relate the concepts meaningfully. Constructing terraria provides a chance to use the concepts and further explore their relationships and attributes. Working in small groups encourages students to evaluate their understanding and to use the concepts.

Basic Ecology discusses the implications of having an interrelated ecosystem. Constructing terraria enables students to experience and even manipulate and experiment with factors that constitute evidence for the assertion that the ecosystem's subdivisions are related.

The cognitive skill, tracing the energy flow in a food chain, requires the use of information covered in *Basic Ecology* and emphasized in the cognitions. The terraria project serves as a good external prop illustrating the energy flow. A student needs to trace this flow in constructing a viable terrarium, and the success or failure of the terrarium provides feedback. The terraria project also serves as a motivational device.

Overall, the instructional foci and the principles and strategies of instruction are combined in Unit II to form a general teaching strategy that should facilitate attainment of the ILOs.

EXAMPLE 7.2: UNIT IV, MANIPULATIONS THROUGH LANGUAGE. *Rationale:* This unit provides the student with the skills and knowledge needed to be a wise and intelligent consumer, voter, and information processor. Preceding units stress the mechanics and the extent of language. This unit begins a part of the course dealing with the effects of language. It deals with the effects of language on what we think, buy, and believe. The next unit stresses language's effects on what we feel.

ILOs:
1. The student will know that language is a powerful manipulative tool. "Know that" in this ILO refers to the student believing in the power of language and understanding why language is powerful. (Cognition)
2. The student will be able to recognize words and phrases that often convey misleading meanings. (Cognitive skill)
3. The student will be able to identify the impression an author wants to make on a reader. (Cognitive skill)

Instructional foci: newspapers and magazines.

General teaching strategy. The unit may start with the teacher providing the class with certain Harris or Gallup polls. Aside from using precise figures such as 73 percent, these polls often employ terms like "vast majority." The class should become convinced of the manipulative power of such words. The teacher can scan other magazines and newspapers with the students presenting items they believe are good. The presentations will involve students stating the author's intentions.

NOTE: The rationale for Manipulations through Language indicates that Unit IV is concerned with recognizing how one is affected by language. Two of the ILOs are cognitive skills that emphasize the ability to recognize these effects. A cognition closely related to these skills deals with a belief in this power of language.

The instructional principles and strategies indicate that experience with firsthand evidence and relating an idea to personal experience are useful strategies in teaching students to develop a justified belief in the truth of ideas. Providing models, feedback, practice, and props, as well as guiding the students' thinking, are useful strategies in teaching cognitive skills.

The use of magazines and newspapers provides a focus that is part of a student's everyday experience. Through locating, discussing, and analyzing examples of manipulative language, students should get the firsthand experience, practice, and feedback needed to accomplish the intended learnings.

COURSE-PLANNING STEP 7.1.   Elaborate each of your selected instructional foci into a description of general teaching strategies. This description should be based on your ILOs and on the instructional principles and strategies presented earlier. Pay particular attention to high-priority unit ILOs (asterisked). Avoid using the passive voice in your descriptions (for example, *do not say:* terraria are constructed). Instead, make it clear who is doing what in the strategy (for example, *do say:* students construct terraria by following instructions the teacher hands out).

COURSE-PLANNING STEP 7.2.   For each of your units write a brief (25–100 word) description or rationale of the unit, what it contains, why it is important, how it builds on previous units (if it does), and how (if at all) the succeeding units build on it.

COURSE-PLANNING STEP 7.3.   Reconsider your total instructional plan in the light of your rationale, checking for internal consistency and comprehensiveness. Add to the completed units any ILOs you had not thought of previously.

Questions for Discussion:
General Teaching Strategies

1. Did you add, change, or eliminate any of your ILOs in the process of specifying a general teaching strategy? Which ones, and why?
2. Which of your units at this point seem to be most complete, most appropriate, or simply best? Why?
3. Which unit at this point seems to be least complete, appropriate, or perfected? Can you say why?
4. Compare your brief unit rationales with your course rationale. Do the units as described seem to support the course rationale fully? Does this comparison suggest that the course rationale be rewritten?
5. With your instructional plan in hand, could someone else now teach this course (assuming practical teaching experience and a knowledge of the subject matter)?
6. Of your ILOs, which two or three do you now feel most confident about accomplishing? Are there any you feel uneasy about? Why?

References

Borton, T. *Reach, Touch and Teach*. New York: McGraw-Hill, 1970.

Brown, G. *Human Teaching for Human Learning: An Introduction for Confluent Education*. New York: Viking, 1971.

Brown, G. *The Live Classroom: Innovation through Confluent Education and Gestalt*. New York: Viking, 1975.

Doyle, W. E. "Academic Work." *Review of Educational Research* 53, no. 2 (Summer 1983): pp. 159–199.

Duck, L. *Teaching with Charisma*. Boston: Allyn and Bacon, 1981.

Gagné, R. M. *Conditions of Learning*. New York: Holt, Rinehart & Winston, 1970.

Gordon, W. J. J. *The Metaphorical Way of Learning and Knowing*. Cambridge, MA: Synectics Education Systems, 1966.

Greeno, J. G. "Cognitive Objectives of Instruction: Theory of Knowledge for Solving Problems and Answering Questions." In D. Klahr (ed.), *Cognition and Instruction*, pp. 123–160. Hillsdale, NJ: Lawrence Erlbaum Associates, 1976.

Hawley, R. C., and Hawley, I. L. *A Handbook of Personal Growth Activities for Classroom Use*. Amherst, MA: Educational Research Associates, 1972.

Klausmeier, H. J., and Ripple, R. E. *Learning and Human Abilities* (3d ed.). New York: Harper & Row, 1971.

Morris, J. *Psychology and Teaching: A Humanistic View*. New York: Random House, 1978.

Raths, L. E., Harmin, M., and Simon, S. B. *Values and Teaching*. Columbus, OH: Charles E. Merrill, 1966.

Schmuck, R. A., and Schmuck, P. A. *A Humanistic Psychology of Education: Making the School Everybody's House*. Palo Alto, CA: National Press Books, 1974.

Stevens, J. P. *Awareness: Exploring, Experimenting, Experiencing*. New York: Bantam Books, 1971.

Weil, M., Joyce, B., and Kluwin, B. *Personal Models of Teaching*. Englewood Cliffs, NJ: Prentice-Hall, Inc., 1978.

Weinberg, C. (Ed.). *Humanistic Foundations of Education*. Englewood Cliffs, NJ: Prentice-Hall, 1972.

Chapter 8

Planning a Course Evaluation

After completing this chapter, the reader should be able to:

1. Comprehend the meaning of the terms *actual learning outcomes, main effects,* and *side effects.*
2. Specify appropriate behavioral evidence for any given ILO.
3. Specify likely side effects that may result from a course.
4. Gather and analyze behavioral evidence using a troubleshooting approach to course evaluation

Perspective on Evaluation

To this point, course planning has been concerned with setting up a focused, justifiable, interesting, feasible, and coherent course. But a course must also be effective, and as planners we need to know how effective it is. Typically we need information about the course's effectiveness in order to make decisions about the course. Such information gathering and subsequent decision making comprise an evaluation aimed at course improvement.

The Uses of Evaluation

Evaluations can be used for many types of decisions. For instance, Cronbach (1963) identified three uses for evaluation: (a) course-improvement decisions, (b) decisions about individual students, and (c) administrative regulation. Evaluation for course improvement involves gathering information that will be useful in deciding which aspects of a course can and should be improved. Evaluation aimed at decisions about individual students consists in gathering information to be used in assessing student needs or in the grading, grouping, or selection of individual students. Evaluation for administrative regulation is directed toward assessing the merit of schools, curricula, materials, teachers, and so forth.

Cronbach (1963) argues that using evaluation for course improvement contributes more toward improving education than do the other uses of evaluation. This argument has been debated, most eloquently by Scriven (1967), who points out that decisions on the merit or worth of a course ("summative" decisions) are as important in improving education as decisions aimed at course improvement ("formative" decisions).

As mentioned, this chapter deals with course evaluation aimed at gathering and analyzing information that will be used for course-improvement decisions. That is, a formative evaluation is emphasized. This emphasis was not chosen because summative decisions are unimportant. But if the course is irremediably bad, this fact should become evident during the formative evaluation. The course can be abandoned on the basis of such data. On the other hand, courses can almost always be improved.

Range of Outcomes

Cronbach (1963), in discussing evaluation for course improvement, emphasizes the need for an evaluation to describe the broadest possible range of course outcomes. On this point Cronbach is in substantial agreement with others such as Scriven (1967), who also emphasize the description of course consequences.

Scriven (1967) elaborates further on the *range* of course outcomes to be examined. He distinguishes between two related but distinct enterprises, which he labels *evaluation* and *goal estimation*. Goal estimation (goal-based evaluation) focuses entirely on the extent to which a course has achieved its *stated goals or objectives*. Evaluation, on the other hand, requires gathering information on the *full range of course outcomes or consequences*. Goal estimation, as well as being more limited in focus, is viewed as less desirable than evaluation because goals are often unrealistic and thus an inadequate basis for information gathering.

Scriven's (1967) emphasis on evaluations that examine a full range of course outcomes has led him to propose *goal-free evaluation* as a radical alternative to goal estimation or goal-based evaluation. Goal-free evaluation views a course as an educational or instructional "treatment" and attempts to gather data on *likely consequences* of that treatment irrespective of stated goals and objectives. In contrast, a goal-based evaluation focuses only on stated goals and objectives.

This chapter combines goal-free and goal-based approaches in attempting to identify the important course consequences. ILOs are used to guide the collection of evidence that will determine whether or not intended learnings are actually achieved. The extent to which the course's ILOs are actualized are referred to as the *main effects* of the course. A second aspect of the evaluation is an examination of materials, methods, and other factors likely to result in consequences or effects that we did not intend or even consider. These unintended (and sometimes undesirable) outcomes are referred to as the *side effects* of the course. Once we collect information regarding both main and side effects, we can use it to make course-improvement decisions.

Using Information for Course Improvement

It may be helpful to think about course evaluation in the same way a TV repairman thinks about a broken TV. If the repairman wants to know whether or not the set works, he plugs it in, turns it on, and evaluates the quality of picture and sound. Assuming there is something wrong with the set, the repairman is faced with troubleshooting the problem. This process consists in setting up a series of probes that result in evidence pertaining to the operation of particular components of the set. The troubleshooting procedure allows him to isolate that aspect of the system which is malfunctioning.

While troubleshooting a course is analogous to electronic troubleshooting, it is far more complex. The likelihood of identifying a single course component as *the* problem is slight. But if we want to be able to use the information gathered in an evaluation to improve the course, we have to relate particular kinds of information to particular course components.

The troubleshooting scheme presented in this chapter is largely based on the intended learning outcomes of the course. Guidelines for gathering evidence are presented first, followed by questions that facilitate the processing of this evidence.

To summarize, actual learning outcomes (ALOs) are those things learned by students during, or as a part of, the course. These ALOs consist of those learnings that were considered important and were thus stated as ILOs (that is, main effects) and those learnings that were not considered important or were thought to be undesirable and were thus not stated as ILOs (that is, side effects). These main and side effects together with an assessment of educational results form the basis of course evaluation presented in this chapter. The kinds of considerations important in this evaluation include the following:

> Do all the intended learning outcomes turn out to be actual learning outcomes?
> If not, which ILOs were and which were not achieved?
> What ALOs were not planned for in the course?
> Are the side effects desirable or undesirable?
> To what extent were the educational goals achieved and were the ILOs relevant to the achievement of those goals?

The answers to these questions must then be applied in a troubleshooting approach in order to make course-improvement decisions. Applying the evidence for decision making involves thinking about the relationship between the evidence gathered and the various course components (for example, teacher behaviors, instructional foci, and the organization of units). To do this, evidence of learning must first be gathered.

Gathering Evidence on Main Effects

The course's ILOs refined in Chapter 4 are of four types: cognitions, cognitive skills, affects, and psychomotor-perceptual skills. The task of evaluation planning for these ILOs is one of specifying what will constitute acceptable evidence, that is, evidence that will indicate whether or not an ILO has actually been learned. Evidence is defined as an outward sign; therefore, by definition, evidence of learning must be observable. Since the evidence will be gathered from students, we look for this evidence in observable student behaviors or observable products of student work.

In the ensuing discussions we will focus the evaluation on high-priority ILOs. We believe that a course evaluation should emphasize these ILOs over less important learnings. Typically, time and resources limit the scope of an evaluation; evidence of highest-priority ILOs may be all the evidence one can gather. These ILOs have been identified and asterisked in Chapter 4 (Course-Planning Step 4.6).

One way to conceptualize the differences between the types of ILOs from the standpoint of evaluation is to consider the extent to which the content or behavior is circumscribed or defined in a particular ILO. A useful rule of thumb is: whatever portion of the ILO was not circumscribed in Chapter 4 now receives the greatest attention in specifying behavioral evidence. For a cognition, the content was highly circumscribed when stating the ILO; therefore, we now focus on the specification of sample behaviors that will serve as evidence. For a cognitive or psychomotor-perceptual skill, the behavior or performance was probably highly circumscribed when stating the ILO, and we must now specify sample contexts (that is, content) for those behaviors. Each type of ILO is treated separately in the following sections.

Cognitions

A cognition is an understanding and has no *directly* observable referent. Therefore, no *one* behavior constitutes acceptable evidence of understanding. The understanding of an idea has numerous and varied exemplifications. The evaluation task, therefore, is to specify a set of behaviors that together will constitute acceptable evidence of understanding. A useful question to ask is, "If someone demonstrates these specified behaviors, would I be willing to say that the person has achieved the intended understanding?"

When faced with the problem of gathering behavioral evidence on the extent of knowledge acquisition, caution is advised. The ability to verbalize an idea (for example, to give a definition or give a label for an object) does not mean that the learner has necessarily understood the idea. It is possible to both recite definitions of ideas that have never been understood and to be unable to formulate a definition of an idea that has indeed been understood.

Indicators that students have learned ideas that are classes or categories of objects or events (see p. 68) include the ability to identify an object by placing it into a category and the ability to recognize a nonexample (that is, an object that bears a "family resemblance" but is not a member of the set; for example, recognizing that a frog is not a reptile). Other behaviors such as defining, stating attributes, and describing relationships serve as evidence for these cognitions. The selection of behavioral indicators for cognitions depends, in part, on whether the cognition requires memory, comprehension, or justified belief:

1. The primary kinds of observable behavior that may indicate memory are stating (either wholly or partially) and recognizing the idea.
2. The primary kinds of behavior that may indicate comprehension include translating, paraphrasing, and explaining. Other behaviors that may be used include comparing, describing, and distinguishing.
3. Behaviors indicating justified belief include verbally justifying, defending, supplying evidence, arguing, and choosing an appropriate course of action based on specific information.

Knowing which properties relate to a particular cognition is a first step toward the specification of evidence. For each relevant property several behaviors should be specified.

The examples that follow illustrate the specification of indicators or evidence.

EXAMPLE 8.1.   *ILO:* The student should understand that regular medical checkups are an essential aspect of good health. (This ILO involves the properties of memory, comprehension, and justified belief.)

Evidence of memory (recalls the assertion): When asked, "What is an essential aspect of good health?" the student responds, "Regular medical checkups."

Evidence of comprehension (comprehends the assertion): The student can explain in his or her own words some aspects of good health.

Evidence of justified belief (has evidence for the assertion): The student can argue the benefits of regular checkups. The student can explain the consequences of not having these checkups. The student can explain the reasons regular checkups are beneficial.

EXAMPLE 8.2. *ILO:* The student understands the idea of gravitational force.

Evidence of understanding the idea. The student defines "gravitational force." The student describes the relationship between gravitational force and other forces. The student points out phenomena that cannot be explained by gravitational force. The student explains relevant phenomena using the idea of gravitational force.

EXAMPLE 8.3. *ILO:* The student understands the relationship between an organism and its environment.

Evidence of understanding the relationship: The student is able to create a map showing how the following terms are related. The student can label relationships where appropriate. (Note: There will be differences between your map and student maps as well as differences among student maps themselves. This evidence should be interpreted with an emphasis on the relationships depicted. A sample answer is included.)

organism	decomposer
reproduction	food chain
niche	food
producer	environment
shelter	survival needs
adaptation	consumer

(See Figure 8.1.)

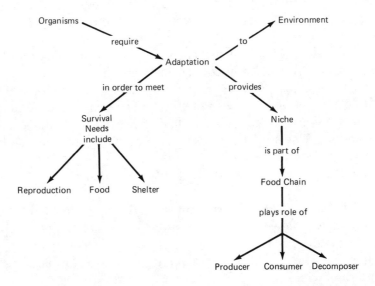

Figure 8.1.

COURSE-PLANNING STEP 8.1.   If one or more of your high-priority ILOs are cognitions, write them down on a separate sheet of paper entitled "Evidence of Main Effects." Then, for each of these ILOs write down two or more observable behaviors that will count as evidence that the student has acquired these cognitions.

Affects

How an individual manifests an affective skill or understanding varies greatly from person to person and situation to situation. It may not always be reasonable to expect a person who has learned an affect to supply behavioral evidence of that affect on demand. Therefore, a useful strategy of course evaluation for affects is to keep your eyes open and observe behavior unobtrusively. The following guidelines should be helpful in using this strategy:

1. Describe what behaviors would evidence an individual's having a particular affective skill or understanding.
2. Consider the context or circumstance in which these behaviors would be likely to occur. That is, during what occasions, and in what places or situations, might a person behave in the desired manner?
3. Consider which of these circumstances arise in the educational setting and would thus permit you to observe a student demonstrating that affect-related behavior.

With these guidelines, you can become sensitive to the opportunities that arise where manifestations of these affects can be observed. The following examples illustrate how you might use these guidelines.

EXAMPLE 8.4.   *ILO:* The student should act in a caring and sound manner toward the environment. (Affective skill)

Evidence of affect (behaviors, actions): The student doesn't willfully disturb any aspect of the environment. The student leaves natural conditions as they are found. The student instructs or reminds others of proper actions. The student states valid reasons for any intrusion he or she makes on a natural setting.

Circumstances: school grounds, field trips (nature hikes).

EXAMPLE 8.5.   *ILO:* The student should recognize his or her tendency to either believe or disbelieve statements made by others. (Affective understanding)

Behaviors: The student can give an accurate description of his or her reaction to others.

Circumstances: When the student accepts outlandish arguments without questions, is being overly argumentative, and questions all statements made by others during class discussions and during interactions with peers outside of class.

Some affective skills and understandings can be evaluated more straightforwardly. That is, a means of gathering evidence can be devised that can be administered to students in a direct manner. The examples that follow illustrate this.

EXAMPLE 8.6.   *ILO:* The student should understand how commercials and advertisements affect consumer behavior. (Affective understanding)

Evidence of affect: The student can explain how commercials try to appeal to individuals. The student can point out examples of consumer behavior where consumers pay more for an advertised product that is entirely equivalent to a less expensive unadvertised product. The student can give examples of how his or her own consumer habits are personally affected by commercials. The student can explain the difficulties in overcoming commercial "hype" surrounding certain types of consumer goods.

EXAMPLE 8.7.   *ILO:* The student should be able to respond to another person's comments with empathy and without altering the content of the message. (Affective skill)

Evidence of affect: Given several transcripts of client comments, the student will write down responses. These can be judged for degree of empathy and how closely the client's meaning was understood.

COURSE-PLANNING STEP 8.2.   If one or more of your high-priority ILOs are affects, write them down on a sheet of paper entitled "Evidence of Main Effects." Then for each of these ILOs write down two or more observable behaviors that will count as evidence that the student has acquired the affect. Finally, write down a set of circumstances or contexts in which the behaviors are most likely to be observed.

Cognitive Skills

Cognitive skills are typically stated in terms of specific though not directly observable behaviors. Because the behavior is often circumscribed, which leaves less room for varied interpretations, the specification of behavioral evidence is generally more straightforward than for cognitions or affects. Two ideas that are helpful in thinking about the specification of appropriate content (or context) in which to demonstrate a skill are *difficulty* and *transfer*. Difficulty refers to the complexity of the content. For example, outlining a long and complex article is more difficult than outlining a shorter article; constructing a convincing argument is more difficult for a position with which you disagree rather than for one you agree with.

Transfer, while related to difficulty, refers to the degree of similarity between the content used for learning the skill and the content used for supplying evidence of the skill. For example, outlining a story or scientific article involves transfer if the learning tasks focused only on outlining newspaper items; having students use *Psychological Abstracts* to locate information when their learning tasks focused on the *Current Index to Journals in Education* also requires transfer. Whenever possible the kinds of evidence you gather for a cognitive skill should vary in terms of difficulty and transfer. This will provide more useful information for making decisions aimed at improving your teaching. The following examples illustrate the process of specifying evidence for cognitive skills.

EXAMPLE 8.8. *ILO:* The student should be able to plan a nutritionally balanced meal.

Evidence of cognitive skill: The student should be able to plan a nutritionally balanced meal for: a person with a large caloric requirement, a very hot and humid summer day, or a child on a cold winter morning.

EXAMPLE 8.9. *ILO:* The student should be able to propose ways to test a hypothesis.

Evidence of cognitive skill: The student should be able to explain, in writing, two different experiments to test a given causal hypothesis. The student should be able to state verbally the qualities of a testable hypothesis. The student should be able to describe empirical and nonempirical modes of hypothesis testing.

COURSE-PLANNING STEP 8.3. If one or more of your high-priority ILOs are cognitive skills, write them down on a sheet of paper entitled "Evidence of Main Effects." Then write down two or more descriptions of behavioral evidence or indicators for each of these ILOs.

Psychomotor-Perceptual Skills

Psychomotor-perceptual skills are skills and abilities of a behavioral nature. The concern in specifying acceptable evidence is again in the *context* of the behavior. As with cognitive skills, students must be given sufficient opportunity to exhibit the behavior.

EXAMPLE 8.10. *ILO:* The student should be able to discern the sounds of orchestral instruments.

Evidence of psychomotor-perceptual skill (aural discrimination): The student should be able to match the names of fifteen different instruments to the sound of each instrument (assumes the student has previously memorized the names. The student should be able to name the instruments he or she hears used in a particular symphonic piece (specify the piece or criteria for selecting the piece).

COURSE-PLANNING STEP 8.4. If one or more of your high-priority ILOs are psychomotor-perceptual skills, write them down on a sheet of paper entitled "Evidence of Main Effects." Then write down two or more descriptions of behavioral evidence or indicators for each of these ILOs.

Gathering Evidence of Educational Results

Educational results are overall course outcomes; they are due to the complex and cumulative effects of actual learning outcomes and other factors acting on students. Educational results are attributes, conceptions, or characteristics of the well-educated person. Anticipated or intended educational results are described by the course goals. Assessing and evaluating educational results are extremely difficult. Results may not be readily observable; or, being broad, they cannot be judged by a single behavior. Typically, results cannot be exhibited on demand. In fact, many results do not materialize until after the course is over. In spite of all these difficulties, if we are serious about our educational goals, we have an obligation to evaluate the educational results of our course.

Evaluating results for some courses means actually gathering evidence of these effects. The results of a driver education course can be assessed by looking at the driving records of students. A course aimed at helping teenage drug abusers can keep track of the students to see if they get and keep employment, succeed in school, and otherwise cope with life more successfully. Evidence of results for high-school honors courses can be gathered by looking at what students take in college, what they major in, and how well they do. The results of many courses may be found in how well prepared students are for subsequent learning and by seeing how they fare in these courses.

Short of actually looking for course results, teachers should be receptive to the kinds of evidence that would indicate the effects a course has had. It is, after all, the anticipated results (that is, goals) that justify a course. We owe it to both our students and ourselves to try to determine how sound our justification is.

Although we have not included a course-planning step concerned with gathering the evidence of educational results, we wish to alert you to the importance of this aspect of course evaluation. If evidence is available, it should be gathered. The poetry course in Appendix B provides an example of the way in which this aspect of evaluation can be planned in designing a course.

Gathering Evidence on Side Effects

Another important kind of evidence is that of side effects. To reiterate, side effects are those outcomes that were not intended and perhaps not even considered when planning the course. Gathering evidence on side effects is difficult because there are no statements that serve as guides for the evaluation. It is doubtful whether the full range of course side effects could ever be assessed. Even if it were possible, the effort necessary to accomplish such an assessment would be enormous. Therefore, only the most likely or probable side effects must be identified in order to guide the evaluation.

Moreover, since time and resource constraints are great, the side effects examined should be limited to those deemed undesirable. Given the goal of course improvement and the constraints typical of an evaluation, the probable undesirable outcomes are most in need of attention. If the situation permits, however, you may also want to assess desirable side effects in order to plan for and optimize their occurrence (in which case they may become intended learning outcomes).

Considering side effects is important when viewing your course because the discovery of potential side effects will probably change what you do in the course. It is particularly important to consider how likely the side effects are to occur and how undesirable they will be if they do occur. For example, a common side effect of an introductory psychology course is a sense of power on the part of the student. Some students may begin to "analyze" their friends and the social interactions in which they take part. Students might also decide that they can become "amateur therapists." If these side effects are likely and viewed as sufficiently undesirable, you might make changes in the course to head them off. For example, maybe all students should experience the discomfort of being "analyzed."

It is conceivable that some side effects are unavoidable and are so undesirable that the course should be abandoned. On the other hand, you might want to go through with the course but with an increased sensitivity toward the probable side effects. In the consideration of side effects you get a chance to "stand outside" your course and become your own critic.

The most effective method for identifying side effects is to examine the instructional plan carefully. The instructional plan is comprised of planned interactions between learner and teacher, instructional foci, and the organization of course units in the context of various institutional factors. A few of these course components are examined in the following sections.

Learner interaction with teacher refers to what teachers do in the course, how they interact with, or behave toward, their students. There are many descriptors of teacher behavior; they include authoritarian, child-centered, and traditional. The important question is: What might students be learning as a result of the exhibited teacher behaviors? From a teacher who constantly emphasizes right and wrong answers, for example, students might learn that a particular subject is clearly defined with no gray areas or areas of debate, that knowledge is factual and either true or false.

There are almost always affective consequences of any prolonged type of interaction between teacher and students. Attitudes about self, school, and subject matter should be examined as possible side effects.

Instructional foci constitute the focal points of the learning experiences in the course. As focal points they can limit as well as enrich learning and can produce biased views of the content with which the course deals.

For example, learning entirely through the use of printed materials, a student might learn that a particular subject (or even learning in general) is a passive enterprise and that personal efforts of experimentation, discovery, or discussion do not lead to legitimate knowledge or learning. (This may apply to the exclusive use of any *one* kind of instructional focus.)

Instructional foci may also lead to undesirable learnings in that they are biased. Bias is evidenced by a particular treatment of certain societal groups (for example, minorities) or by stressing a particular ideology (for example, environmentalist views of the environment to the exclusion of other views).

Organization of course units may result in unintended learnings stemming from the relationships among the course's units. Considerations here focus on the sequence and grouping of units, that is, relationships implicit in the course organization.

For example, a history course organized on a chronological basis may lead the student to a cause-effect relationship. That is, a particular event occurred, which caused the following event, and so on. A chronological organization may hinder the student's learning of recurrent themes in history or important historical ideas (for example, nationalism). Or a botany course organized around plant parts in such a way that a student learns about the root, then the stem, seeds, leaves, and flowers in that order may result in the student's viewing a plant as a group of individual structures rather than as a single organism with specialized tissues forming its various parts.

Other factors bear on course outcomes. Such factors range from how students are seated (possibly the mere fact that they are seated) to the scheduling of units (for example, are interesting units lumped together or interspersed with other less interesting units?).

Examining the instructional plan in order to assess likely side effects is a complex task. The examples above should be helpful in pointing out the range of areas to investigate. Two general guidelines may be of further use in assessing side effects.

1. Examine the attitudes of students toward the subject, toward how it is being taught, and possibly toward school in general.
2. Examine the course for those features that are stable (that is, significant strategies, materials, or behaviors that the student experiences daily). These features should form the basis for answering the question: What might students be learning as a result of this?

Focusing the search for side effects on attitudes and other outcomes likely to result from the prominent aspects of the course places this search in a realistic perspective. The examples that follow may help prepare you to gather evidence of side effects.

EXAMPLE 8.11.   Mr. Harris is teaching the senior honors section in world history for the first time. Mr. Harris values this opportunity highly and spends an entire summer preparing for the course, which will focus on "Revolutions of the World." His goal is to have students understand the historical forces that caused people to revolt and to relate these forces to current societal forces.

Rather than use available books, which Mr. Harris feels are inadequate, he bases the course on a carefully prepared series of lectures. Outside readings will be employed occasionally. The course focuses on the American, French, and Russian revolutions.

What effects might a lecture presentation have on students? How might students characterize revolution as a result of using the American, French, and Russian cases as examples? Are there other kinds of revolution that are not violent or not political? Do revolutions occur in non-Western countries? Do revolutions always result in stable political-social arrangements? Do the rebels always win? What role does ideology play?

EXAMPLE 8.12.   Ms. Cole had taught junior English for several years. The course had always focused on a set of novels and plays read by the class in the same sequence. Ms. Cole had led discussions about the books and had found herself doing most, if not all, of the discussing. To remedy this she decided to take a nondirective role in the course. She provided a long list of readings to students on the first day of class. Students were free to read any six books they selected. During class, small groups were formed in which students discussed common readings. Often these groups were made up of only two or three students. One large group of students (about 17 pupils) always read the same book and were thus in the same group. Ms. Cole did not intervene and required only a written synthesis in which students described their reaction to the reading and group discussion.

By being nondirective, might Ms. Cole give students the impression that "expert opinion" has no place in discussions of literature? Is a student's choice of reading always a wise choice? Are aspects such as style and genre likely to be considered in these types of discussion? Can students distinguish good or great literature from lower-quality work?

These questions and those accompanying Example 8.11 illustrate a few side effects that seem likely as a result of these courses. These examples should point out the perspective needed when looking for side effects.

COURSE-PLANNING STEP 8.5. Examine your course's planned interactions between the learner and (a) the teacher, (b) the instructional foci, (c) the organization of course units, and (d) the institutional setting of the course. On a sheet of paper entitled "Possible Side Effects," list unintended undesirable learnings that you as a teacher and course planner should be wary of as you teach the course.

Troubleshooting

Course planning has, at this point, ended. Troubleshooting, which consists of using the information gathered during evaluation for making course-improvement decisions, is done after the course has actually begun.

In evaluating a course, you should know whether the course's high-priority ILOs have been achieved. You should also be aware of any major undesirable consequences of the course. You may have some evidence that bears on the educational results of your course. The task now is to use this information to improve the course.

Pinpointing the aspect of a course in need of improvement presents many problems. Assume, for example, that as a result of an evaluation you determine that one or two important ILOs have not been achieved. Does this mean that the instructional focus was inadequate? the teaching strategy faulty? the ILO unlearnable or unteachable? a prerequisite was unprovided for? Any number of these factors could be involved. The following is a scheme for systematically trying to determine which course aspects need improvement:

1. *Gather all the evidence you can.* How many students failed to achieve a particular ILO? What students were they? What did these students do differently? Did anything else distinguish these

students from those who did learn the ILO? How "close" did these students come to learning the ILO? *If you have evidence of an unachieved ILO, then*

2. *Examine the ILO.* Are prerequisites provided for? Does the ILO fit in with the other ILOs that were achieved? *If the ILO appears satisfactory, then*

3. *Examine the course organization.* Did the ILO receive proper emphasis in the unit? Was it preceded and followed by appropriate ILOs? Was the instrumental content appropriate for teaching the ILO? *If the course organization is satisfactory, then*

4. *Examine the general teaching strategies for the ILO.* Did the instructional focus provide the focus necessary for this ILO? Was the instructional focus interesting? Was the teaching strategy appropriate? Was enough time spent on this ILO? Was the ILO emphasized sufficiently? *If the instructional plan is satisfactory, then*

5. *Examine the instruction.* Was the instructional plan actually carried out? What details may have changed? Was the plan adequate to hold students' attention and interest? Did outside disturbances, unexpected events, scheduling changes, or other factors interfere with instruction?

If you have gathered evidence on your course's educational results, you will want to include this information in your troubleshooting. Since educational results are due to a variety of interacting factors (some of which are entirely outside the course), improvement decisions are difficult. However, depending on the importance of an unachieved goal or the undesirableness of an obtained result, course changes may be very necessary. Troubleshooting here will have to include external factors. Has something occurred in the school, city, or neighborhood that could affect course results? What other sorts of things are students involved in at this time? Much of the troubleshooting you have already done will apply here. Perhaps the problem is several unachieved ILOs or possibly discipline problems in the class caused you to employ unusual or harsh measures. If all your high-priority ILOs were achieved, and the course went smoothly, but yet the results were disappointing, you will have to ask some questions about whether your intended learnings are as appropriate for your goals as you had initially thought.

One further useful way to troubleshoot a course is to administer a questionnaire to the students. Questionnaires can ask students about a wide range of topics. The questions can be specific and detailed or they can require general and overall views. They can ask about the effectiveness of administrative and instructional procedures or about the students' reaction to personal characteristics of the teacher; they can inquire about ratings of current practices or they can ask for suggestions of new practices. Obviously, it is difficult to know what to ask and where to stop. A useful criterion in developing questionnaires is to limit them to questions that will help inform course-improvement decisions.

As you develop questions, center the questions on those areas in which you are willing and able to make changes. Then design your questions so that they solicit information useful in making those decisions. Don't waste your students' time with questions that do not or cannot lead to course improvements. For example, asking students to rate your overall performance as a teacher gives information too general to be useful and has the potential only to inflate or deflate egos. On the other hand, the students' reaction to the size of their within-class group may well be valuable information.

By carefully and systematically making changes and continuing to evaluate the course each time it is taught, the course should become more and more refined. As noted, troubleshooting cannot be carried out while a course evaluation is being planned. But when the course is actually taught, troubleshooting should be incorporated as a useful scheme that aids course improvement.

Summary

This brings to a close the planning of your course. In a sense, course planning never stops but continues to evolve. Unless a course is scrapped or radically altered, however, further planning often takes the form of refinements based on the evidence gathered during evaluations as well as on "gut" reactions. To some extent we can only know what we want to accomplish as we try to implement preliminary plans. Thus, ILOs, educational goals, and other course components will be altered as you or others actually teach the course.

We hope that you have worked through, rather than around, the book to arrive at this summary. Much of what you have read and what you have been asked to do may have seemed highly technical. We recognize that a considerable amount of actual course planning also involves common sense and a great deal of creativity. What needs to accompany these two ingredients, however, is the talent for asking the right question at the right time and having the understandings and skills necessary to answer (and ask) these questions.

Questions for Discussion: Course Evaluation

1. Troubleshooting involves using evidence to think about course components. The links between various course components are often important to consider when deciding where to make course changes. In what ways are each of the following course compo-

nents linked: (a) rationale-general teaching strategies, (b) ILOs-instructional foci, and (c) unit organization-ILOs?

2. Discuss any course you may have taken in which side effects or unintended learnings were of greater significance than the espoused aims of the course. What may have contributed to this?

3. In trying to improve a course, what is the benefit of making systematic improvements instead of "wholesale" course revisions?

4. What type of information would lead you to abandon a course?

5. What are the differences and similarities between course evaluation as presented in this chapter and pupil evaluation as you have experienced it?

References

Cronbach, L .J. "Evaluation for Course Improvement." *Teachers College Record* 64 (1963): 672–683.

Scriven, M. "The Methodology of Evaluation." In R. W. Tyler, R. M. Gagné, and M. Scriven (eds.), *AERA Monograph Series on Curriculum Evaluation. Volume 1: Perspectives of Curriculum Evaluation*. Chicago: Rand McNally, 1967.

Epilogue

Our central message in this book has been that when we teach we should teach with a purpose. Further, our purposes should be made explicit in the form of educational goals and intended learning outcomes. There are no hard-and-fast rules for explicating our purposes; we must think for ourselves about our students, our subject matter, and our assumptions about education, and then express our purposes appropriately. We have to discipline ourselves to take our purposes seriously so as not to lie to ourselves. If we want students to learn to solve problems, mere content coverage just won't suffice. Our instructional planning must be appropriate for our purposes. These are the major lessons to be learned from this book.

Although the major purpose of designing a course has been to learn how to develop a curriculum, this was not our only concern. An unstated but nevertheless important benefit of working on this project was to learn what to look for in a curriculum, to begin the process of becoming a curricular "connoisseur" (Eisner, 1985). Developing a curriculum gives us a different perspective on curricula developed by others. This perspective enables us to look at curricula and talk about them more intelligently, precisely, and profoundly.

Often educators compare the educational enterprise to another activity, that of travel. In such an analogy the student does the traveling, teachers serve as travel guides, educational goals and intended learning outcomes are considered destinations, and instructional plans specify the means of transportation and the itinerary.

But there is a constant danger inherent in the planning of educational itineraries and the means of transportation; there is much more to a journey than arriving at the destination on time and unharmed. People also embark on journeys for the experience of traveling. A trip through France is not undertaken just to arrive in Paris. The French countryside, the French people, the French wine and food, and the enjoyment of a traveling companion are all as important for the "success" of the journey as the arrival in Paris. Nor should a kindergartener embark on an educational journey merely to receive a high school diploma or to learn the three R's. Thus, there are compelling reasons for expecting the educational process not only to help children become "well educated," but also to meet a set of criteria relating to the intrinsic, rather than instrumental, aspects of the process. The educational process should not only accomplish goals but also be humane, rational, engaging, enjoyable, and personally gratifying, to mention just a few such criteria. The most compelling reason for this requirement is not that such humane education is most efficient or effective (it may not be), but, instead, that schooling constitutes a substantial portion of people's lives and life should be lived in such a manner.

One final caveat in using this guide must be mentioned. In all our planning, research, and evaluation it is easy to forget that educational journeys are for the student-traveler, not for their teacher-guides, nor for the travel-agent administration. The educational travel industry is simply intended to help the student-traveler along on an educational journey; as much as we want to, we cannot make the journey for the student. We can only act as guides. It is in this spirit that this book is intended to be used.

Reference

Eisner, E. *The Educational Imagination: On the Design and Evaluation of School Programs* (2d ed.). New York: Macmillan, 1985.

Appendixes

The two course designs that follow represent the wide range of educational levels and subject matter appropriate for the principles of planning set forth in this text. The first is a unit on the metric system developed for use with a first- or second-grade class. The second is a course on poetry developed for college students but suitable for high-school students with high verbal ability. Both designs employ most of the principles proposed in this book. Both designs also make use of some devices not suggested here. Creative curriculum development entails using a set of standard principles and techniques in a flexible way, molding them to a particular planning situation, and combining these structures with new design approaches invented for that situation. The designs bear witness to the principle that departures from the standard approach should be not only tolerated but even encouraged.

A Metric Measurement Unit for Grades One and Two

Prepared by Susan M. Etheredge

RATIONALE

At one time junior and senior high-school students learned metrics to aid them in their study of chemistry. It now seems imperative that the study of metrics should begin in elementary school classrooms to prepare students for the swing toward metrics that is reaching into every facet of American life. Metric conversion is seen in the goods we buy, the material we read (textbooks, newspapers, cookbooks, road maps, and signs), and the leisure activities we pursue.

Complete transition to the metric standard may or may not happen in the United States, but the influence that metric conversion has on our daily life provides sufficient reason for metric education in the elementary classroom. This unit plan, designed for first and second graders, introduces children to the concept of measurement in general and then, more specifically, to metric measurement.

Children at this age, although still somewhat egocentric, are beginning to show interest in the world around them and are ready to learn new things not directly related to themselves. The egocentricity still evident at this age can be appealed to in a study of measurement by using familiar topics, for example, height, weight, and body measurements or the weights and volumes of food and liquid children consume.

Six- and seven-year-olds just beginning to learn about measurement should acquire some basic knowledge about the need for standard units of measurement. They should know that they are learning a form of communication that enables people to understand one another. Above all, the children should have many practical experiences with linear, weight, volume, and temperature measurement. These experiences should combine actual measurement with estimation.

This metrics unit is designed to be taught separately from any teaching of our measurement system as it now exists. It is not to be taught as a comparative unit with the American system. Conversion from one system to the other is not at all important in this unit. I have found that there is less confusion and better understanding when metric measurement is taught separately from our present measurement system.

Throughout this unit the children should become aware of the presence of metrics around them. They should begin to understand that they are learning a special language important to universal communication. Their study of metrics from unit to unit and year to year will become increasingly meaningful and valuable as they begin to relate it to their world outside of school.

CENTRAL QUESTIONS

1. What is measurement?
2. What do we measure?
3. How do we measure?
4. What are units of measurement?

INTRODUCTION

This metrics unit is designed for first and second graders. The unit can be adapted for any number of children, but the primary consideration would be the availability of measuring equipment. It is suggested that there be a centimeter ruler, a tape measure, and a meter stick for each child; a metric balance or scale for every two children; and a set of liquid measuring equipment for every two children. The suggested time block per day is about forty minutes for actual teaching and practice. More time should be allowed on days when the children are expected to set up and put away their own measuring materials.

The prerequisites are few in number, but important: (1) The children should have a facility with numbers. They should be able to read and write numbers from 1 to 100 satisfactorily. For this reason, it is best, especially with a mixed first- and second-grade group, to plan this unit for the end of the year. They should also be able to compute simple addition and subtraction problems. (2) The children should have a clear understanding of the meanings of greater than, more than, less than, bigger than, larger than, smaller than, higher than, and lower than. (3) The children should have had some previous experiences and instruction in nonstandard measurement and informal measuring. This unit is designed on the assumption that the children have had experiences measuring with rods, books, clips, cards, balances, and so on (nonstandard forms).

This metrics unit is outlined into subunits. There are four subunits: Linear Measurement, Weight Measurement, Volume (Liquid) Measurement, and Temperature. There is also a "get ready" day outline to briefly review nonstandard measurement and to prepare the children for the first day's discussion.

The sequence of the subunits is intentional and serves a purpose. The child begins with a form of measurement that is the easiest to measure and read—linear measurement. Next come weight and liquid measurements which are somewhat more difficult and abstract for young children just beginning a study of precise measurement. Finally, there is temperature, a form of measurement that the children do not really interact with in the same way they do with the other forms. The understandings in this subunit are the most abstract.

This sequence might be described as going from the concrete to the abstract.

The understandings and the skills grow more complex and sophisticated as the unit progresses.

The closing statement in this introduction is a personal one. So often measurement units are taught with a pure skill emphasis. Children may become precise measurers, but they don't understand why they measure or even what can be measured. In designing this unit, the cognitive-psychomotor skills seemed to continually reoccur as high-priority learning outcomes. I was at first disturbed about this, thinking that some of the cognitions should receive first priority, but through the unit planning I came to the realization that for those final learning outcomes to happen the children would first have to understand many of the cognitions.

INTENDED LEARNING OUTCOMES FOR
THE UNIT IN ORDER OF PRIORITY

1. *Cognitive-psychomotor skill.* The child should be able to measure in the metric units:
   a. Measure and record length, width, height, and perimeter in metric units and state measure as whole units or combination of units, for example, 1 meter and 6 centimeters.
   b. Measure, record, and compare weights of two or more objects and order up to three objects by weight.
   c. Measure and record volume of a container using liter and milliliter, compare volume of two or more containers, and order up to three containers by volume.
   d. Measure and record daily temperature, compare temperature of two or more days, and order up to three recordings by temperature.
2. *Affect.* The child should have confidence in his ability to measure in the various metric units.
3. *Cognition.* The child should understand the concept of measurement.
4. *Cognition.* The child should know what a standard unit of measurement is.
5. *Cognition.* The child should understand the need for and importance of standard units of measurement.
6. *Cognitive skill.* The child should be able to explain what a standard unit of measurement is and why it is important.
7. *Cognition.* The child should be aware of the present uses of metric measurement in all areas of daily life: shopping, cooking, travelling, weather, work, recreation, and so on.
8. *Affect.* The child should appreciate the practical application of metrics in everyday life.
9. *Cognition.* The child should understand that the metric system is the system of measurement used by most countries in the world.
10. *Cognition.* The child should understand that we in the United States are presently using another form of measurement, but need to know (and possibly practice) the metric system since it is being used in the United States.

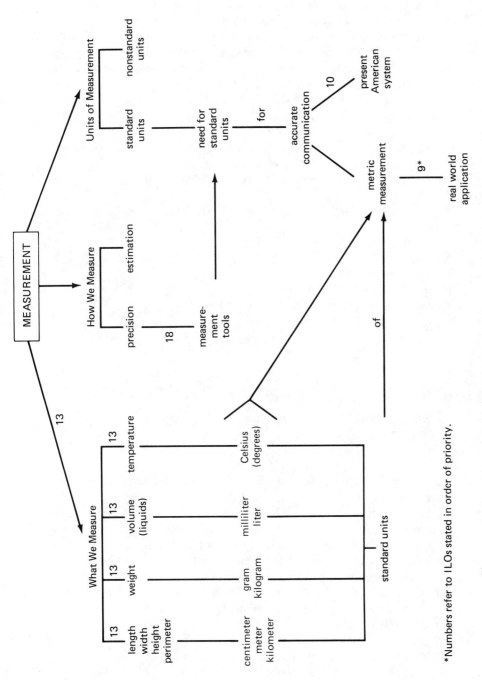

Figure A.1. Conceptual Map for "A Metric Measurement Unit for Grades One and Two."

*Numbers refer to ILOs stated in order of priority.

11. *Cognitive skill.* The child should be able to explain why he or she is learning metric measurement.
12. *Psychomotor-perceptual skill.* The child should be able to
    a. Measure accurately with a centimeter ruler, a tape measure, a meter stick, and a trundle wheel to the nearest whole number.
    b. Measure accurately with a balance scale using gram and kilogram weights to the nearest whole number.
    c. Operate a metric scale, using the sliding weight, to the nearest gram or kilogram.
    d. Read a metric scale.
    e. Measure the volume of liquid, using metric spoons and flasks, always to the nearest milliliter or liter.
    f. Read the thermometer in degrees Celsius, to the nearest whole degree.
13. *Cognition.* The child should understand that we measure the following things:
    a. length, width, height, perimeter
    b. weight
    c. volume (liquids)
    d. temperature
14. *Cognition.* The child should understand the meanings of
    a. length, width, height, perimeter (linear measurement)
    b. weight
    c. volume
    d. temperature
15. *Cognitive skill.* The child should be able to discuss what things are measured and define each term:
    a. length, width, height, perimeter
    b. weight
    c. volume
    d. temperature
16. *Cognition.* The child should know the basic units for the different measurement forms:
    a. Centimeter, meter, and kilometer are all units for linear measurement.
    b. Gram and kilogram are units for weight measurement.
    c. Milliliter and liter are units for liquid volume measurement.
    d. Degrees Celsius are units for temperature measurement.
17. *Cognitive skill.* The child should be able to name the basic units of measurement for each type of measurement:
    a. Centimeter, meter, and kilometer for linear.
    b. Gram and kilogram for weight.
    c. Milliliter and liter for volume.
    d. Degrees Celsius for temperature.
18. *Cognition.* The child should understand what the word precision means and what tools are needed to measure precisely in metrics:
    a. Centimeter ruler, meter stick, tape measure, and trundle wheel are

      used to measure the length, width, height, and perimeter of something.

    b. Scale and balance are used to measure weight.

    c. Measuring spoons, cups, and graduated flasks are used to measure liquid volume.

    d. Celsius thermometer is used to measure temperature.

19. *Cognitive skill.* The child should be able to identify which measurement tools are used to precisely measure a specific thing:
    a. Centimeter ruler, meter stick, tape measure, and trundle wheel for linear measurement.
    b. Scale and balance for weight.
    c. Measuring spoons, cups, and graduated flasks for liquid volumes.
    d. Celsius thermometer for temperature.

20. *Cognition.* The child should know the approximate amounts the following units represent:
    a. centimeter, meter, kilometer
    b. gram, kilogram
    c. milliliter, liter
    d. 0°C, 30°C, 100°C

21. *Cognitive skill.* The child should be able to represent the approximate value of these units either with "real world" examples or physical demonstration:
    a. centimeter, meter, kilometer
    b. gram, kilogram
    c. milliliter, liter
    d. 0°C, 30°C, 100°C

22. *Cognition.* The child should understand what the word estimation means and what it means to estimate in measurement.

23. *Cognitive skill.* The child should be able to estimate measurement in the various metric units, within a reasonable scale for each unit.

24. *Cognition.* The child should understand what it means to compare, more specifically, to compare the results of an estimate and a precise measurement.

25. *Cognitive skill.* The child should be able to compare his estimations with precise measurements.

"GET READY" LESSONS AND DISCUSSION

This is a brief review of nonstandard units. As stated in the Introduction, the children should already have had measurement experiences of the type described in the Teaching Strategy below. It is hoped that the children have acquired some knowledge from their earlier study of measurement. The purpose of the "get ready" lesson and discussion is to reactivate that knowledge and to prepare the children for the new information to follow.

    Intended Learning Outcomes: Numbers 3, 4, 5, 6, 9, 10, 11.

    Instructional Foci: Books, Cuisenaire rods, paper clips, pieces of string of various lengths, beans, pencils, straws, tiles, pieces of paper, file cards—any items you can use to measure something. Paper and pencil for each child.

Teaching Strategy: Each child will be given one item with which to measure. Most of the items are different. The teacher will tell them to use their item to measure the following things: the length of a chalkboard, a doorway, the top of a desk, and so on. They will record their measurement of each object.

A discussion will then follow. The ideas to be highlighted and emphasized are as follows: everyone got different answers—their measuring devices are called nonstandard units of measurement—everybody needs to use the same unit of measurement—otherwise we will have a confused group of people—won't understand each other—need for standard units—what are some standard units of measurement—why do we need these standard units—what is accurate communication—why is it important—awareness that there are two types of standard measurement units for accurate communication—metrics and the system we use now—we're going to study metrics—most of the world is using the metric system of measurement—we don't, but it is being used more and more in our country and we should understand it. This "get ready" activity should close with a discussion of "What are we doing when we measure?"

SUBUNITS

The intended learning outcomes that will appear under each subunit are those particular to that subunit. At this time the ILOs that are common to all *four* subunits are 2, 3, 4, 5, 6, 7, 8, 9, 10, 11, 22, 23, 24, and 25.

The reader is asked to remember that the ILOs listed above are included in every subunit. The wording of these ILOs is of a general nature. It is up to the teacher to see that these learnings are reinforced and understood in the context of each subunit's topic or theme.

Subunit I: Linear Measurement

The concepts of length, width, height, and perimeter will be explored and defined in this unit. We will talk about length as the longest side of an object, width as the shortest side of an object, height as the distance from the bottom to the top of an upright object (often synonomous with length), and perimeter as the distance around an object. The metric units centimeter, meter, and kilometer will be introduced and used throughout the unit. The measuring tools presented will include the centimeter ruler, the centimeter tape measure, the meter stick, and the trundle wheel. Both estimation and precision will be discussed and stressed in this unit.

Intended Learning Outcomes: Numbers 1a, 12a, 13a, 14a, 15a, 16a, 17a, 18a, 19a, 20a, and 21a.

Instructional Foci: Centimeter rulers, centimeter tape measures, meter sticks, trundle wheels; teacher-made posters with linear units and abbreviations written out; series of worksheets; classroom objects to measure (pencils, pens, books, paper clips, staplers, paper, file cards, blocks, crayons, and so on); Metric Measuring License (to be discussed in Teaching Strategy).

Teaching Strategy: The terms length, width, and height will be introduced and discussed. The children and teacher will spend time identifying the lengths, widths, and/or heights of various objects.

Then the standard metric units of linear measurement—centimeter, meter, and kilometer—should be presented. These units should be presented one at a time, not as a group. The organization and sequence is important here. First the centimeter should be introduced and discussed. Then the measuring tools to measure a centimeter should be presented. The estimation and measurement of items under 100 centimeters is necessary before presenting the meter. It is essential to perform the same sequence with the meter before discussing the kilometer.

The children should be given a frame of reference for each linear unit. For instance, a centimeter is about the width of your baby finger, the thickness of a slice of bread, or the width of a popsicle stick. A meter might be the distance from the floor to a six-year-old's chin (use a meter stick to determine this), the width of a standard-size door, or the width of a newspaper opened up. A kilometer might be the distance from the school to the local movie theatre or the Y.M.C.A.—use a locality with which the children are familiar. These estimates will provide the children with some concrete, familiar ground before their actual measuring experiences begin. Teacher-made posters accompanied by pictures illustrating these metric units would be useful at this point.

The word estimation is to be defined and discussed. What does it mean to estimate? Why do we estimate? When might we make estimations? How do we estimate? Motivating questions at this stage might include: About how many centimeters long do you think this pencil is? About how many meters wide do you think this chalkboard is? Let the children actually use their pinkies and other visual or physical aids for rough estimates.

This will lead into the presentation of the linear measurement tools: the centimeter ruler, the tape measure, the meter stick, and the trundle wheel. The word precision should be introduced here. What does it mean to measure precisely? Why and when would we need precise measurements? Provide the children with hypothetical situations and ask, "Would it be better to estimate or measure precisely in this situation?"

Instruct the children in the use of each tool. Allow for many measuring experiences using classroom objects and any personal belongings the children may want to measure.

Worksheets should include both estimation and precise measurement and a comparison of results. How close was I? Did I estimate too much or too little? Actual problem solving using simple addition and subtraction could be integrated here. How many centimeters (meters) off was I? How much longer (wider) is the book than the paper? Perimeter should be introduced once the children have successfully estimated and measured lengths, widths, and heights.

Accurate measurement should be stressed. Estimation is of secondary importance. Accurate measurement, the ease with which it's done, and the written recording of measurements are of primary importance. An understanding of which measurement tool is best to measure various dimensions is also of high priority (use a centimeter ruler for a smaller length, a centimeter tape measure for distances around an object, a meter stick for a longer length, and a trundle wheel for very long distances). The children should also be able to measure and record distances as a combination of units, for example, 2 meters and 4 centimeters.

The Metric Measuring License is an activity that can be included in the complete Metrics Unit. (See the example below.) It can act as a thread that runs through each subunit, unifying the Metric Measurement theme. It reflects the learnings of each subunit. The children work in pairs, helping each other with the measuring and recording of their personal data.

METRIC MEASURING LICENSE

for centimeter, meter, gram, kilogram, milliliter, liter,
and degrees Celsius

cm = centimeter	m = meter	g = gram
kg = kilogram	ml = milliliter	l = liter

This license entitles _____, upon completion of the form below, to be an **OFFICIAL METRIC MEASURER**, authorized to measure, at any time, using **OFFICIAL METRIC UNITS**, anything than can be measured either with **OFFICIAL MEASURING TOOLS** or by **ESTIMATION**: height ____ arm spread ____ nose to fingertip ____ hand span ____ palm ____ thumb ____ index finger ____ middle finger ____ ring finger ____ pinkie ____ knee to floor ____ foot length ____ foot width ____ shoe length ____ shoe width ____ plain step ____ giant step ____ around head ____ around neck ____ around chest ____ around wrist ____ around waist ____ around thigh ____ around ankle ____ weight ____ weight of shoe ____ weight of relaxed hand ____ weight of favorite book ____ volume of lunch milk or juice ____ your body temperature ____ outside temperature today ____ .

age ____ years ____ signature _____ date ____

All of the measurements will change—Keep your Metric Measuring License up-to-date!

The centimeter and meter are worked with more often than the kilometer in this subunit. The kilometer is discussed in more abstract terms. The children and teacher may take a "Kilometer Walk" someday, but it is introduced as the unit used to measure very long distances, like a distance you may walk, run, drive, or fly. It can be used in the problem-solving sense—How many kilometers did Pat run if she ran 1 kilometer on Monday and 2 kilometers on Wednesday? Or, Would you use meters or kilometers to tell someone how far it is to Amherst? The kilometer is to be taught in a more abstract way—there are no actual measurement experiences with the kilometer at this level.

The teacher should provide time for discussions of practical, real-life applications of linear measurement. Children should have ideas about possible situations when precise measurement would be essential and when estimation would be sufficient. They should understand clearly how precision is different from estimation.

The final lesson(s) should combine the three linear units: centimeter, meter, and kilometer. The children are to understand what unit and what tool is used to measure what linear dimension. The teacher is expected to check this understanding with observations of their interactions with the measuring equipment and their daily written and oral work.

Suggested time to spend on this subunit: 5 days, 30 to 40 minutes each day.

Subunit II: Weight Measurement

What is weight and the way it's measured in the metric system is the topic of this subunit. We will talk about weight as the amount of heaviness something has. This type of measurement is to be contrasted with linear measurement. How is it different? How are they alike? The gram and kilogram are the measurement units introduced. Precision and estimation are important elements again in the subunit.

Intended Learning Outcomes: Numbers 1b, 12b, 12c, 12d, 13b, 14b, 15b, 16b, 17b, 18b, 19b, 20b, and 21b.

Instructional Foci: Balances, sliding weight scales, metric scales, weights of assorted sizes (grams and kilograms), dollar bill, nickel, piece of chalk, magic marker, golf ball, tennis ball, stick of butter, softball, loaf of bread, two-pound box of sugar cubes, pencils, paper, series of worksheets.

Teaching Strategy: This subunit will begin with a discussion of weight. What is weight? Does anyone know how we measure it? How is weight measurement different from linear measurement? How are they similar?

The gram is introduced as the basic unit of measurement of weight. Items that weigh various amounts are passed around for the children to hold: dollar bill (1g), nickel (5g), new piece of chalk (10g), large magic marker (25g), tennis ball (50g), stick of butter (100g), softball (200g), and a loaf of bread (500g). A chart is made with the children to record these amounts.

The children then estimate the weights of various objects under 500g using the above items to compare. They record their estimations.

The next lesson will be devoted to precision measurement. Gram weights are introduced and explained. The children are taught how to use a balance and sliding weight scale. They work in pairs or alone, depending on the number of scales and children. They weigh the objects they had previously estimated, record the precise weights, and compare their estimates with final results.

The kilogram is then introduced as the unit used for weights larger than a thousand grams. A two-pound box of sugar cubes, a kilogram weight, and any other items weighing about a kilogram are given to the children to handle. Estimation of items and precision measurement are again done, this time with the kilogram. Each child is weighed on a metric scale at this time.

The children will be asked to measure, record, and compare the weights of at least two or more objects and then order those objects by weight. They will also graph *or* order (heaviest to lightest) the weights of all the children in the group, providing that it does not cause any child undue embarrassment. They will also need to complete the sections of their Metric Measuring Licenses that apply to weight.

In order to relate metric weight measurement to the real world, the children will be asked to make a list of at least five packaged goods they can find in their homes that have a designated gram or kilogram weight. Together, the teacher and children can make a composite list. Discussion of weight application to other daily experiences is also important.

Suggested time to spend on this subunit: 5 days, 30 to 40 minutes each day.

Subunit III: Volume (Liquid) Measurement

Volume is the key word in this subunit. Volume will be presented as the amount of liquid that is needed to fill a particular amount of space. Amounts of water will be estimated, measured, and compared. The distinction between weight and volume will be an important point of discussion. Once again, estimation and precision will be emphasized. The milliliter and the liter will be introduced as the basic units of liquid measurement.

Intended Learning Outcomes: Numbers 1c, 12c, 13c, 14c, 15c, 16c, 17c, 18c, 19c, 20c, and 21c.

Instructional Foci: Measuring spoons, liter flasks, milliliter eye droppers, containers of various shapes and sizes, water table if possible, pencils, paper, series of worksheets.

Teaching Strategy: The first lesson will begin with a discussion of liquids the children drink. Containers (bottles, glasses) will be available for illustrative purposes. Do you usually drink this much orange juice? How many glasses of juice would we need to fill this bottle? Do you know how we measure liquids?

The distinction between solid weight measurement should be clarified in the children's minds. It should be demonstrated that we are not trying to find out how much the liquid *weighs*, but how much *space* it takes up in the container.

A milliliter will be introduced as a very small unit of liquid measurement. Together, with milliliter eye droppers, we will find out how many milliliters of water it takes to fill up various sizes of small containers. They will see that a common size cup is 250 milliliters. Precision measurement is stressed here.

The liter is introduced as the next unit of liquid measurement after the milliliter. The children will be told that it takes 1000 of those milliliter drops to fill the one-liter container. The children will be asked to estimate the amount of liters needed to fill various large-size containers, to precisely measure the amounts of liquids, and then to compare the volume of two or more containers, ordering up to three containers by volume. They will record their findings.

The children will look at home to see if they can find liquids packaged or bottled in milliliter and liter containers. A class list will be made. They will also complete the liquid volume section of their Metric Measuring Licenses.

Before starting the temperature subunit, the teacher and children will bake a sweet. They will follow a very simple recipe using both weight and liquid measurements. (See page 187 for cookbooks with metric recipes.)

Suggested time to spend on this subunit: 4 days, 30 to 40 minutes each—1 day for the cooking activity.

Subunit IV: Temperature

Temperature—what is it? We will talk about temperature as the amount of hotness or coldness as measured on a definite scale. Degrees Celsius will be presented as the metric unit for measuring this amount. The Celsius thermometer will be introduced as the instrument, or scale, used to measure these degrees of hotness or coldness. Reference points on a Celsius thermometer will be established to help the children see the comparative nature of understanding temperature.

Intended Learning Outcomes: Numbers 1d, 12f, 13d, 14d, 15d, 16d, 17d, 18d, 19d, 20d, and 21d.

Instructional Foci: Inside Celsius thermometer, outside Celsius thermometer, numerous Celsius thermometers—at least one to measure human body temperature—pencils, paper, series of worksheets, one large-scale model of a Celsius thermometer with "movable" parts.

Teaching Strategy: The topic of temperature will be introduced with a discussion of everything the children already know about it. What is temperature? How do we measure temperature? Why do we need to know temperatures?

The children will learn how to read a Celsius thermometer by using a large-scale model with movable parts that can be changed to many different temperature readings. We will talk about the different places thermometers can be used and the different types there are (outside, inside, freezer, refrigerator, meat, body, and so on).

Working in pairs or small groups, the children will take readings of various temperatures: outside, inside the classroom, a bucket of ice, a pot of boiling water, tap water (hot and cold), a refrigerator, a freezer, and body temperature. They will record their readings. Together the group will discuss their findings and will make a chart of the various readings. We will order them from coldest to hottest. We will talk about the degrees that represent very cold things, lukewarm things, and hot things. The following chart will then be presented.

$-20°C$	very cold
0	freezing
10	cool spring day

20	nice spring day
25	good room temperature
30	nice summer day
35	swimming weather
37	heat wave
40	normal body temperature
100	boiling water

A daily temperature reading will be taken. At the end of this subunit the children will order the readings from hottest to coldest and will answer questions pertaining to them. On what day was it the hottest? the coldest? How much hotter was it on Tuesday than on Wednesday? They should work with five readings. The teacher will need to supply two of them since this is a three-day subunit.

As a final lesson, the children will need to give approximate temperatures in degrees Celsius for various situations. Here are a few examples. It's a hot summer day. How many degrees Celsius do you think it is? I want to make a cup of tea, but I need boiling water. How many degrees Celsius will the water need to be? If it's winter and there's ice on the ground, it's probably _____°C. What would you wear outside if the thermometer read 10°C? −20°C? What would you do outside if it was 25°C? Where would you be if your mom or dad took your temperature and it read 40°C? Those children who need to use the chart may do so.

The children should complete their Metric Measuring Licenses at the end of this subunit.

Suggested time to spend on this subunit: 3 days, 30 to 40 minutes each day.

Note: A final activity that might be interesting to try at the end of this subunit would be to construct a concept map with the children. Give them the headings What We Measure, How We Measure, and Need for Standard Units of Measurement. See what ideas they can come up with to fit under each heading.

It may illustrate the structure of their thinking, the "chunks" of learning they've acquired from the unit, and the connections they have made among the "chunks."

UNDESIRABLE LEARNING OUTCOMES
POSSIBLE FROM THIS UNIT

1. The child who has already had some experiences with metric measurement or learns the material quickly may become bored and uninterested in the unit.

Possible solution: Enrichment! The child could learn more of the basic units in each measurement area: millimeter, decimeter, dekameter, milligram, and kiloliter. The child could begin doing some simple conversions within metrics. For example, 20 centimeters = _____ decimeters; _____ milliliters = 4 liters; 3000 grams = _____ kilograms. The child could be exposed to a number of application problems that involve more advanced computational skills or reasoning, for example, How many meters of fencing are needed for a rectangular playground that measures 11 meters wide by 22 meters long? The height of a ceiling is 300 centimeters. How many meters is that?

The concept of area could be introduced and explored with square centimeters, square meters, and square kilometers.

2. A younger child in the group or a child who is not grasping the concepts may become frustrated and self-conscious because of unsuccessful attempts.

Possible solution: Remedial attention! Don't expect the child to learn all the measurement units presented. Allow the child to work only with the meter, gram, and liter. Stress measurement over estimation if that's the child's strength. Simplify the material. Pair the child with another slower learner so they may work together at their own pace rather than feel the pressure from a faster worker.

3. If a child has a good understanding of our present measuring system, he may want constantly to "talk conversion." This may confuse the child who is unable to understand that this is a measurement system unrelated to the one he or she already knows. The child may become frustrated with the teacher's unwillingness to compare centimeters with inches, for instance.

Possible solution: The teacher does not have to ignore the child's desire to know comparable amounts in our system. It can be done on an individual basis, so that the other children will not be confused with the information. The teacher should make it clear to the child that they are studying metrics as a measurement system by itself and are trying not to compare it with our system.

4. A child who consistently estimates poorly may feel as though he or she is not doing well or succeeding. Even though accurate estimation is not of the highest priority, it is included in many lessons. The child may feel like a failure if he or she is a poor estimator.

Possible solution: As stated in the remedial ideas section, deemphasize estimation with this child. Give the child more experiences with precision measurement. Have the child estimate more spacious dimensions that allow for "physical" aids—hands or feet, for example. Or allow them to have examples (liter flask, kilogram weight) by their side for constant comparison. Allow the child to estimate with the help of concrete aids, rather than with mental-visual pictures.

EVALUATION OF HIGH PRIORITY INTENDED LEARNING OUTCOMES

Evidence of Main Effects of the Five High Priority ILOs

1A–D. COGNITIVE-PSYCHOMOTOR SKILL

Evidence of cognitive skill/psychomotor skill: The child is given hypothetical situations and asked to solve them. Here are some examples:

Situation #1: There's a wall in my living room that is 2 meters long. I want you to measure that desk to see if it will fit against that wall. The child will have to figure out what measurement tool to use, measure the length of the desk, record the length, and then explain whether it will fit or not. (The desk should be straight edged and easily measurable.)

Situation #2: I have three objects: an apple, a mug, and a golf ball. (Try to have items that weigh about the same as the gram weights.) I want you to measure them, write down the measurements, and then tell me which one is heaviest, next heaviest, and then lightest. The child will have to decide what measurement tool to use to find out how heavy or light an object is, weigh it, record, and then order the objects by weight.

Situation #3: I have three containers: A, B, and C. They're all filled with different amounts of water. (The containers should all be different sizes, but not obvious as to how much liquid they hold.) I want you to measure each one, record the measurements, and then order them to show which container has the smallest amount to the largest amount. The child will have to choose the correct measuring instrument, measure the amount of water in each container, record, and then order them by volume.

Situation #4: I have three containers. One is filled with ice, one is filled with water that's been sitting here for awhile, and the last one is filled with very hot water. I want to know the exact temperature of each container and then I want you to order the temperatures from highest to lowest. The child will need to take a temperature reading of each container, record them, and then order the readings.

2. AFFECT

Evidence of affect (behaviors actions): The child attacks the problems stated above in a confident, comfortable manner. The child doesn't hesitate when given measurement tasks; he or she doesn't need constant direction while measuring. The child is able to quickly decide what measurement tool is necessary to solve a problem. The child offers to help other children who are having difficulty with precision measurement or estimation. The child exhibits little difficulty in the recording of measurement results.

Circumstances: group activities in the classroom, written work, testing situation.

3. COGNITION

Evidence of understanding: The child describes what sorts of things we measure, why we might want to measure these things, and how we measure each particular thing. The child is able to contrast the various types of measurement: linear, weight, volume, and temperature. The child is able to compare precision measurement with estimation.

4. COGNITION

Evidence of understanding: The child is able to give examples of standard and nonstandard units of measurement. The child is able to categorize a list of words into standard units of measurement and nonstandard units of measurement.

5. COGNITION

Evidence of understanding: The child should be able to explain, in his or her own words, why we need to have standard units of measurement. The child should be able to give examples of confusing situations when nonstandard units are used.

The daily written work and a final worksheet that would combine the four subunit topics of metric measurement would also be useful evaluative tools. Daily observation of the children interacting with the materials and the measuring equipment is the best way to assess the psychomotor-perceptual ILOs.

A final worksheet that combines linear, weight, volume, and temperature measurement would serve as a means to evaluate once again the children's learnings of some of the cognitions and cognitive skills. The worksheet could look something like this:

I would need to find	Unit I'd choose	Measuring tool I'd choose
length of this room		
outside temperature		
width of a book		
body weight		

The following are some ideas for questions. Directions would be to choose the best estimate. They could be done orally for nonreaders or beginning readers.

The height of a ceiling in a home is
a) 3 meters   b) 1 centimeter   c) 4 grams

The length of an ant is
a) 5 meters   b) 1 centimeter   c) 2 liters

The weight of a newborn baby is about
a) 3 kilograms   b) 2 meters   c) 10 grams

Your thermos might hold
a) 5 liters   b) 30°C   c) 500 milliliters

BOOKS THAT MAY BE USEFUL IN PLANNING A METRICS MEASUREMENT UNIT

Mathlab Metric Edition, Grades 1–2, Action Math Associates, Inc. *Series of activities—editions for grades 1 through 6.*

Metric Can Be Fun!, Munro Leaf, Scholastic Book Services, 1976.

Metric Puzzles, Tricks, and Games, Steve Morgenstern. Sterling Publishing Co., Inc., 1978.

Desserts and *Cakes and Cookies*, cookbooks printed by Playmore, Inc., New York, 1978. *Many easy recipes given in metric measurement—good for classroom use.*

Comments

This excellent example of a unit plan for young children has some features worth noting. The author includes an introduction in addition to a rationale. This was an excellent opportunity for her to express her thoughts on the unit immediately after planning it. ILOs are stated in order of priority and not by type of learning category. This has advantages and disadvantages. While readers get a good picture of the overall course emphasis, they do not ever get "talked through" the conceptual map or see the skill development sequence.

If the work is to be used by others, stating the ILOs by priority and by type of learning outcome is probably worthwhile.

The introductions to subunits and the description of general teaching strategies are easy to read and address themselves to sequence, emphasis, and children's thinking, although the use of the passive voice tends to obscure who is doing what in the classroom.

These are matters of central concern; they convey a sense of enthusiasm and they show evidence of thoughtfulness, of having grappled with difficult issues and decisions. They are characteristic of a plan that will be truly useful to teachers. A good plan captures something of the planner, something intangible but clearly recognizable in course designs such as this one.

A.N.R.

American Poetry: Female Voices

Prepared by Mary Gilliland

RATIONALE

Words are an interface between humans and the world. Each of us might be said to create her/his reality with the words we choose and the way we say them. People learn language in two ways: by exposure to it and by invention of it. Words are coined for specific uses, and individuals constantly rearrange them to convey a new sense of the world. Familiarity with poetry, where the arrangement of words is of keen importance, allows the individual to describe experience. S/he is able to make comparisons, to say what is like what else, and to note the distinguishing details of objects. S/he is familiar with the emotions and thoughts of other individuals, who may have a different perception of reality. With the power of language, s/he can use words to effect changes in the surrounding world.

Society loses an immeasurable amount of potential development through the silence of its members. Poetry arose from a practical need: the need to voice one's thoughts and feelings. Its earliest expressions included work songs, lullabies, laments for the dead, love lyrics, protest ballads and geneology tables. In the twentieth century, particularly in America, poetry has been pushed off to the side, considered esoteric, become read instead of spoken, and often read only by other poets. Poetry has become less democratic, and spoken of as useless. Yet the nuclear accident at Three Mile Island brought scores of protest poems to the readers of local and national newspapers. Articulating our experiences and communicating with each other is an important balance in a culture which views itself as specialized, alienated, and escape-oriented. No less beneficial is the joy of the singing, however sad the subject.

Many poets have been overlooked during the sweeps of the critical pendulum. A majority of the ignored or forgotten American poets are women. When one uncovers their writing, from the musty library stacks, one finds very good poetry and a side or perspective of life that has been discounted by most established critics. Here, women readers can find role models and confirmation of their own experience as valid. Men can find new light and a broader range for the questions they turn over in their own lives. These awarenesses will give the entire audience more chances and choices to make their own lives round and full. They will also decrease the loss in sensibility to society that comes with turning our backs on vital areas of life.

The contemporary women's movement has affected American poetry. It has vastly increased the amount of words in print written by women, past and present. Increasingly, this poetry receives popular attention and response. Also, the variety of subject matter has broadened to include topics particular to women (e.g., childbirth, female bonding, combining work and homelife) as acceptable themes for poems. For these reasons, and because women are still underrepresented in most college curricula, the syllabus consists of female writers.

The first European-American poet was a woman. From the seventeenth century on, female voices have added to that lineage; there is a tradition, strong and emerging. Many of these poets have addressed themselves, in prose, to the question of the practicality of poetry: its use in society, the function of the poet in the world. These essays are a valuable bridge between the texts of the poems and the everyday lives of the audience.

Two assumptions this course makes are that there is no single definition of poetry and there are no experts on the subject. A poem is not just words that conform to a certain structure; one can argue that the blues is of greater worth than a sonnet, and vice versa. The course is an introductory one, and hence does not require students to be familiar with a large body of poetry, but it does expect their level of sophistication in reading and writing to be that of the student entering college. This prerequisite is necessary because the weight of instructional foci often falls as much on the individual's verbalized experience of poetry as on the texts themselves. The course of study is designed to expand or explode previous notions of poetry, and includes the learning of poetic terms alongside poems in order to establish a common ground for discussion and expansion. The diversity of poems selected makes the course suitable either as a terminal survey for those who have satisfied their interest, or as a springboard for further academic exploration.

A Note on the Texts

The World Split Open: Four Centuries of Women Poets in England and America, 1552–1950. Edited by Louise Bernikow. New York: Random House, 1974.

Rising Tides: 20th Century American Women Poets. Edited by Laura Chester and Sharon Barba. New York: Simon & Schuster, 1973.

Poetry Handbook: A Dictionary of Terms, 3rd edition. Babette Deutsch. New York: Funk and Wagnalls, 1969.

The tacit dismissal of women writers by book reviewers and professors is a volatile subject, one which the instructor of the course must be aware of and capable of discussing. If the contrast between Deutsch and Bernikow prompts students to investigate the history and tone of established criticism, they will be encouraged to pursue the subject for their class presentations. But it must be

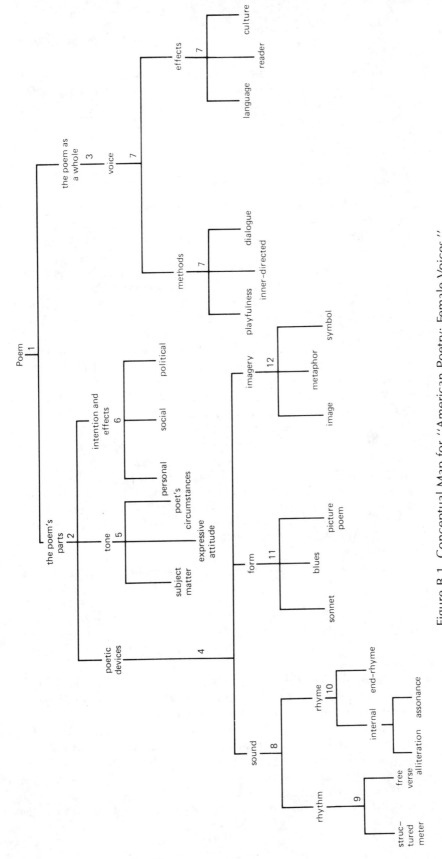

Figure B.1. Conceptual Map for "American Poetry: Female Voices."

remembered that although this course takes a step towards adjusting the im-balance of literary history, it is not focused on defensiveness or reparations. The poets selected for study have something to say, and they say it well. Focusing on their work, the course's central question is: What is poetry? What can we say about poetry?

Intended Learning Outcomes

These can be stated in three general categories of synthesizing intended learning outcomes that underlie the specific ones of every unit. Each of the six topics is meant to add a further dimension to what students have already learned.

1. Students will command some of the equipment necessary for analyzing how a poem means what it does. As well as comprehending poetic ter-minology, they will be able to find examples of definitions in the poems they read. They will be familiar with poets who shared the experience of being female in America, but lived in diverse circumstances and chose to write of many different themes in their poetry. For this reason, and because of the variety of forms and techniques studied, students will have a technical and historical basis for comparing other poems they may read.
2. Students will acknowledge and state their emotional and intellectual re-actions to poetry. They will play with their own senses in order to un-derstand how poetry makes sense of experience. They will appreciate how language is a vehicle that transmits thoughts into changes in the individ-ual and in society.
3. Students will be prompted to ask questions about poetry. They will be able to justify their interpretation of a poem and respond to viewpoints that differ from their own. They will understand that some answers are definite and others are tentative, but all are shaped by the accumulated knowledge and skill of the questioner.

The following statements summarize the major relations depicted in the con-ceptual map.

1. A poem can be experienced in at least two ways: by analyzing its parts and by responding to it as a whole.
2. An analysis of a poem can be in terms of its poetic devices, its tone, and its intention and effects.
3. The reader initially reacts to the poem's voice; one can further under-stand one's response to a poem as a whole after analyzing its parts.
4. Sound, form, and imagery are the major poetic devices.
5. Tone is an amalgamation of subject matter, expressive attitude, and the poet's circumstances. The attitude the poet displays toward subject mat-ter and reader affects the reader's response to the poem. The choice of subject matter and expressive attitude is shaped by a poet's social and personal circumstances.
6. Reasons for writing poems vary, but often the intention is to change

individuals or society. The function of poetry may be personal expression, social commentary, or political change. If the message of a poem is strong, poetic devices may have less prominence in the presentation.

7. The individual voice may be playful, inner-directed, or a dialogue implying a response. Interacting with these methods, the voice may be directed towards affecting language (the medium of communication), individual readers, or the general culture.
8. Sound is built from rhythm and rhyme.
9. Rhythm ranges from structured meter to free verse.
10. Rhyme can occur within lines and at the end of lines.
11. Form ranges from strictly structured poems (sonnets) to poems with songlike qualities (blues) to poems wherein the visual shape is part of the poem's effect (picture poems).
12. Imagery expands the physical sense with the imagination. Imagery can be small (image) or large (symbol), and can make a comparison (metaphor).

In addition to these major relationships, other important relationships among the ideas should be noted. Although making each of these explicit on the map would have produced undue clutter, these other relationships are represented in the following statements:

Sound + message = meaning.
There are various degrees of structure in both rhythm and form.
Immediate physical environment (foreground) + socioeconomic background shapes the choice of imagery.
Poet's intention may or may not match reader's perception.
Poets influence each other, forming a tradition.
Reader may be involved in poem either as observer or as participant, depending on how much distance the author creates.
One function of poetry is modernizing myths and fairy tales (reworking material that previous authors have created).
Another function is actively creating a personal and/or universal mythology.
Tone combined with poetic devices causes revolution in thinking and acting.
The dialectic between methods and effects allows the individual voice to do what a poet does: to make the familiar new.

UNIT ORGANIZATION

A standard unit is two weeks long, but the course is designed to be flexible enough so that the length can vary from one to three weeks, depending on difficulty of subject matter and student interest. Poems are read aloud in class, and discussion of assigned poems is the primary focus. Other instructional foci were developed to concretize the students' experience of poetry and to enable them, in their own words, to react to the unit's theme. Each cluster of poets was chosen for the difference of their poetic expression and outlooks on life within the context of their time. The sequence is not chronological; the topics move from components of poetry that are readily nameable to those that are more abstract.

Although the outline appears to be organized in discrete units, during class discussion of any topic there will be references to poems previously studied. At some point during each unit, the instructor will state the unit theme, answer questions, and add relevant information that is not found in the textbooks.

INTRODUCTION (one session)

The introductory session will be partly a lecture on the background against which to view the material of the course. The instructor will discuss the earliest forms of poetry, poetic traditions, and the relevance of applying poetic terminology to the poems which will be analyzed during the course.

Intended Learning Outcomes (in order of priority)

Students will understand that a question about poetry can have many answers, depending on the background, socioeconomic class, and values of the questioner.

Students will acknowledge their initial response to a poem.

Students will understand that the roots of poetry are oral expression and communication.

Students will remember how they have reacted to poetry in the past.

Teaching Strategies: Students will be asked to discuss their earliest memories of poetry and current reactions to it. The introductory lecture will follow. The instructional focus of this session is a short written response to two poems that will be discussed later in the course: Teasdale's "Central Park at Dusk" and Levertov's "Enquiry." This is a benchmark for progress in the understanding of poetry. The class will then discuss some unanswered questions: (1) What is poetry? (2) Why does a woman write poetry? (3) What are the uses of poetry?

Because of the novelty of our approach to poetry, the course rationale will be explained. Then, a short introduction to the texts.

UNIT I: SOUND

Because words are the medium of poetry, we first focus on the way poems sound. The earliest poetry was sung, or chanted to musical accompaniment. Anglo-Saxon verse, which was the beginning of the English tradition, was performed in this way, and was structured with a steady stress rhythm and alliteration of consonants. Although most poetry today is printed, its basis is still its musical appeal to the ear. The individuality of poets is evident in the principles of rhyme and meter that they choose to stress. The chosen sounds interact with the sense of the words to emphasize meaning.

Intended Learning Outcomes (in order of priority)

Students will understand that the words a poet selects are chosen as much for their effect on the ear as the message they convey to the mind, and that sound and sense interact with each other to produce the meaning of a poem.

Students will be able to pinpoint examples of alliteration, assonance, and different types of end-rhyme within a poem.

Students will be able to describe the difference between free verse and set meter.

Students will enjoy their own experiments with sound and be able to judge if a particular sound is a natural response to a physical activity or emotion.

Instructional Foci:

Bernikow/Chester: Emily Dickinson, Gwendolyn Brooks, Judy Grahn
Deutsch: accent, connotation, free verse, metre, parallelism, phoneme, rhyme, rhythm
Breathing exercise
Poems read round the room
Essay
Writing a sound poem

Teaching Strategies: Because many people have the impression that poetry is meant to be silently, passively read, this unit will demonstrate how each person can pay attention to her/his breath and how poetry evokes an active response from the listener. We begin with breathing exercises in order to find out how humming one sound feels different from humming another and how one phoneme (smallest unit of sound) means something different from another one. The exercise consists of short, long, deep, shallow breaths; then sound is added, experimenting with the effect of different vowels and consonants.

To increase our familiarity with each other's voices, and to see how the meaning of a poem changes depending on the way it is read, we will go round the room with one of the shorter assigned poems, experimenting with emphasis on a particular sound, varying lengths of breaths, and reading to a metronome. The assigned poems will be analyzed with these emphases:

Dickinson: assonance (vowel rhyme) and hard consonants to create a mood of openness or coldness

Brooks: rhymes that do/do not correspond to a formal scheme

Grahn: unmusicality; repetition, and the occasional appearance of the jingling form of nursery rhymes

To maintain the emphasis on sound as a bodily sense with which we take in impressions and give out expressions, students will write a poem made of sounds (not words). This will convey the feeling of up to three minutes of a physical activity such as cross-country skiing or kneading bread. When they read these aloud in class, they will be encouraged to demonstrate the activity, so they can feel and we can see how sounds involve the whole body.

This unit is the most flexibly long of the course because of the assumption that sound is the primary poetic sense and because of the extent of the technical reading assigned. The definitions in Deutsch are basic ones, and it is important that students understand them in order to establish a common vocabulary. They will write a short analysis of the meter and rhyme of one poem.

UNIT II: FORM

Unspoken poetry is available at public readings and on recordings, but the form in which it is most readily accessible is on the printed page. To communicate feelings or thought, they must be given form. Units of form range from syllables to an entire poem. Keeping in mind the previous exploration of sound, this unit turns to the impact of a poem's visual organization. It will encourage students to hear a poem as they read it.

Intended Learning Outcomes (in order of priority)

Students will be able to compare two poems in terms of the emotional and intellectual responses they inspire in the reader, and argue for the validity of different forms of poetic expression (sonnet, blues, picture-poem).

Students will have an understanding of standard poetic forms against which to compare modern and more experimental verse. They will see how a poet who stretches the rules can still be technically within them.

Students will recognize blatant and subtle repetition in a poem, and be able to analyze its effect.

Students will compare the effect of a poem when it is heard to the same poem when it is read.

Students will be able to translate one art medium into another, reflecting the representation that poetry (or any other art) makes of life.

Instructional Foci:

Bernikow/Chester: Edna St. Vincent Millay, Bessie Smith, May Swenson

Deutsch: ballad, calligramme, concrete poetry, couplet, elegy, form, logopoeia, sonnet

Listening to a Bessie Smith record

Draw an outline of a poem

Essay

Teaching Strategies: To strengthen students' comprehension of the literary definitions, questions, disagreements, and applications to the poems of the course will be aired. Because we are moving into the subcategories of poetic form (ballad, elegy), *Poetry Handbook* will be referred to quite frequently in class.

The assigned poems will be analyzed with these emphases:

Millay: standard sonnet form and its expansion into lines of irregular length; ballad form; the use of conversation in a poem

Smith: repetition of lines in a poem set to music; the blues; blues/ballad

Swenson: presentation of the theme of a poem by playing with its typographical arrangement on the page; repetition of words

In order to compare the visual and auditory effects of a poem, we will listen to a recording of Bessie Smith: is it the same poem in both instances?

After the instructor reads a short passage about the shapes of novels (by Virginia Woolf), students will draw a shape (an outline, not a picture) of Millay's "Sonnet XXXI." We will compare them, and discuss how the shape is a representation of the poem and how a poem is a representation of an experience.

Because of the diversity of the poems studied so far, it is likely that questions of worth and personal preference will arise. Students will write a short paper comparing two poems in terms of their success within their own genre, and stating what types of audience and feelings each appeals to.

UNIT III: IMAGERY

The various forms of imagery—image, metaphor, symbol—represent the thing described in words. This can be done by painting a verbal picture. But imagery is not necessarily visual; it can appeal to any one of the senses, and it can also link the senses together by associating an image perceived by one with an image perceived by another. The poet uses imagery to make the thing (person, scene) concrete or tangible for the reader. She can do this by playing with the symbolic overtones, as well as the colors or sounds, which the imagery suggests. She can also add depth to the poem or broaden its appeal by inserting images/symbols from past traditions or other cultures. Unit I enabled us to examine the smallest part of a poem, the individual phoneme; unit II moved through larger parts: lines, stanzas, and the appearance of the total poem. One focused on the sense of hearing; the other on sight. This unit integrates these two, and adds the other sensory levels at which imagery operates. Rather than fragmenting the works discussed, an effort will be made towards finding how imagery contributes to the unity of a poem. Unit III closes the first block of the course, the examination of the tools the poet uses.

Intended Learning Outcomes (in order of priority)

Students will be able to distinguish an image from a symbol, and a metaphor from an allegory, and to discuss the common root of these terms: their foundation in the sensory or imaginary world, and their aim of describing what the perceptible world is like.

Students will be able to make connections and comparisons of their own sensory experiences, and describe how an object/feeling is like something else.

Students will compare their perception of an unfamiliar poem with the meaning which the poet expected them to perceive. This is a yardstick which they will apply to other poems they read, so that they test their conclusions after the first reading of a poem.

Students will understand that one poem can influence another. This poet can be either a contemporary or someone from another time or culture.

Instructional Foci:

Bernikow/Chester: Amy Lowell, H.D., Louise Bogan, Denise Levertov
Deutsch: classical, haiku, image, imagism, imitation, lyric, metaphor (including allegory), pastoral poetry, polyphonic prose, synesthesia
Outdoor walk
Essay
Poetry reading

Teaching Strategies: Because so many poetic images are taken from nature, and in order to show that one of the main functions of imagery is to make relationships among experiences through the senses, the class will take a short outdoor walk. Students will be asked to describe what an experience (watching a waterfall, smelling it, sticking their hands in it) is like: what color it is, what it reminds them of, what other experiences it brings to their minds.

Assigned reading will be discussed with these emphases:

Bogan: linking of the senses; symbol; modern shaping of old myths
H.D.: color imagery; relevance of themes from Greek mythology; creating a figure: description vs. personification; imagism
Levertov: clothing imagery; personal relationships described in images; modern day fairytales
Lowell: animal imagery; imagism; images and rhyme in prose poems; Chinese & Japanese poetic forms

Since H.D. and Lowell were guiding members of early twentieth century Imagism, we will spend some time discussing this movement, and the legacy it has bequeathed to modern poets, particularly Levertov.

To integrate their understanding of units I, II and III, students will write an essay analyzing a poem from one unit in terms of the topic of another unit.

A local poet will be invited to visit the class (or we will attend a poetry reading). Hearing poems which they haven't seen will re-emphasize the oral aspect of poetry. Students will have the opportunity to ask the poet questions about the writing process and topics we have discussed in class. They will also be able to check out any discrepancies between the information the poet intended to convey and what they actually heard.

During this unit, the course's emphasis will shift from memory-learning to application of what the students know. Readings from Deutsch will continue to be assigned, but most of them are short and will be mentioned only as they bear upon poems under discussion.

UNIT IV: TONE

The author's stance within a poem is often bypassed in an analysis of what it means. Yet a grouping of words can have a distinct flavor, and tell us something about the author's attitude towards herself, society, and even her poetry. With this unit, we progress to an area which is more abstract than poetic devices; in the second half of the course we will examine the poet's choice of subject matter and the way she chooses to present it, as well as how a poet's social and personal circumstances shape her self-perception. The purpose of this unit is to see what consensus or disagreement arises about the authorial stance, and to question whether a poem can be toneless, or objective. Because the chronology of this course spans several centuries, we will also examine the hypothesis that the tone a poet chooses is indicative of the time in which she lives.

Intended Learning Outcomes (in order of priority)

The student will be able to explain how the tone of different poems/poets creates different reactions to the subject in the reader, and experience this through experimentation.

The students will be able to state what they feel about a poem whose tone seems to exclude the reader from the poet's universe, and one which invites the reader to participate in it.

Students will continue to apply poetic terminology to their reading, while considering the poet's sincerity, wit and judgment about her subject matter.

Students will be aware of different ways of studying poetry: individually or compared with other poems, chronologically or grouped according to theme or common technique. They will be aware that their own feedback on a poem is the sum of these different ways of viewing it.

Instructional Foci:

Bernikow/Chester: Sara Teasdale, Sylvia Plath, Marge Piercy
Deutsch: ambiguity, confessional poetry, irony, light verse, poetic diction, pure poetry, romantic, tone, wit
Unanswered questions
Class presentations
Essay

Teaching Strategies: Students will write a short list of attitudes which an author might adopt, e.g., authoritative/submissive, complaining/rejoicing. They will then read aloud one of Teasdale's and/or one of Plath's poems with a stance of their choice, and determine which one was intended.

Poems will be discussed in these ways:

Teasdale: sarcasm (exultation); exaltation; conventionality
Plath: despair; manipulation of the reader; self-pity
Piercy: irony; invitation to comraderie; disgust

These categories are not as easily separable as they appear; we will compare poems as often as study them individually.

At this point, a common vocabulary of terms has been established, American poets of varying times and outlooks have been studied, and attention to the individual voice of a poet has begun through the study of tone. It is a good time to collect any questions which students may have. These can be examined in class discussion, and explored further by individuals for the purpose of class presentation. Each student will give a 10–15 minute talk during the remainder of the course. Besides their questions, other possible topics are: Bernikow's introduction, Deutsch's poems and her preface, interview with the visiting poet, tone of male criticism, and a poet who is anthologized but not on the syllabus.

Students will write an essay describing how the tone of one of the assigned poets indicates her feelings about herself, her society and her reader, and speculating on the reasons why the poet writes.

UNIT V: INTENTION

Although popular belief holds that inspiration takes one by storm, most poets decide what they're doing, at least by the time they've finished a poem. Thought is involved in writing, and poets are at least subliminally aware of the audience they write for. This concept was presented embryonically in the assigned paper of unit II and developed in discussion during unit IV. Now we will consider it from the perspective of the personal, social and political effects of poetry. Unit III presented many beautiful poems which talked about various forms of war. This unit also presents reflections on society, but these poems are stripped of crisp symbolism and imagistic overtones; they are written in long narrative lines or ballads of protest. A central question in this unit is whether the song-power of poetry need be beautiful, or whether the music of a poem can be less important than its message.

Intended Learning Outcomes (in order of priority)

Students will appreciate the personal, social and political applications of poetry, and be able to discuss where these overlap.

Students will express their preference for plain or elaborate poems ("bald" or "beautiful"), and be able to ask if this preference indicates assumptions (about what poetry should be) that need to be examined.

Students will be able to say how a poem makes a difference in the way they feel, about themselves or about its message.

Students will recognize that traditionally female experiences are as valid subjects for poetry as those traditionally considered male.

Students will understand that a poem can either tell a whole story or give clues to the story by presenting a moment of life, rather like the difference between a movie and a photograph.

Instructional Foci:

Bernikow/Chester: Ann Bradstreet, The Mills and the Mines: Worker Poets,
   Muriel Rukeyser
Deutsch: decorum, didactic verse, epic, metonymy, poem, satire, sensibil-
   ity, verse paragraph
Photocopies of essays from Levertov's *The Poet in the World* and Rukeyser's
   The Life of Poetry
Freezing exercise
Benchmark essay
Class presentations

Teaching Strategies: Poets often articulate their thoughts about writing in
modes other than verse. We will begin this unit with a study of excerpts from
two books of essays: *The Poet in the World* and *The Life of Poetry.* These essays
address such topics as: the function of the poet and poetry, the impact poetry
has on societal change, and aspects of American culture that have caused poetry
to be minimized.
   The assigned poems will be discussed with these emphases:

Bradstreet: autobiography; sense of historical tradition; mothering; isola-
   tion of female writers
Worker Poets: working; protest of employment conditions; hard times and
   song; female bonding
Rukeyser: female mythology; her story; writing the biographies of workers
   and other artists in poetry

In order to clarify students' understanding of the conscious and unconscious
ways poetry works, several of them will be stopped during reading or discussion
and asked questions like: "Who are you now?" "What do/don't you know?"
"Was that a poem?"
   To evaluate how their understanding of poetry has changed, students will
write a short response to the two poems presented at the first class. They will
use as many technical terms as possible in elaborating their exposition of the
meaning of each poem.

UNIT VI: VOICE

A poet's voice is the synthesis of her self-perception (unit IV) and her perception
of the world (unit V). It is the personal prism through which she filters her
tone, intention, and the poetic devices she chooses. One might say that her voice
is a poet's art. This unit integrates threads of the three preceding ones: the effect
of the poem/poet on language (III), effect on the reader (IV), and effect on the
world (V). One of the earmarks of poetry is that it makes the familiar world
new. We will examine experiments with language (relating back to sound and
form) which revolutionize the way we speak (and think), and poems which

attempt to revolutionize the way we think/act with ourselves and each other. We will also explore how a poet's voice creates a personal and/or universal mythology.

Intended Learning Outcomes (in order of priority)

Students will be able to describe the way in which the poet combines her self-awareness and awareness of society in a particular poem.

Students will state the ways in which poetry has made their view of the world new.

Students will be aware of the voices which have been raised against sexism, racism (and thus, classism) in poetry.

Students will appreciate their own imaginative power.

Students will understand that changes in language bring about changes in society.

Instructional Foci:

Bernikow/Chester: Gertrude Stein, Diane DiPrima, Nikki Giovanni

Deutsch: abstract poetry, cubist poetry, mythopoesis, neologism, objective correlative, poet, symbol

Class presentations

Fantasy

Dialogue

Essay

Teaching Strategies: To grasp how a voice which is both self and other can be created, students will imagine that they are one of the poets of this unit and complete such sentences as; How I perceived the outdoor walk is . . . , What I do in New York City is . . . , How I feel about people hearing my poetry is . . . , My keenest observation about life is. . . .

Assigned poems will be discussed with the following emphases:

Stein: 3rd person voice; using language in new ways; playfulness; repetition; prose in poetry

DiPrima: 2nd person voice; informality; internal dialogue; the poem as a letter to the reader; political activism

Giovanni: 1st person voice; Black English; dialogue in poetry; political activism

These poems address the problem of sexism and racism, in general and in literature. One of the final discussions will focus on this, and on women and the literary world.

Students will select two or three poems from the course that made a difference in their lives or in the way they look at the world. In the final essay, they will explain how the poems did this.

Having been exposed to a number of poets, and having talked with one in real life, students will engage in an imaginative exercise with one of the poets (or persona created in a poem) of this course. Using the Intensive Journal technique developed by Ira Progoff, they will be guided through a written dialogue with this person. They will be encouraged to ask for answers to any questions that they still have, for, finally, the answers will be found within themselves.

COURSE EVALUATION

1. Evidence of Main Effects

The three synthetic intended learning outcomes have to do with

  a. Analysis of poetry
  b. Affective response to poetry
  c. Refining the universe of questions about poetry

Judging how well these intentions are actualized, we note

(1) The primary evidence is found in students' participation in class discussion and depth of analysis in their essays. They can paraphrase the meaning of a poem. They can say definitions in their own words, and find examples of poetic terms within the poems studied. They can express their thoughts coherently. They can note details, as well as summarize the entire poem and place it within a social, historical context. Their vocabulary, enriched by new uses of language, can vary and improve.

(2) The evidence is observation of body language, although words are also accepted. Students can value the worth of their emotional (and physical) response to poetry as well as their intellectual reactions. They can say how one of their senses works with another, and thus make their own analogies of the world of things. They can measure how their response to poetry has varied at different times in their lives, enjoy sharing this with others, and vicariously put themselves in the place of a person with a differing attitude or environment who is reading the poem. They can read poems aloud with feeling and care.

(3) This evidence can be gathered during class discussion and from reports of conversations outside class. Students can define a question from different angles and be able to make general questions specific. They can formulate personal questions and place them in the context of society, history, and literary criticism. They can persuade others that their point of view is valid.

2. Possible Side Effects

(1) A certain amount of synthesizing of the concept will occur during each unit, but complete integration of the topic is not always possible or desirable. Each cluster of poets was chosen to highlight that conceptual aspect of their work, but many of them could as easily serve in another

unit of the course. Sometimes the poets of a unit are polar opposites or people who move in different worlds, so a student seeking a unified interpretation of the theme may be disappointed.

(2) The level of sophistication of the reading assumes that the audience is motivated. Students who are not enthusiastic about poetry may tire of the depth of discussion.

(3) The choice of texts sets up a dialectic between traditional (so-called "objective") criticism and feminist criticism. Students may find this confusing. Truly feminist criticism balances the traditional interpretation of a literary work by examining the subjective assumptions of critics who deny that they have any. But the word is often misinterpreted to mean partisanship or a prejudiced approach to literature. Misunderstanding creates self-consciousness, defensiveness and hostility; students may experience these feelings. They may also feel resentment for past literary oppression of women rather than openness to the texts and attitudes that we can work with now.

(4) Students may trust their own interpretation of a poem before examining it fully. The assumptions that there are no experts and no simple definitions in poetry does not mean that there are no standards of judgment, or that there are excuses for vagueness.

(5) Unless the exercises are guided with some degree of spontaneity and naturalness, students may think they are contrived. Students who identify themselves as total intellectuals may think it's silly to play with their senses.

(6) Because we are studying so many good writers, students may doubt their own writing ability.

(7) Students may think that solutions to all societal problems begin with or come from poetry, instead of viewing poetry as one form of protest or change among many.

(8) Although *Poetry Handbook* mentions writers from other cultures and occasionally quotes from their work, we will not study them in class. Because the course's concern is American poets, students will not be exposed to the functions of poetry in other countries (many of them very different from America, and very rich), and many formulate narrow ideas of its boundaries. Likewise, since we do not discuss any male poets, students many think their work is unimportant or irrelevant.

3. Realization of Educational Goals

Students who have learned to be appreciative critics of poetry will find that their own words mediate between themselves and the world. They pay attention to their choice of words. Like the poet, they can make connections among sensory objects, and between things and an abstract understanding of life. They pay attention to their own voice, being aware of how deep within the body it originates (mouth, throat or abdomen). Thus, they judge the sincerity of their own words from their physical origins, and are aware of the unresolved doubts that a shallow voice indicates. Their attitude toward poetry is the natural enthusiasm of the child. Poetry moves beyond the classroom and students attend public readings, write or publish their own poetry, subscribe to a poetry magazine, read poetry outside of class, or support a poetry reading benefitting a public cause. They have an overview of poetry, and can distinguish shortcomings in poets whose work they identify with or admire. Vice versa, they can point out good technique in poets who are not to their taste. They listen to other people's opinions instead of hastily criticizing them. Students are not able to generalize about American female poets. Some students may challenge the course assumptions and suggest other ways to approach the subject. All these are indicators that the concern that poetry be an integral part of students' lives has been realized.

COMMENTS

This design for a poetry course has many strengths. It is clearly written and quite creative. We particularly applaud the nonsexist way the designer addresses an imbalance in the teaching of poetry by focusing her instrumental content on the work of female poets. Her course is first and foremost a solid conceptual approach to the teaching of poetry, regardless of the poet's gender.

In addition, there are some nice touches in this design. For example, the design's use of general ILOs for the course and specific ILOs for each unit maximizes the benefit of both levels of specificity. The general ILOs capture the course's focus and coherence. The specific ILOs add the detail necessary for planning and teaching actual lessons.

Further, the notes on the texts and on the unit organization are important statements for understanding her approach. Although the designer does not follow "the letter of the law" in her evaluation plan, she certainly provides a sensible way to conduct an evaluation in a subject traditionally characterized as difficult to evaluate.

G.J.P.

Glossary

Actual learning outcome A change in a person's capability or state of mind that results from interaction with people, ideas, or objects. Changes such as physical injuries, physiological maturation, and those that are drug-induced are excluded from this concept.

Affect An umbrella term for two types of intended learning outcomes: affective understandings and affective skills.

Affective skill A type of intended learning outcome dealing with the ability to behave in ways that reflect certain attitudes.

Affective understanding A type of intended learning outcome dealing with self-knowledge or knowledge about the interaction of self with others.

Assertion An idea that can be stated as a proposition, that is, asserting something to be true—facts, principles, generalizations. Assertions constitute one set of ideas for students to learn.

Central question One of the fundamental questions with which a course deals and which identifies the focus of the course.

Clustering ILOs The grouping of ILOs into unit-sized chunks.

Cognition An idea that is intended to be learned.

Cognitive skill The ability to use or apply cognitions.

Conception A type of cognitive intended learning outcome. Conceptions entail a way of looking at the world; that is, a person's theory or belief system regarding some set of phenomena.

Conceptual map A chart depicting the relationship among the important ideas with which a course deals. The map describes the organization of understandings in the course.

Curriculum An organized set of intended learning outcomes presumed to lead to the achievement of educational goals.

Curriculum development The process by which intended learning outcomes are selected and organized.

Educational goal A desirable attribute of a person (for example, literate, tolerant, or creative) that is expected to result from the educational process. These goals are "educational" (rather than societal or institutional) if they are achievable through learning.

Educational result A description of the kind of person that develops as a consequence of the complex interactive and cumulative effects of formal and informal education, as well as maturation. These may or may not correspond with the intended educational results, that is, the "educational goals."

Evaluation The collection and analysis of data for the purpose of making a judgment or rendering a decision.

206

Flowchart A diagram depicting the components of a complex skill in terms of subskills and understandings.

General teaching strategy The instructional events that are planned around an instructional focus for the accomplishment of ILOs. These strategies are described at a level more general than daily lesson plans but more specific than a list of materials to be used.

Goal setting The process by which goals are formulated.

Instruction Providing experiences for learners with the intention of bringing about particular learnings.

Instructional focus A theme, problem, activity, stimulus, or vehicle for communicating ideas designed to facilitate the learning of a set of ILOs. They are termed "foci" because they serve as focal points for learning and lend coherence to a set of ILOs.

Instructional plan An outline for a course specifying its units and the means for teaching each unit. For each unit in the plan, intended learning outcomes for the unit, the unit rationale, and general teaching strategies should be described.

Instructional planning The process of forming and organizing unit-sized chunks of a course, specifying an instructional focus for each unit, and designing a set of instructional events around each focus.

Intended Learning Outcome (ILO) Something that the student is expected to learn. A course's ILOs may consist of cognitions, cognitive skills, psychomotor-perceptual skills, or affects.

Main effect An actual learning outcome corresponding to a course's ILOs.

Psychomotor-perceptual skills Physical or perceptual competencies and abilities intended to be learned.

Rationale There are two kinds of rationales: (a) *Course Rationale,* a statement justifying a course in terms of the course's educational goals. These goals are discussed in the context of the planner's conception of the learner, the society, and the subject matter. (b) *Unit Rationale,* a statement describing what a particular unit is about, how it builds on previous units, and how subsequent units build on it.

Sequencing principle The reason behind, or the basis for, ordering course units in a particular manner.

Side effect An unintended and often undesirable learning outcome resulting from a course's methods, materials, organization, as well as other factors.

Skill A gross category of intended learning outcomes comprising the things a teacher wants students to be able to do as a consequence of instruction.

Understandings A gross category of intended learning outcomes including ideas a teacher wants students to acquire as a consequence of instruction.

Unit A coherent chunk of a course.

Value An ideal or a state of affairs toward which one or more persons has a high affective regard, for example, equality of educational opportunity.

Selected Bibliography

Bransford, J. D., and Stein, B. S. *The Ideal Problem Solver*. New York: W. H. Freeman, 1984. Describes a problem-solving model. Problem solving is broadly conceived and includes learning through understanding, intelligent criticism, generating new ideas, and effective communication. Very useful for designing instruction for these and other high-level cognitive outcomes.

Doyle, W. E. "Academic Work." *Review of Educational Research* 53, no. 2 (Summer 1983): 159–199. A perspective of classroom life that focuses on academic tasks, that is, the intellectual work in which students are actually engaged. The relationship between academic tasks, learner processing, and learning outcomes is explicated. This should prove useful in instructional design. The article also includes a description of the social context of classrooms and how this influences academic endeavors.

Gagné, R. M., and Briggs, L. J. *Principles of Instructional Design*. 2d ed. New York: Holt, Rinehart & Winston, 1979. A detailed account of one school of design theory.

Gall, M. D. *Handbook for Evaluating and Selecting Curriculum Materials*. Boston: Allyn and Bacon, 1981. The only comprehensive guide to curriculum materials. Contains useful checklists of criteria, lists of catalogues, bibliographies, and suggested procedures.

Golby, M., Greenwald, J., and West, R. *Curriculum Design*. New York: John Wiley, 1975. A collection of readings. Important selections by Benjamin, Hirst, Dewey, Phenix, Schwab, Kilpatrick, Bloom, Eisner, Macdonald-Ross, White, Cronbach, Bruner, and others, many of which have been cited in *Course Design*.

Goodlad, J. *A Place Called School*. New York: McGraw-Hill, 1984. A descriptive study of schools intended to be used in efforts to improve schools. The study is inspired, in part, by the fact that while we know about certain specific features of schools, we know little about schools in a holistic sense. Useful information about what is covered in the school curriculum as well as a set of comprehensive goal statements for schools is included.

Gow, D. T. *Design and Development of Curricular Materials*. Vol. 1, *A Self-Instructional Text*; Vol. 2, *Instructional Design Articles*. University Center for International Studies, University of Pittsburgh, 1976. A highly detailed approach to the development of individualized instructional materials following an approach based primarily on the work of Glaser, Lindvall, Gagné, and Bloom. Offers a very different perspective from *Course Design*.

Hartley, J., and Davies, I. K. (Eds). *Contributions to an Educational Technology*, Vol. 2. New York: Nichols Publishing (London: Kogan Page), 1978. An anthology of articles on educational "means," that is, educational technology in the broad sense. Includes classic articles by Markles (on teaching concepts), Hartley and Burnhill (on writing texts), Papert (on teaching thinking), and Keller (on the Keller Plan for individualized instruction).

Johnson, M. *Intentionality in Education: A Conceptual Model of Curricular and Instructional Planning and Evaluation*. Center for Curriculum Research and Services, 63 Northgate Drive, Albany, NY, 1977. A highly detailed presentation of the "Johnson Model." (See our Chapter 1). Although this book is usually considered difficult reading by students, it is highly recommended for its careful specification of terminology, invention of a symbol system, and identification of logical relations among concepts.

Miller, J. P. *The Educational Spectrum: Orientations to Curriculum*. White Plains, NY: Longman, 1983. An analysis of seven different "orientations" to curriculum ranging from the behavioral to the disciplines to the humanistic. Provides a useful overview of options in curriculum development.

Novak, J. D., and Gowin, D. B. *Learning How to Learn*. New York: Cambridge University Press, 1984. An extensive treatment of concept mapping, among other useful techniques. Contains many examples.

Popham, W. J., and Baker, E. L. *Systematic Instruction*. Englewood Cliffs, NJ: Prentice-Hall, 1970. A simplified presentation of design theory as represented in the work of Tyler, Popham, Bloom, and Gagné.

Posner, G. J. "Tools for Curriculum Research and Development: Potential Contributions from Cognitive Science." *Curriculum Inquiry* 8, no. 4 (Winter 1978): 311–340. The beginnings of an attempt to relate "network representations" of content (a detailed version of conceptual maps) to the analysis of disciplines, content organization decisions, learning objectives, content, analysis, and evaluation of student learning. Also contains a brief review of the then current state of knowledge in cognitive science.

Pratt, D. *Curriculum: Design and Development*. New York: Harcourt Brace Jovanovich, 1980. A basic text on curriculum development which elaborates many of the points made in *Course Design*.

Schaffarzick, J., and Hampson, D. H. (Eds). *Strategies for Curriculum Development*. Berkeley: McCutchan, 1975. A collection of essays by directors of curriculum projects describing the procedures of each project.

Senesh, L. *Our Working World: New Paths in Social Science Curriculum Design*. Chicago: Science Research Associates, 1973. An excellent example of the relationships among conceptual maps, major assertions, intended learning outcomes, unit organization (scope and sequence), and activities for a K–6 social studies program.

Wigginton, E. *Sometimes a Shining Moment: The Foxfire Experience*. Garden City, NY: Anchor Press/Doubleday, 1985. Includes a complete description of a course in English composition taught using the Foxfire approach. More importantly, the book contains a stimulating discussion on how to design and redesign courses to serve "double-duty," that is, to accomplish state or district goals and also to help students understand their roots and their responsibilities.

Zais, R. S. *Curriculum: Principles and Foundations*. New York: Harper & Row, 1976. An excellent general text on curriculum. It includes very readable and comprehensive discussions of curriculum history and curriculum foundations (that is, philosophy, social issues, human nature, and learning theory), as well as extensive treatment of topics contained in *Course Design*.

Please remember that this is a library book,
and that it belongs only temporarily to each
person who uses it. Be considerate. Do
not write in this, or any, library book.